WORLD
WAR I

VOLUME 2
1914-1918

WORLD WAR I

INTRODUCTION BY
J. M. WINTER

HAMLYN

Project editor Peter Furtado

Project art editor Ayala Kingsley

Text editors Robert Peberdy, Mike March, Sue Martin

Cartographic manager Olive Pearson

Cartographic editor Zoë Goodwin

Designers Frankie Wood, Janet McCallum, Wolfgang Mezger, Gill Mouqué, Niki Overy, Linda Reed, Nicholas Rous, Tony de Saulles, Dave Sumner, Rita Wütrych

Picture research manager Alison Renney

Picture research Jan Croot, Diane Hamilton, Rebecca Hirsh, Angela Murphy, Diana Phillips, Linda Proud, Christine Vincent, Charlotte Ward-Perkins

Editorial assistants Elaine Welsh, Monica Byles

AN EQUINOX BOOK

Planned and produced by
Andromeda Oxford Ltd
9–15 The Vineyard
Abingdon
Oxfordshire OX14 3PX

Main text © Copyright
JM Winter 1988

© Copyright Andromeda Oxford
Ltd 1993

This edition published by
Hamlyn, part of Reed
Consumer Books Ltd, Michelin
House, 81 Fulham Road, London
SW3 6RB

ISBN 0 600 57990 5

Printed in Germany by
Mohndruck Graphische Betriebe
GmbH. Gutersloh.

ADVISORY EDITORS

Alan Borg
Imperial War Museum,
London

Asa Briggs
Worcester College, Oxford

Carlo Cipolla
University of California,
Berkeley, USA

Sir Napier Crookenden
Formerly Lieutenant of Her
Majesty's Tower of London

Andrew J. Goodpaster
US Army (retired)

Wolfgang Krieger
Ebenhausen, Germany

David Landes
Harvard University, USA

William McNeill
University of Chicago, USA

Peter Pulzer
All Souls College, Oxford

**Hartmut Pogge von
Strandmann**
University College, Oxford

Philip Waller
Merton College, Oxford

Geoffrey Warner
Open University

M.L.H.L. Weaver
Linacre College, Oxford

Charles Webster
All Souls College, Oxford

EDITORS

John Campbell
Freelance writer, London

John Harriss
London School of Economics

Richard Maltby
University of Exeter

C. S. Nicholls
St Antony's College, Oxford

Sidney Pollard
Formerly of University of
Bielefeld, Germany

J. M. Winter
Pembroke College,
Cambridge

CONTRIBUTORS

Gerold Ambrosius
University of Bremen,
Germany

Duncan Anderson
Royal Military Academy,
Sandhurst

Ian Beckett
Royal Military Academy,
Sandhurst

Geoffrey Best
Formerly of University of
Sussex

Robert Bideleux
University of Swansea

Simon Boughey
Corpus Christi College,
Cambridge

Gail Braybon
Freelance writer

Sir Julian Bullard
All Souls College, Oxford

Kathleen Burk
Imperial College, London

Angus Calder
Open University

Peter Carey
Trinity College, Oxford

Jane Carmichael
Imperial War Museum,
London

Malcolm Cooper
Formerly of Newfoundland
University, Canada

P. L. Cottrell
University of Leicester

Robert Dare
University of Adelaide,
Australia

Martin Dean
Formerly of University of
Cambridge

Anne Deighton
University of Reading

John Erickson
University of Edinburgh

David Fletcher
The Tank Museum, Wareham

CONTENTS

James Foreman-Peck
University of Hull

Brian Foss
Freelance writer

Michael Geyer
University of Chicago, USA

Robert Gildea
Merton College, Oxford

Anthony Glees
Brunel University

Roger Griffin
Oxford Polytechnic

Jennifer Hargreaves
Roehampton Institute,
London

Nathaniel Harris
Freelance writer

Nigel Harris
University College, London

Gundi Harriss
Birkbeck College, London

David Horn
University of Liverpool

Julian Jackson
University College of
Swansea

Keith Jeffrey
University of Ulster

Matthew Jones
St Antony's College, Oxford

Paul Kennedy
Yale University, USA

Ghislaine Lawrence
National Museum of Science
and Industry, London

Peter Lowe
University of Manchester

Keith Lyons
London School of Economics

Dermott MacCann
Brunel University

Peter Martland
Corpus Christi College,
Cambridge

Roger Morgan
London School of Economics

Lucy Newton
Leicester University

A. J. Nicholls
St Antony's College, Oxford

David Penn
Imperial War Museum,
London

Brian Holden Reid
King's College, London

Catherine Reilly
Freelance writer

Denis Ridgeway
Formerly of Royal Navy
Scientific Service

Gowher Rizvi
University of Warwick

Keith Sainsbury
University of Reading

Harry Shukman
St Antony's College, Oxford

Penny Sparke
Royal College of Art, London

Jill Stephenson
University of Edinburgh

Stanley Trapido
Lincoln College, Oxford

T.H.E. Travers
University of Calgary,
Canada

S.B. Whitmore
Formerly British Army of the
Rhine, Germany

Paul Wilkinson
University of Aberdeen

Elizabeth Wilson
North London Polytechnic

Roger Zetter
Oxford Polytechnic

Ronald Tamplin
University of Exeter

Ruth Pearson
University of East Anglia

Peter Lambert
University of East Anglia

INTRODUCTION

First let us consider the politicians' war. At the center of power in 1914 were the political leaders of the major European states. Since their words and deeds set off the catastrophe of World War I, a history of the war must begin with them. To do so is to address these questions: first, why did war break out in 1914? Second, what did the political leaders of Europe understand was happening when they went to war? And third, how did they react when the war itself took control of their lives and fortunes?

To understand the decisions made in 1914, we must bear in mind the situation, aims and aspirations of the major political leaders of the time. They operated within both an international power system, dominated by alliances, and domestic political structures of equal or even greater complexity. In 1882 Germany, Austria-Hungary and Italy had formed a Triple Alliance, according to which the parties would be defended by the others, if attacked. This agreement was renewed at regular intervals until 1914. On the other side, Russia and France had concluded a pact in 1892 to resist any aggression by the Triple Alliance. In 1904 an Anglo-French understanding (the so-called Entente Cordiale) added another plane to the circle of alliance and hostility in which diplomatic events were determined.

The divisions within European domestic politics were as deep and at times seemed to be as threatening as those in the international sphere. Partly this was a result of the basically undemocratic character of all major regimes of the pre-1914 period. In 1914 both the nature of the franchise and the rules of political power were very remote from those of the late 20th century. Modern parliamentary systems now taken as the norm, in which the executive is responsible to a legislature elected by universal suffrage, existed nowhere in Europe in 1914. That this should have been the case in autocratic Russia, even after the 1905 revolution, should cause no surprise. But few realize that the "mother of parliaments" – the center of the British political system – was in no sense a democratic institution in 1914. There were only two countries which did not have universal manhood suffrage in Europe in 1914. One was the United Kingdom; the other, Hungary. Other states had introduced manhood suffrage in parliamentary elections earlier – Austria in 1907, Italy in 1912, and states in Germany as early as 1867. But such measures were often more symbolic than real, especially in light of the limitations on parliamentary power in the Habsburg (Austro-Hungarian) and Hohenzollern (German) monarchies. Furthermore, while New Zealand and Australia had introduced votes for women in 1893 and 1902 respectively, no European state had done so before 1914. Indeed women were unenfranchised in the UK until after World War I; in France, until after World War II.

The British system had the advantage of making the government of the day answerable to an elected legislature, which could dismiss it, should a vote of confidence fail in the House of Commons. The German system operated on different assumptions. The Kaiser appointed the chancellor, who was answerable to him and not to the German parliament or Reichstag. It was said that the only major requirement for the chancellorship in pre-1914 Germany was that the candidate should have no party political experience at all. In addition, the Kaiser appointed the chief of the imperial general staff. Should his choice be eccentric, there was no constitutional way to change it.

The best way to characterize pre-1914 political life in Europe is to suggest that political power was exercised by a small circle of men drawn from the upper-middle class and the aristocracy. Some were appointed; others were elected; but most acted without the constraint of a system of checks and balances between the executive and legislative arms of government. Politicians and the civil servants who staffed their offices and ministries were also recruited from a tiny minority of the populations they ostensibly served. Their knowledge of the conditions and hopes of their people varied considerably; their desire to preserve power in the hands of their nationality or class did not.

On both grounds – nationality and class – political leaders in prewar Europe were under threat. It is important to note that every major European country was a mix of nationalities. The British had the Irish problem (see p.57): Ireland became independent only in 1922. The Germans and Russians both had a Polish problem: Polish independence dated from 1919. The Russian and Austro-Hungarian monarchies were kaleidoscopes of nationalities. Even in France it was difficult to speak of a national identity before 1914: a majority of recruits to the army did not speak French in the generation before the war.

The challenge to established political power on grounds of social class was equally problematic. The emergence of an industrial proletariat, a central feature of 19th-century industrialization, led inevitably to the appearance of a mass labor movement dedicated to securing economic, political and social rights for ordinary working people. Different national labor movements adopted different forms of political action. In Germany the political struggle overshadowed the industrial struggle. The key institution was the Marxist German social democratic party. In France industrial power predominated, through the general federation of labour (*CGT*) though the socialist party (*SFIO*) had substantial working-class support.

These groups acted internationally too. In the 1860s and then again in the 1880s an international association of socialist groups was formed, known as the First and Second Internationals. They encompassed a wide array of political parties, some reformist, some revolutionary, but all were dedicated to the transformation of capitalism into a more just and equitable social order. The European socialist movement threw up leaders of outstanding ability and integrity, men and women of deep humanistic convictions. Jean Jaurès in France and August Bebel in Germany stood for a future in which inequality and poverty would be but memories of a distant past.

The issues of nationality and class deeply divided European society after 1918, but in ways very different from those of 1914. First, the war broke up the Austro-Hungarian Empire, and created the states of Austria, Hungary, Czechoslovakia and Yugoslavia. Secondly, Poland regained its independence, after a century of domination by Russia, Austria and Germany. Thirdly, nationalist politics within the defeated powers as well as in the victorious powers intensified after the war, as was evident in the postwar rise of fascism first in Italy and then in

The socialist challenge to European regimes: Jean Jaurès in 1913.

Germany. World War I reordered but did not resolve the nationalities problem.

Similarly the problem of class conflict deepened after the war. At first, there was collaboration across class lines in war production and in the ranks of the armies. But after the onset of war weariness in 1916–17, class conflict recurred in new and more ominous forms. This was due in part to the overthrow of the Russian czar, and the seizure of power in 1917 first by a provisional government of liberals and moderate socialists, and then by the Bolsheviks under Lenin (see p.60). But internal pressures within each combatant country also made the challenge of labor in 1917–18 more powerful than it had ever been before. That it could be contained was not at all clear when the Armistice was signed in November 1918. World War I first blunted and then sharpened class conflict in Europe, and presented an ominous threat to the capitalist system at the end of the war. By 1919 the overlap between war and revolution was clear to all who had eyes to see. Inflation bred strikes, and revolutionary groups attempted to seize power in many cities in central Europe. In most places they failed completely; occasionally they succeeded for a brief period, before being swept away by a counterrevolutionary tide, which grew in the interwar years. By the 1930s millions had succumbed to the temptation of fascism.

By 1919 a new generation of socialist leaders had emerged. Bebel died peacefully in 1913. Jaurès was murdered in July 1914. Gone too were Rosa Luxemburg and Karl Liebknecht, murdered in 1919. In their places stood the men of the Bolshevik revolution, above all Lenin and Trotsky. They took part of the socialist movement into a communist international organization. The remainder retained their commitment to democratic socialism.

The German general Paul von Hindenburg came from the Prussian Junker class of large landowners; his French opponent in 1918, Philippe Pétain, came from a farming family in the north of France; John J. Pershing, who led the American Expeditionary Forces, came from a small town in Missouri. A military career was the natural choice of sons of such families, whose contact with the complexities of urban and industrial life was at times tenuous or nonexistent. Many passed through the high military academies of their countries – Sandhurst in the UK, Saint-Cyr in France, West Point in the USA – and progressed through the chain of command in the relatively peaceful decades before 1914. Some saw service in colonial wars, and were schooled in the arts of maneuver in which cavalry had traditionally played an important part.

The very expansion of armies in the prewar period necessitated a change in the social composition of the officer corps. More and more men were required to process the annual crop of recruits, leading to an infiltration of middle-class men into the army as professional soldiers. Between 1860 and 1913 the nobles' share in the German officer corps had dropped from 60 to 30 percent.

This "democratization" of the officer corps was accompanied by a deepening of the significance of the military in the political and social life of the nation. As imperial power grew in the late 19th century, nation and army had grown closer together. This was not true in all countries – witness the turmoil over the Dreyfus affair (1896–1905) and the evidence it disclosed of incompetence, corruption, and worse in the higher reaches of the French high command (see p. 32). But even under these difficult circumstances, the prestige of the army survived the disgrace of a few of its most senior men.

Many of those in positions of command in European armies in 1914 were wedded by temperament and training to a belief, first, in military action as the solution to political problems and, second, in the offensive as the answer to all military problems. In many way, an emphasis on the offensive suited the needs of military planners in the prewar period. First, political support could be secured more easily for creating weapons of attack rather than defense. Secondly, if these weapons were seen as the cutting edge of a short, decisive war, then offensive strategies appeared cheaper than defensive ones. Thirdly, offensive strategies were intellectually more attractive. They could be worked out on drawing boards and in war games with some degree of precision; defensive strategies were clouded in uncertainty, and thereby threatened the organizational unity of armies. In effect, developments in strategy helped to weaken the hand of diplomats who wanted to threaten the use of force rather than to resort to it, and thereby made war more likely in the years before 1914.

The shadow of World War I fell over military planning long after the Armistice in 1918. The failure of a short, sharp, decisive offensive, in which the infantry was the key element, led in two contradictory directions: first, toward new theories of armored warfare, pioneered by those who knew the ghastliness of trench warfare, such as Basil Liddell Hart or Charles de Gaulle; secondly, toward defensive strategies, such as the ill-fated Maginot line, a series of concrete fortifications built by the French in the interwar years, which were easily overcome by the Germans in 1940. Ironically, the failure of the war of movement in 1914 prepared the way for a more successful war of movement 25 years later, in which tanks, artillery and air power produced the decisive breakthrough which had eluded the generals of World War I until the very end of the conflict.

Generals

The second concentric circle of power in World War I was composed of the men who directed military and naval affairs. The boundaries between this circle and that of the political elites were never clear and occasionally nonexistent. "The Generals' War" follows the failure of the original strategy of the German general staff, and considers the various attempts made by the generals of all armies to break the stalemate in the following four years. Here we also explore the protracted struggle between generals and politicians for control of strategy. By and large the generals won.

The social composition of the general staffs of the major European armies was remarkably similar. Most men who made the army their career and who rose to the top were raised in the country among the titled or untitled gentry.

Soldiers

In discussing the soldiers of World War I there are two central questions to be answered. Why did they go to war? Why did they stay once they knew the war they had expected was not the war they had to fight?

An answer to the first question requires some consideration of the history of the draft. In most continental countries (but not in the UK or the USA) conscription was established in law in 1914. The origins of conscription can be located in the Revolutionary and Napoleonic Wars (1793–1815), when the success of French mass recruitment led the defeated powers to emulate the methods of the victors. Austria and Prussia adopted conscription after defeats at the hands of the French at Austerlitz in 1805 and at Jena in 1806 respectively. In the 19th century the French army largely reverted to a professional corps, due to a provision in the law whereby citizens could buy themselves out of military service. Prussia's victories against Austria-Hungary in 1866 and against France in 1870 reset the model just as Napoleon's had done 60 years earlier. In 1872 "buying out" was abolished in France, as it was in Italy and Russia in 1873 and 1874. But some privileges remained: Frenchmen with higher education retained the right to a reduction in length of military service until 1905.

For those of more modest means, the major method of avoiding military service before 1914 was emigration. In Italy conscription was adopted in 1873, but in the following years, young men preferred to seek a new life overseas rather than to join the army. A law was passed in 1888 with the intention of preventing men below age 32 from leaving the country, but the outflow of young potential recruits continued unabated in the following decades. The same happened in the Austro-Hungarian and Russian Empires.

If emigration reduced military manpower in one way, poverty did so in another. It was simply impossible for the bulk of the urban proletariat to pass the usually lax medical examinations of the major armies. Peasants did better, and thereby constituted the majority of land armies in 1914.

In absolute terms, Russia had most men under uniform among the great powers in 1914. Its 1.3 million-man standing contingent exceeded the military and naval personnel of France and Germany by about 400,000 men. In turn these dwarfed the smaller armies of Britain, Italy, and Austria-Hungary, numbering between 250,000 and 500,000 men. Further afield, the Japanese boasted 300,000 men under arms; the USA around 160,000. Of course, quantity and quality were by no means identical, among both professional soldiers and the reserve forces of former conscripts which theoretically stood ready to serve in the event of a national emergency.

The vast expansion of regular forces when that emergency came is a story told later in this book. The fact that mass armies were already in existence in 1914 and that millions of Europeans – however reluctantly – had already spent a part of their youth in them may help to account for the relative ease with which manpower was mobilized after the outbreak of war.

Civilians

Behind the armies were the home fronts, the concentric circle of widest dimensions, from which soldiers and sailors were drawn and supplied. Again, this account will chart the progressive disturbance of civilian life in wartime, from the period of illusions in 1914 to the disillusionment, anger, defiance and despair of 1917–18. Questions of propaganda, women's work, strikes, and food dominate the discussion, as they did that of contemporaries. These issues also suggest that the outcome of the war was not solely a function of the bravery and tenacity of fighting men. Victory in war arose out of the economic resources and social cohesion of one side and the progressively more damaging shortages and social divisions within the other. This was true in Russia in 1917, and to a certain extent in Italy and Austria-Hungary in the last year of the war. But the decisive fact was that Germany cracked in 1918, both at home and in the field of battle, and lost the war.

Some believe that, given the economic potential of the two sides, what was remarkable was not Germany's defeat, but that it held out for so long. Together Germany and Austria-Hungary constituted a bloc representing about 19 percent of world manufacturing production in 1913. France, Russia and Britain represented a bigger industrial base, about 28 percent of world manufacture. This advantage became more important the longer the war dragged on. The displacement of Russia by the USA on the Allied side in 1917 only made matters worse for Germany. The British-French-US manufacturing bloc occupied over 50 percent of world production in 1913.

It is true that the German economy was strong in areas essential for munitions production. This gave it an advantage in the first year of the war. But the imbalance in overall industrial power and in financial resources, as well as the greater sophistication of the Allied system of civilian supply, ultimately gave the Allies a decisive superiority, which Germany could not resist in the last year of the war.

The four phases of World War I

World War I was not one continuous struggle but consisted of four separate phases, each with its own character and distinguishing features. Each phase presents major issues, which will be summarized here.

1914: the war of illusions

World War I erupted at the beginning of August 1914, when the two major power-blocs in Europe – Germany and Austria-Hungary on one side (the Central Powers), and the UK, France, and Russia (the Entente Powers), on the other – declared war on each other. This was the first general war to break out for a century, and its initial phase was dominated by a series of illusions as to its likely duration and character. There had been wars between *industrializing* states before: witness the Crimean War of 1853–56, the Franco-German War of 1870–71 and the Russo-Japanese War of 1904–05, as well as the real prototype of the bloodbath of 1914–18, the American Civil War. But never before had there been a conflict between all the *industrialized* nations of Europe. It is perhaps understandable that most political and military leaders, as well as the populations they led, grossly underestimated the time and the exertions necessary to win such a war.

1915: stalemate and stagnation

The invasion of France by the German army in 1914 was the first of four military gambles which determined the course of the war. By late autumn 1914 it was apparent that the first gamble had failed, and that the kind of lightning military victory won by the Prussian army in the early stages of the Franco-Prussian War had eluded the Germans. Consequently battle lines hardened in the west to produce a series of linked fortifications across southern Belgium and northern France from the English Channel to the Swiss border – the Western Front. In the east a war of movement continued, but soldiers became entrenched in most theaters of operation in the second year of the war, as shown by the fighting in Gallipoli in Turkey

▶ German strength in munitions: a Krupp factory in the early 20th century.

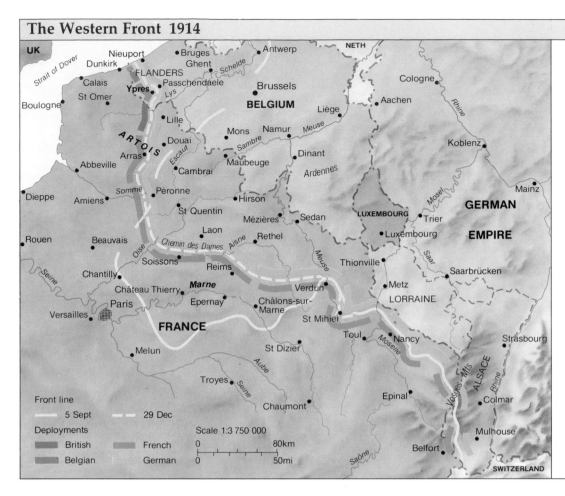

The Western Front 1914

UK
NETH
Strait of Dover
Nieuport · Bruges · Antwerp
Dunkirk · Ghent
Calais FLANDERS
St Omer Passchendaele
Boulogne Ypres Lys
Lille
ARTOIS Douai
Abbeville Arras Cambrai
Dieppe Péronne
Amiens Somme St Quentin
Rouen Beauvais Laon
Chantilly Chemin des Dames Soissons
Château Thierry Marne Reims
Paris Epernay Châlons-sur-Marne
Versailles
FRANCE
Melun St Dizier
Troyes Aube Seine
Chaumont

Schelde Brussels
BELGIUM Liège Aachen
Mons Namur Meuse
Sambre Dinant
Maubeuge Ardennes
Hirson
Mézières Sedan
Rethel
Aisne

Cologne
Rhine
Koblenz
Mainz
LUXEMBOURG Trier
Luxembourg GERMAN
EMPIRE
Thionville Saar Saarbrücken
Verdun Metz
LORRAINE
St Mihiel
Toul Nancy
Moselle Strasbourg
Epinal ALSACE Colmar
Vosges Mts Rhine
Mulhouse
Belfort
SWITZERLAND

Front line
—— 5 Sept
– – 29 Dec
Deployments
British French
Belgian German
Scale 1:3 750 000
0 — 80km
0 — 50mi

August 4
(to Sept. 4) Main weight of the German army swings through Belgium and into France, pushing back the small Allied force in front of it. Meanwhile the main weight of the French army is being thrown (unsuccessfully) against German positions in Lorraine.

September 5–10
Battle of the Marne. French Fifth and Ninth Armies and the British Expeditionary Force stop the German invasion along the River Marne.

September 13
(to Oct. 18) With deadlock on the newly established front along the River Aisne, the Allies try to turn the Germans' northern flank. The Germans, however, have exactly the same idea and the moves of each side merely extend the front (and the deadlock) all the way to the sea.

October 18
(to Nov. 22) Battle of Ypres. The Germans attempt to bludgeon their way through the new Allied line so as to reestablish a war of movement, but find it impossible.

December 17–29
Battle of Artois. The French try to break the German line, and fail.

The Western Front 1915

UK
NETH
Strait of Dover
Nieuport · Bruges · Antwerp
Dunkirk · Ghent
Calais Passchendaele
St Omer FLANDERS
Boulogne Ypres Lys
Aubers Lille
Festubert Neuve Chapelle
Loos
ARTOIS Douai
Arras Cambrai
Abbeville
Dieppe Péronne
Amiens Somme St Quentin
Rouen Beauvais Laon
Chemin des Dames
Chantilly Soissons
Château Thierry Marne Reims
CHAMPAGNE
Paris Epernay Châlons-sur-Marne
Versailles
FRANCE
Melun St Dizier
Troyes Aube Seine
Chaumont

Schelde Brussels
BELGIUM Liège Aachen
Mons Namur Meuse
Sambre Dinant
Maubeuge Ardennes
Hirson
Mézières Sedan
Rethel
Aisne

Cologne
Rhine
Koblenz
Mainz
LUXEMBOURG Trier
Luxembourg GERMAN
EMPIRE
Thionville Saar Saarbrücken
Verdun Metz
LORRAINE
St Mihiel
Toul Nancy
Moselle Strasbourg
Epinal ALSACE Colmar
Vosges Mts Rhine
Mulhouse
Belfort
SWITZERLAND

Front line
—— 10 March
– – 14 Oct
Deployments
British French
Belgian German
Scale 1:3 750 000
0 — 80km
0 — 50mi

March 10–13
Battle of Neuve Chapelle: a limited British and Indian attack captures the village of Neuve Chapelle.

April 22
(to May 27) Second Battle of Ypres. The Germans use gas against the French for the first time, but by the end of the battle they have moved only 5km (3mi).

May 4
(to June 18) Second Battle of Artois. Despite the diversionary attacks by the British at Aubers Ridge (May 9–10) and Festubert (May 15–25), the French again take heavy casualties. Frustration sets in among the generals of both sides.

September 25
(to Oct. 14) Third Battle of Artois. After a period of rest and recovery, simultaneous attacks are launched in Artois and Champagne by the French and at Loos by the British (to Nov. 4). Although some gains are made, French losses reach staggering proportions.

The Western Front 1916–17

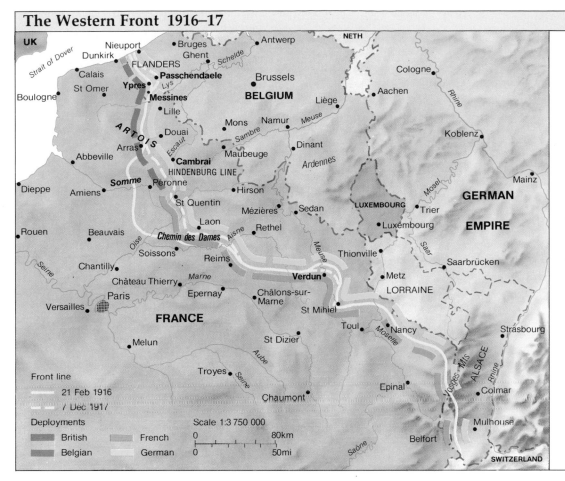

UK · Strait of Dover · Nieuport · Dunkirk · FLANDERS · Bruges · Ghent · Antwerp · NETH
Calais · St Omer · Ypres · Passchendaele · Schelde · Brussels · Cologne
Boulogne · Messines · Lys · BELGIUM · Liège · Aachen · Rhine
Lille · Mons · Namur · Meuse · Koblenz
ARTOIS · Douai · Sambre · Dinant · Ardennes · Mosel · Mainz
Arras · Cambrai · Maubeuge · GERMAN
Abbeville · HINDENBURG LINE · Escaut · LUXEMBOURG · Trier
Dieppe · Somme · Péronne · Hirson · EMPIRE
Amiens · St Quentin · Mézières · Sedan · Luxembourg
Rouen · Laon · Rethel · Thionville · Saar · Saarbrücken
Chemin des Dames · Aisne · Meuse · Metz
Beauvais · Soissons · Reims · LORRAINE
Chantilly · Oise · Verdun · Strasbourg
Seine · Château Thierry · Marne · Châlons-sur-Marne · St Mihiel
Paris · Epernay · Toul · Nancy · Moselle
Versailles · FRANCE · St Dizier
Melun · Aube · Vosges Mts · ALSACE
Troyes · Seine · Epinal · Colmar · Rhine
Chaumont · Mulhouse
Belfort
SWITZERLAND

Front line
— 21 Feb 1916
-- 7 Dec 1917

Deployments
■ British   ■ French
■ Belgian   ■ German

Scale 1:3 750 000
0 — 80km
0 — 50mi

1916

February 21
(to Dec. 18) Battle of Verdun. Germans attack Verdun.

July 1
(to Nov. 19) Battle of the Somme. British and French infantry mount assaults on the German lines. Eight km (5mi) are gained.

1917

March 16
A section of the German line is moved back to the Hindenburg Line.

April 9–14
British and Canadians attack at Arras. Canadians take Vimy Ridge.

April 19–29
Nivelle's Chemin des Dames offensive against the German lines. French gains are negligible; mutinies follow.

June 7–14
Battle of Messines Ridge. After a great mine explosion, British forces clear ground for the next major offensive.

July 31
(to Nov. 10) Third Battle of Ypres. The British, Australians and Canadians grind forward to the village of Passchendaele.

November 20
(to Dec. 7) Battle of Cambrai. British tanks break the German line, but soon lose captured territory.

The Western Front 1917–18

UK · Strait of Dover · Nieuport · Dunkirk · FLANDERS · Bruges · Ghent · Antwerp · NETH
Calais · St Omer · Ypres · Passchendaele · Schelde · Brussels · Cologne
Boulogne · Lys · BELGIUM · Liège · Aachen · Rhine
Lille · Mons · Namur · Meuse · Koblenz
Arras · Douai · Sambre · Dinant · Ardennes · Mosel · Mainz
Abbeville · Cambrai · Maubeuge · GERMAN
Dieppe · Somme · Péronne · Hirson · Escaut · Sedan · LUXEMBOURG · Trier · EMPIRE
Amiens · St Quentin · Mézières · Luxembourg
Rouen · Laon · Rethel · Thionville · Saar · Saarbrücken
Beauvais · Chemin des Dames · Aisne · Meuse · Metz
Oise · Soissons · Reims · Verdun · LORRAINE
Chantilly · Château Thierry · Marne · Châlons-sur-Marne · St Mihiel · Strasbourg
Seine · Paris · Epernay · Toul · Nancy · Moselle
Versailles · FRANCE · St Dizier
Melun · Aube · Vosges Mts · ALSACE
Troyes · Seine · Epinal · Colmar · Rhine
Chaumont · Mulhouse
Belfort · Saône
SWITZERLAND

Front line
— 8 Aug   -- 11 Nov

Deployments
■ British   ■ French
■ Belgian   ■ American
■ German

Scale 1:3 750 000
0 — 80km
0 — 50mi

1917

December 5
New Bolshevik government in Russia signs an armistice with Germany, enabling German forces on the Eastern Front to be moved west for a major offensive on the Western Front.

1918

March 21
(to July 17) The Spring offensive. The German army launches a series of attacks, and gains huge areas of France. The German advance toward Paris is stopped by the Allies at the Second Battle of the Marne (July 15–17).

July 18
With the Germans visibly losing cohesion, Foch (appointed overall Allied commander during the worst of the German attacks) declares the time is right for an Allied offensive.

August 8
(to Nov. 10) The Allied armies manage to restore a war of movement, and roll back the exhausted Germans toward their own borders. The German army is saved from disintegration only by the Armistice (Nov. 11).

and in Italy, which had entered the war in late 1914 and early 1915 respectively.

1916–17: the great slaughter

The scale of the war on the Eastern Front was monumental, but it was never at the heart of the war. Whatever happened in the vast operations in Poland and the Balkans, the conflict would be won and lost on the Western Front. The effort to do so dominated events in 1916–17.

If the first military gamble made by Germany in the war was the invasion of France in 1914, the second was the Battle of Verdun. The first was an attempt to win a war of annihilation; the second, a war of attrition. Starting on 21 February 1916 the German army tried to "bleed the French army white", by an assault on the salient of Verdun in eastern France. This battle turned into a ten-month bloodbath for both sides.

While the fighting around Verdun raged, the British opened a major offensive further west in France, near the River Somme. This gigantic assault, launched on 1 July 1916, was renewed periodically throughout the following six months, but without any success in its primary objective, which was to break through the German lines in order to fight the war of movement everyone had been waiting for since October 1914.

In late July 1917 the British tried again, this time in southern Belgium, near the city of Ypres. This cluster of offensive operations, which dragged on remorselessly until November, is called the Third Battle of Ypres, or simply Passchendaele. It was a complete failure. In the three major military operations of this phase of the war – Verdun, the Somme, and Passchendaele – the defensive positions held out, but at a cost to both sides of approximately two million casualties.

There were other major military and political events in 1916: for instance, the Russian army achieved a major military victory in the Brusilov offensive and in the Battle of Jutland, despite its inconclusive outcome, the British navy kept control over the North Sea. This meant that the blockade of German ports continued, putting a strain on the German economy which was deepened by a series of poor harvests leading to the "turnip winter" of 1916–17. These difficulties forced the Germans to press home a submarine war – their third major gamble of the war. This aimed to cut essential supplies and force the UK to the conference table, but at the risk of widening the conflict by killing neutral citizens.

1917–18: revolution and peace

In April 1917 the United States responded to the German U-boat campaign by declaring war on the Central Powers. This was one of the two major events which fundamentally changed the character of the war. The other was the Russian Revolution of March 1917, which toppled the czar's imperial regime and placed a Provisional government in its place. The new regime was made up of liberals and moderate socialists who were still committed to throwing the German army off Russian soil. But the failure of their offensive undermined the basis of popular support for the new government. In November power was seized by Lenin and the revolutionary Bolshevik socialists – the only group that had been committed to taking Russia out of the war at whatever the price.

The price was high, but the Russians had no alternative. At the Treaty of Brest-Litovsk, signed on 3 March 1918, the Russians handed over a vast territory, including Poland, the Ukraine, the Baltic states and Finland, thereby creating a huge satellite empire for Germany in the east. The price for the Allies was heavy too. The defeat of Russia meant that Germany could concentrate its efforts on the Western Front and reinforce its position in Belgium and France in order to launch an offensive to win the war before the weight of American manpower and materiel would be felt. This offensive came on 21 March 1918, and very nearly achieved its objective. Within a few weeks the German army was within 80 km (50 mi) of Paris, but could not capitalize on its initial gains.

But that was the end of Germany's fourth and last gamble of the war. It ran out of reserves of manpower and materiel just as the United States was beginning to play a major role in the conflict. By the summer of 1918, the tide had turned. The German army started to retreat, and the high command began to see that the war was lost. All of Germany's allies collapsed, and to prevent further slaughter and the invasion of their country – by this time torn by dissension and incipient revolt – the German high command informed the Kaiser that Germany could not win an outright victory. In effect they had to accept the bitter fact that the war was lost. The Kaiser abdicated, and an armistice took effect on 11 November 1918.

The first "people's war"

This description of the four phases of the war presents only the outlines of the conflict. But it does suggest a number of points which help to account for its outcome. Again it may be useful to encapsulate this argument.

It is possible to see World War I as a series of gambles taken by Germany: the Schlieffen Plan, Verdun, the U-boat campaign, and the March 1918 offensive. Each nearly brought victory; each ultimately failed. The reasons for failure are complex. But one important part of the story is social and economic. In other words, military front and home front stood together and collapsed together during World War I, as the hungry populations of German and Austria recognized by 1918. The Allies won the war primarily because they were able to field their armies without starving their civilian populations. In this respect, the first "people's war" was won by the "people's democracies" in more than just the obvious sense. This is the appropriate context in which to place America's contribution to the war. Both before 1917 and after, the United States helped the Allies win the "people's war".

The aftermath of the war

This account will present an image of the war as a man-made shock wave spreading out from an epicenter to various peripheries. This is a useful way of describing the war, as it moved from the centers of political power, to the general staffs, to the armies they led, and to the populations they defended, with varying degrees of success. But this approach has one serious drawback; it neglects the factors that made people call it the "Great War": first, its gigantic scale; and second, the deep and indelible mark it left on the cultural life of the 20th century. In the final chapters we attend to aspects of the aftermath of World War I.

The aftermath of the war was a time of reckoning and a time of mourning for millions of people throughout the world. This indeed is another way of seeing the conflict as a "people's war". They paid the price. The casualty lists which grew and grew as the war continued preclude any conclusion other than that the war was one of the most miserable chapters in human history. The fact that much bravery and some good came out of it is beside the point; the war was an abomination. Being so many, the victims of the war became one: the Lost Generation. Their shadow is cast wherever one looks in Europe. If this book succeeds in suggesting some of the dimensions of the catastrophe, and some of its enduring consequences, then it will have achieved its purpose.

The Eastern Front 1914–15

The Eastern Front 1916–17

1914

August 17–26
Russians launch a two-pronged offensive into lightly-held East Prussia and beat off an initial German counterattack at Gumbinnen (Aug. 20).

August 26–30
Battle of Tannenberg. Germans crush the southern prong of the Russian advance.

September 5–9
Battle of the Masurian Lakes. Germans turn back the eastern prong of the Russian advance.

September 28
(to Oct. 27) First Battle of Warsaw. The Germans and Austro-Hungarians attack the huge concentrations of Russian troops in Poland, south of Warsaw, head on. The Russians stop the opposing armies and force them back.

November 11–25
Second Battle of Warsaw. The Germans and Austro-Hungarians renew their attack on the Russians; this time to the west of Warsaw. The Russians are caught off guard and the Germans and Austro-Hungarians advance as far as Lodz.

November 16–29
The Austro-Hungarians attack in the Krakow sector. The attack is blunted by the Russians. In the Carpathians, denuded of Austro-Hungarian troops for the Krakow battles, the Russians make substantial gains.

December 3–15
Battle of Limanowa. The Russians attack Krakow, which is successfully defended by the Germans and Austro-Hungarians.

1915

January 23
(to mid April) Both sides launch attacks in the Carpathians. Since 11 November 1914 the Russians have besieged the city of Przemysl. Austro-Hungarian attempts to relieve the city fail with heavy losses. Przemysl falls to the Russians on March 22.

February 8–22
Winter Battle of Masuria (to the east of the Masurian Lakes). The Germans and Austro-Hungarians force the Russians to retreat but they fail to break through.

May 2
(to Sept. 30) Central Powers' Summer offensive. The Germans lead a breakthrough at Gorlice which throws the Russians back from the Carpathians. Further north, under strong German and Austro-Hungarian pressure, the Russians retreat to shorten their line and abandon the vast "bulge" of Russian Poland.

1916

June 4
(to Aug. 10) Brusilov offensive. The Russians attack on the relatively open ground between the Pripet Marshes and the Carpathians and roll back the Austro-Hungarian line. The Germans stabilize the situation by sending reinforcements to the Austro-Hungarians.

1917

January-February
Sporadic fighting in the Carpathians.

June 18
(to July 13) The Kerensky offensive. The Russians launch a series of weak offensives along the Eastern Front, which are easily repulsed.

July 19
(to Aug. 4) The Germans launch a counteroffensive and push the Russian line further east. The effort stalls for want of reserves and supplies.

September 1–5
After intensive training of their assault units, the Germans capture the Russian port of Riga (at the extreme northern end of the Front), but fail to trap the defending Russian army, which escapes.

December 5
Armistice is signed on the Eastern Front between the Germans and the new Bolshevik government of Russia.

FROM BALKAN CONFLICT TO WORLD WAR

Why did armed conflict in southeastern Europe engulf the world? The first reason is that the European alliance system converted a localized conflict into a general European war. In 1879 Germany and Austria-Hungary had formed the Dual Alliance; in 1893–94 France and Russia had become allies. Hence an Austro-Russian military conflict was bound to become a Russo–German one, which in turn touched off Franco–German conflict, leading to the invasion of Belgium, which ensured Britain's entry into the war. Thus once war was declared between Austria and Serbia on 28 July, and Russia mobilized its armies, a general war broke out. An alliance system conceived as a deterrent to European war helped precipitate one.

Secondly, a European war became a world war because it was waged between imperial powers, able to summon the manpower and resources of colonies and dependencies throughout the world. The Senegalese joined the French; an Indian army supplemented the British in Mesopotamia and on the Western Front. In German East Africa German troops led British and African soldiers on a wild goose chase for four years. Portugal joined the Allies in part to defend or extend its African empire. In August 1914 Japan seized former German possessions in China. The Allies put pressure on China formally to enter the war, which it did on 14 August 1917. After the USA joined the Allies in April 1917 (see page 59) American diplomacy brought Central American satellite states into the conflict: within 24 hours of the US declaration of war, Panama and Cuba followed suit. Brazil, Guatemala, Nicaragua, Costa Rica, Haiti and Honduras joined in later. In addition, extra-European colonies and dependencies were populated by European immigrants. Many Canadians, Australians and New Zealanders who joined up in 1914 were indeed defending their country – Britain. Anglo–American family ties were also strong.

Thirdly, the conflict became worldwide because the economic interests of the major powers were spread throughout the globe. Britain had built a vast international trading network in the late 19th century. This was both its strength and its vulnerable point, at which Germany's U-boats struck. They failed in every respect. The UK blockade of Germany was more successful in stripping it of vital supplies.

The economic side of the war touched neutrals in many ways. All were affected by wartime inflation. Some, like Denmark or Holland, had to consent to trading arrangements with Germany which were distinctly unfavorable. To feed German families, Danes went without milk. Sweden introduced food rationing to deal with severe shortages. Other economic effects of the war were less deleterious. Many countries were starved of European finished goods, and had to produce their own. The economies of Brazil, Argentina, Japan, China and India "took off" during a war which was both the apogee and the end of European dominance of the world.

- ● Major land conflict
- ■ Important sea battle
- ✳ Bombed area

August 1914
- Allies and Associates
- Central Powers
- Neutral
- Neutral, later joining Allies
- Neutral, later joining Central Powers

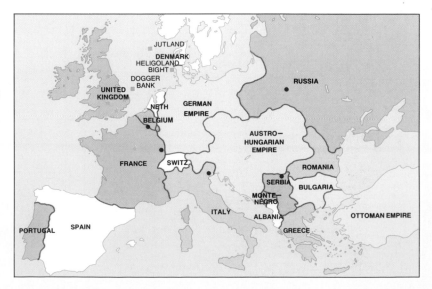

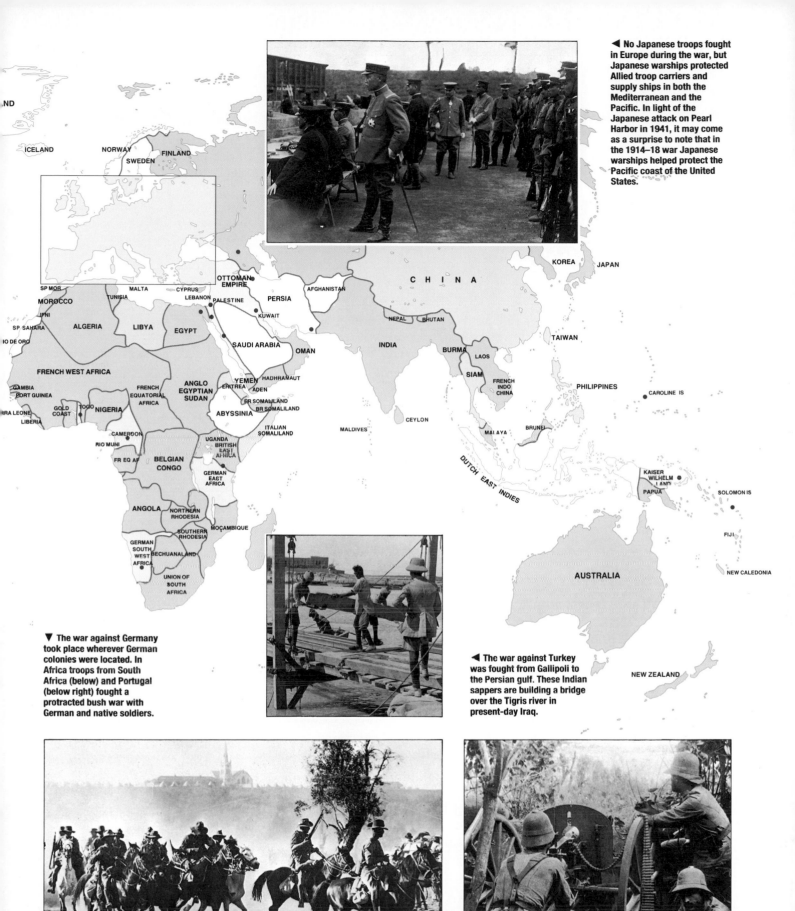

No Japanese troops fought in Europe during the war, but Japanese warships protected Allied troop carriers and supply ships in both the Mediterranean and the Pacific. In light of the Japanese attack on Pearl Harbor in 1941, it may come as a surprise to note that in the 1914–18 war Japanese warships helped protect the Pacific coast of the United States.

▼ The war against Germany took place wherever German colonies were located. In Africa troops from South Africa (below) and Portugal (below right) fought a protracted bush war with German and native soldiers.

◄ The war against Turkey was fought from Gallipoli to the Persian gulf. These Indian sappers are building a bridge over the Tigris river in present-day Iraq.

17

Time Chart

	1914	1915	1916
Politicians	• **28 June**: Assassination of Franz Ferdinand at Sarajevo • **28 July**: Austria-Hungary declares war on Serbia • **1 Aug**: Germany declares war on Russia • **3 Aug**: Germany declares war on France • **4 Aug**: UK declares war on Germany • **4 Aug**: Germany declares war on Belgium • **2 Nov**: Russia declares war on Turkey • **6 Nov**: UK and France declare war on Turkey	• **26 Apr**: Italy and Allies agree Treaty of London • **23 May**: Italy declares war on Austria-Hungary • **25 Aug**: Italy declares war on Turkey • **26 Aug**: Italy declares war on Germany • **14 Oct**: Bulgaria joins Central Powers • **30 Nov**: France, UK, Russia and Japan sign Pact of London	• **24-29 Apr**: Easter Rising in Dublin, Ireland • **5 June**: UK minister of war, Kitchener, dies when HMS *Hampshire* is sunk • **27 Aug**: Romania enters the war on the side of the Allies • **7 Nov**: Woodrow Wilson is reelected president of the USA • **21 Nov**: Death of Austro-Hungarian emperor, Franz Josef • **Dec**: Lloyd George becomes prime minister of the UK
Western Front	• **4 Aug**: Germans invade Belgium • **7-16 Aug**: British Expeditionary Force lands in France • **23 Aug**: Battle of Mons • **24 Aug**: Main German armies enter France • **5-10 Sep**: First Battle of the Marne: German invasion halted • **15 Sep**: The first trenches are dug • **17 Sep–18 Oct**: Race to the sea • **12 Oct–11 Nov**: First Battle of Ypres	• **10-13 Mar**: Battle of Neuve Chapelle • **22 Apr–27 May**: Second Battle of Ypres • **4 May–18 June**: Second Battle of Artois • **9-10 May**: Battle of Aubers Ridge • **15-25 May**: Battle of Festubert • **25 Sep–4 Nov**: Battle of Loos • **25 Sep–14 Oct**: Third Battle of Artois • **25 Sep–6 Oct**: French offensive in Champagne	• **21 Feb–18 Dec**: Battle of Verdun • **1 July–19 Nov**: Battle of the Somme
Eastern Front	• **20 Aug**: Battle of Gumbinnen • **26-30 Aug**: Battle of Tannenberg • **6-15 Sep**: Battle of the Masurian Lakes • **11 Nov–early Dec**: Germans push Russians further east	• **3 Jan**: Germans make first use of gas-filled shells • **8-22 Feb**: Winter Battle of Masuria • **2-4 May**: Battle of Gorlice-Tarnow	• **4 June–10 Oct**: Brusilov offensive
Balkan	• **8-12 Sep**: Battle of Lemberg • **2 Dec**: Austro-Hungarians capture Belgrade • **11 Dec**: Serbians recapture Belgrade	• **5 Oct**: Allied troops begin disembarking at Salonika • **7 Oct–20 Nov**: Austro-Hungarians invade Serbia	• **8-17 Jan**: Central Powers knock Montenegro out of the war • **Sep–Dec**: Central Powers invade Romania
Turkish	• **22 Dec–18 Jan 1915**: Russians repulse Turkish attacks in the Caucasus	• **Feb**: Allies bombard Turkish forts at entrance of Dardanelles • **Feb–Nov**: Allied attack along River Tigris, Mesopotamia • **18 Mar**: Allies attempt naval attack on Dardanelles • **25 Apr–9 Jan 1916**: Allied land operations at Gallipoli • **5 Dec–29 Apr 1916**: Siege of Kut	• **6 June**: Start of Arab revolt in the Hejaz • **4 Aug–9 Jan 1917**: British drive Turkish forces out of Egypt
Italian		• **23 June–7 July**: Battle of the Isonzo	• **15 May–26 June**: Austria-Hungary's Asiago offensive • **6-17 Aug**: Sixth Battle of the Isonzo
African	• **Aug–Nov**: First campaign in East Africa • **Oct**: Allied conquest of German Southwest Africa	• **June–Jan 1916**: Main Allied campaign in Cameroon	• **4 Sep**: Allies capture Dar Es Salaam in German East Africa
War at sea	• **1 Nov**: Battle of Coronel • **8 Dec**: Battle of the Falkland Islands	• **24 Jan**: Battle of Dogger Bank • **Feb–Sep**: First period of intensive German submarine warfare • **7 May**: Sinking of the *Lusitania*	• **Mar–Apr**: Second period of German submarine warfare • **31 May–1 June**: Battle of Jutland
Generals	• **2 Aug**: Moltke appointed commander of German field armies • **4 Aug**: French appointed commander of the British Expeditionary Force • **21 Aug**: Ludendorff appointed chief of staff of German Eighth Army • **22 Aug**: Hindenburg appointed commander of German Eighth Army • **14 Sep**: Moltke resigns; succeeded by Falkenhayn	• **15 Jun**: Pétain appointed commander of French armies • **5 Sep**: Czar Nicholas II takes command of Russian armies • **3 Dec**: Joffre appointed commander of French armies • **19 Dec**: Haig becomes commander of British Expeditionary Force	• **4 Apr**: Brusilov appointed commander of Russian southern armies • **29 Aug**: Hindenburg is made commander of German field armies with Ludendorff as quartermaster general • **12 Dec**: Nivelle is appointed commander of French northern and northeastern armies

1917	1918	1919
• **15 Mar**: Czar Nicholas II of Russia abdicates; provisional government is formed • **6 Apr**: USA enters the war on the side of the Allies • **27 June**: Greece enters the war on the side of the Allies • **7 Nov**: In Russia Bolsheviks overthrow the provisional government • **16 Nov**: Clemenceau becomes prime minister of France • **3 Dec**: Bolshevik government in Russia signs armistice with Germany	• **8 Jan**: Woodrow Wilson, US president, publishes 14 Points as basis for peace • **3 Mar**: Russia and Central Powers sign the treaty of Brest-Litovsk • **7 May**: Romania and Central Powers sign the Treaty of Bucharest • **30 Sep**: Armistice concluded between Allies and Bulgaria • **27 Oct**: Austria-Hungary asks Italy for an armistice • **9 Nov**: German Kaiser abdicates • **11 Nov**: Armistice between Allies and Germany takes effect	• **5-11 Jan**: Spartacist revolt in Germany • **18 Jan**: Peace conference begins at Versailles near Paris • **28 Jun**: Versailles Treaty signed • **11 Aug**: Weimar constitution comes into force in Germany • **10 Sep**: Treaty of Saint-Germain signed with Austria
• **16-29 Apr**: Chemin des Dames offensive • **31 July–10 Nov**: Third Battle of Ypres • **20 Nov–8 Dec**: Battle of Cambrai	• **21 Mar–18 July**: German Spring offensive • **23 Mar–15 Aug**: Germans shell Paris • **2 Apr**: US troops enter war on Western Front • **18 July–10 Nov**: Allied counteroffensive	
• **Jan–Feb**: Sporadic fighting in the Carpathians • **18 June–13 July**: Kerensky offensive • **3 Sep**: Germans capture Riga	• **May**: Allies intervene in Russian civil war	• **Oct**: End of Allies' intervention in Russian civil war
• **24 Apr–22 May**: Battle of Doiran	• **14-29 Sep**: Allied counteroffensive makes gains from Bulgaria	
• **24 Feb–11 Mar**: British retake Kut and capture Baghdad • **6 July**: T.E. Lawrence and Arabs capture Aqaba • **11 Dec**: British capture Jerusalem	• **19 Sep–25 Oct**: British capture Damascus, Beirut and Aleppo • **30 Oct**: Turkish Sixth Army in Mesopotamia surrenders	
• **24 Oct–10 Nov**: Battle of Caporetto	• **24 Oct–2 Nov**: Battle of Vittorio Veneto	
• **Dec–25 Nov 1918**: Lettow-Vorbeck's long retreat		
• **1 Feb**: Germans recommence unrestricted submarine warfare	• **28 Oct**: Mutiny of German sailors at Kiel	• **21 Jun**: German fleet scuppered at Scapa Flow
• **29 Apr**: Pétain appointed chief of French general staff • **10 May**: Pershing appointed commander of American Expeditionary Forces • **15 May**: Foch appointed chief of French general staff • **4 Jun**: Brusilov appointed commander of Russian armies	• **28 Jan**: Bolsheviks found the Red Army in soviet Russia • **14 Apr**: Foch appointed commander of most Allied forces • **27 Oct**: Ludendorff resigns command • **5 Nov**: Foch given responsibility for Allied strategy	

THE
POLITICIANS'
WAR

Datafile

War broke out in 1914 after a decade of international tension. The decision to go to war was taken by a handful of men. Their understanding of the strategic situation and of the underlying power relationships was flawed. The outcome was a series of miscalculations which converted a local incident in the Balkans into a world war. Some leaders greeted war enthusiastically; but some saw they had opened a Pandora's box.

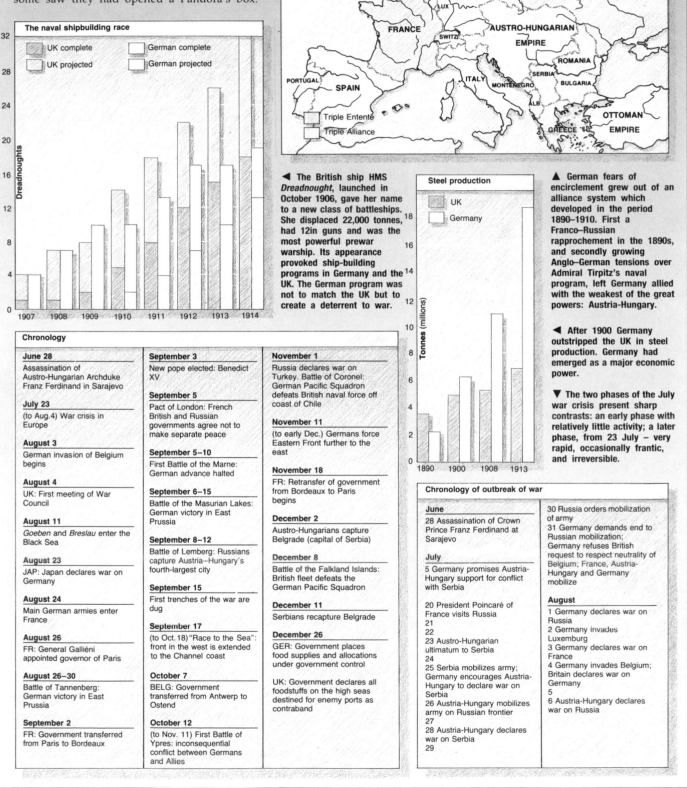

European Alliances 1914

The naval shipbuilding race

- UK complete
- UK projected
- German complete
- German projected

(bar chart, y-axis: Dreadnoughts, 0–32; x-axis: 1907 1908 1909 1910 1911 1912 1913 1914)

◄ The British ship HMS *Dreadnought*, launched in October 1906, gave her name to a new class of battleships. She displaced 22,000 tonnes, had 12in guns and was the most powerful prewar warship. Its appearance provoked ship-building programs in Germany and the UK. The German program was not to match the UK but to create a deterrent to war.

Steel production

- UK
- Germany

(bar chart, y-axis: Tonnes (millions), 0–18; x-axis: 1890 1900 1908 1913)

▲ German fears of encirclement grew out of an alliance system which developed in the period 1890–1910. First a Franco–Russian rapprochement in the 1890s, and secondly growing Anglo–German tensions over Admiral Tirpitz's naval program, left Germany allied with the weakest of the great powers: Austria-Hungary.

◄ After 1900 Germany outstripped the UK in steel production. Germany had emerged as a major economic power.

▼ The two phases of the July war crisis present sharp contrasts: an early phase with relatively little activity; a later phase, from 23 July – very rapid, occasionally frantic, and irreversible.

Chronology

June 28
Assassination of Austro-Hungarian Archduke Franz Ferdinand in Sarajevo

July 23
(to Aug.4) War crisis in Europe

August 3
German invasion of Belgium begins

August 4
UK: First meeting of War Council

August 11
Goeben and *Breslau* enter the Black Sea

August 23
JAP: Japan declares war on Germany

August 24
Main German armies enter France

August 26
FR: General Galliéni appointed governor of Paris

August 26–30
Battle of Tannenberg: German victory in East Prussia

September 2
FR: Government transferred from Paris to Bordeaux

September 3
New pope elected: Benedict XV

September 5
Pact of London: French British and Russian governments agree not to make separate peace

September 5–10
First Battle of the Marne: German advance halted

September 6–15
Battle of the Masurian Lakes: German victory in East Prussia

September 8–12
Battle of Lemberg: Russians capture Austria-Hungary's fourth-largest city

September 15
First trenches of the war are dug

September 17
(to Oct.18) "Race to the Sea": front in the west is extended to the Channel coast

October 7
BELG: Government transferred from Antwerp to Ostend

October 12
(to Nov.11) First Battle of Ypres: inconsequential conflict between Germans and Allies

November 1
Russia declares war on Turkey. Battle of Coronel: German Pacific Squadron defeats British naval force off coast of Chile

November 11
(to early Dec.) Germans force Eastern Front further to the east

November 18
FR: Retransfer of government from Bordeaux to Paris begins

December 2
Austro-Hungarians capture Belgrade (capital of Serbia)

December 8
Battle of the Falkland Islands: British fleet defeats the German Pacific Squadron

December 11
Serbians recapture Belgrade

December 26
GER: Government places food supplies and allocations under government control

UK: Government declares all foodstuffs on the high seas destined for enemy ports as contraband

Chronology of outbreak of war

June
28 Assassination of Crown Prince Franz Ferdinand at Sarajevo

July
5 Germany promises Austria-Hungary support for conflict with Serbia
20 President Poincaré of France visits Russia
21
22
23 Austro-Hungarian ultimatum to Serbia
24
25 Serbia mobilizes army; Germany encourages Austria-Hungary to declare war on Serbia
26 Austria-Hungary mobilizes army on Russian frontier
27
28 Austria-Hungary declares war on Serbia
29

30 Russia orders mobilization of army
31 Germany demands end to Russian mobilization; Germany refuses British request to respect neutrality of Belgium; France, Austria-Hungary and Germany mobilize

August
1 Germany declares war on Russia
2 Germany invades Luxemburg
3 Germany declares war on France
4 Germany invades Belgium; Britain declares war on Germany
5
6 Austria-Hungary declares war on Russia

1914 THE WAR OF ILLUSIONS

How did a local crisis turn into World War I?

Who was responsible for the escalation?

Three schools of thought and their answers

Was the war the culmination of German expansionist ambitions?

Or did Germany risk war to support Austria-Hungary?

Or should European countries collectively be blamed for failure to maintain peace?

One of the most controversial questions of 20th-century history is how did the war crisis of 1914 turn into World War I? The basic chronology is not in dispute. The crown prince of the Austro-Hungarian Empire, the Archduke Franz Ferdinand, chose to visit Sarajevo in Bosnia with his wife on 28 June 1914. Bosnia was an imperial province, but one that had only been incorporated in the Empire in 1908 (after annexation from the Turkish Empire). Most of its inhabitants were Serbs, many of whom felt more affinity with the neighboring kingdom of Serbia. The day of the crown prince's visit was St Vitus' Day: the great Serbian festival that marked the end of medieval Serbia's independence. That day in Sarajevo a handful of students, who were members of a fanatical Serbian nationalist organization, the Black Hand, tried to assassinate the couple. They missed on the first attempt, but succeeded on the second. The Austro-Hungarian response was to label the assassins puppets of Serbian intelligence, whose aim was to challenge Austro-Hungarian sovereignty over all its south-Slavic lands (which today largely form Yugoslavia). After consultations with its German allies on 5–6 July, Austria-Hungary presented Serbia with

▼ Gavrilo Princip, an 18-year-old Bosnian Serb student, was easily apprehended after firing the shots that killed the Archduke Franz Ferdinand and his wife in Sarajevo. Princip was too young to face the death sentence; he received a 20-year prison term but died of tuberculosis in an Austrian fortress near Prague in 1918.

a set of political demands – an ultimatum deliberately designed so Serbia would reject it.

Balkan conflict to international confrontation
The ultimatum was sent on 23 July. It was perceived as a challenge to the status quo in the Balkans by Russia, the protector and promoter of Slav nationalism in the region and the enemy of Austria-Hungary. With Russian backing Serbia met most of the demands, but refused to give in completely. Russia reacted quickly, and ordered a partial mobilization for 29 July.

This changed an Austro–Russian quarrel into a Russo–German one, because Russian mobilization threatened Germany. It also presented Germany with the real possibility of a two-front war, because a conflict with Russia would trigger the intervention of Russia's ally, France. German military planning had anticipated this and took for granted that, in any war against Russia, Germany would have to attack France first.

Even though the Sarajevo crisis did not concern any issue of dispute between Germany and France, German mobilization on 31 July – which was in fact decided upon before the news of the Russian mobilization reached Berlin – was linked

to a military plan that would turn a Russo-German conflict into a pan-European conflict. In this plan Germany would preempt a possible protracted war on two fronts by knocking the French army out of the conflict before Russia was able to occupy the whole of Eastern Germany. This was to be accomplished by a huge operation – based on a modified version of the famous Schlieffen Plan of 1905 – in which the German army would pass through Belgium and northern France in an enormous arc. The aims were to outflank French forces on the German–French border, sweep up the French army near Paris and then take the capital itself, or encircle it, as had been done in 1870.

◄ The "Eastern Question" in the eyes of the cartoonist of the Parisian *Petit Journal*. The reference is to 5–6 October 1908, when Bulgaria declared its independence from Turkey and Austria annexed Bosnia and Herzegovina. The first step led the following year to military conflict between Bulgaria and Turkey. The second step set up a collision course between Austria and Serbia, which vigorously opposed the annexations.

Austria-Hungary and The Balkans

On account of its explosive mixture of peoples and the interest of the great powers in the region, the Balkans was the most volatile area of prewar Europe. The great power most directly concerned was the Austro-Hungarian Empire, because its territory extended into the Balkans and many of its subject peoples belonged to ethnic groups (such as the Serbs and Romanians) who had also set up Balkan kingdoms of their own. Sprawling over a vast area of central and eastern Europe, the Austro-Hungarian Empire was a multinational entity with a population of some 50 million. The only thing that united its various nationalities was that they were subjects of the Habsburgs, one of the great European dynasties, whose chief representative in 1914 was the Emperor Franz Josef.

During his reign, from 1848, defeats by France (1859) and Prussia (1866) had virtually ended Habsburg influence in Italy and Germany, turning Austria into an east European· power. However, these reverses proved a less serious threat to the integrity of the Empire than the growing national consciousness of its various peoples. Of these the magyars (Hungarians) had been the strongest and most restive. The Habsburg solution to the Magyar problem, implemented in 1867, was to convert the Austrian Empire into the dual monarchy of Austria-Hungary. In effect the Hungarians were taken into partnership with the "Austrian" (German) element, and the Empire was divided.

This situation remained unchanged down to 1914, despite its manifest dangers. Some foresaw the eventual collapse of the Empire, but prophecies of Austria's doom were not new, and the Habsburgs had an impressive record for adaptation and survival. Some security was also provided by the alliance with Germany, signed in 1879.

The rulers of Austria-Hungary were naturally afraid that the existence of new nations such as Serbia would cause unrest among minority groups of the same language and culture who lived within the borders of the Empire. But they also entertained ambitious schemes for expansion into the Balkans, possibly in collaboration with Russia. In 1908 a mixture of expansionist and defensive motives impelled Austria-Hungary to annex Bosnia and Herzegovina, Turkish provinces which the Austrians had administered since 1878. Most of the population were Serbs, and the annexation was denounced by Serbia, with the backing of Russia; but both were forced to climb down when Germany supported Austria.

The Austrians were not the only disturbers of the Balkan status quo. Bulgaria, Serbia, Greece and Montenegro coveted the remaining Turkish territory in Europe. They joined forces and secured their various aims. But Austria and Italy intervened to prevent the establishment of an enlarged Serbia on the Adriatic; instead, Albania was created. Differences between Serbia and Bulgaria then led to a second Balkan War (June–July 1913), when an alliance of states stripped Bulgaria of territory won in the first war.

In 1914 Austro-Serbian hostility persisted and Bulgaria nursed grievances. The Balkans were already tension-ridden when, on 28 June 1914, the Archduke Franz Ferdinand was assassinated at Sarajevo in Bosnia.

▼ In Europe only Switzerland was able to create political unity out of linguistic diversity. Lacking the unifying features of geography or tradition, the Austro-Hungarian Empire presented a collage of linguistic cultures, in which nationalist aspirations were expressed. Omitted from the map is the Yiddish language, spoken by millions of Eastern European Jews.

Language Groups 1914

POLAND

GERMAN EMPIRE

Prague •
BOHEMIA
MORAVIA
Danube
Vienna •
AUSTRIA
TYROL
Lake Balaton
Trieste •
Drava
Sava

GALICIA
Lemberg •

HUNGARY
Budapest •

TRANSYLVANIA

ROMANIA

Adriatic Sea
DALMATIA
BOSNIA
Sarajevo •
HERZE-GOVINA

SERBIA

BULGARIA

ALBANIA

- Czech
- German
- Hungarian
- Italian
- Polish
- Romance
- Romanian
- Serbo-Croatian
- Slovak
- Slovenian
- Ukrainian

Scale 1 : 10 000 000

0 ——— 200 km
0 ——— 100 mi

Whatever the military implications of this plan, its political costs were profound. Schlieffen violated the central tenet of Karl von Clausewitz, that war was politics by other means. The Schlieffen Plan was based upon the assumption that German troops would cross Belgium to attack France. But the sovereignty of Belgian territory had been guaranteed by all the major powers, including Britain, in 1839. The swing through Belgium risked bringing the UK into the war. This is precisely what happened. On 4 August Britain declared war on Germany and its allies. The ensuing spiral of conflict, which had started with the murder of two Austrian nobles, ended with the deaths of 9 million men.

Why war in 1914?

By and large historians know what happened in 1914. But since virtually the end of the war they have argued about who was responsible for the escalation of a Balkan quarrel into a world war. Basically there are three schools of thought: first, the "primacy of German responsibility" approach; second, the "calculated risk" approach; and third, the "collective guilt" approach.

The primacy of German responsibility

In order to understand this argument, vigorously promoted by the Hamburg historian Fritz Fischer during the 1960s, one of the basic factors in the political equation of 1914 must first be considered.

Franz Josef 1830–1916

Franz Josef I, emperor of Austria and king of Hungary, came to the throne during the turmoil of one revolution and died on the eve of another. His early days were spent in a rigorous clerical environment, and military service in Italy during the 1848 revolution prepared him for his life-long work: the maintenance of monarchical power and the extirpation of revolution. But eventually, economic difficulties and military and diplomatic setbacks forced him to come to terms with the warring factions within the Empire, in particular Magyar nobles, but also Germans, Czechs, Poles and Slavs. In 1866–67, he recognized these claims by becoming king of Hungary and by instituting a limited constitutional system in Austria. His personal life was equally unfulfilled. His son Rudolf committed suicide in 1889, his wife was assassinated in 1897, and his heir Franz Ferdinand was of a different cast of mind.

Franz Ferdinand 1863–1914

Two untimely deaths made Franz Ferdinand, the nephew of Franz Josef I, heir to the Austro-Hungarian Empire: Crown Prince Rudolf's suicide in 1889 and the death of his father, Archduke Charles Louis, in 1896. Over the next 18 years he was given a wider role in domestic and military affairs, and took a more flexible line in considering reform than the emperor. His commitment to the monarchy was unequivocal, and he spent years in opposition to the Magyar nobles, whose aspirations, he believed, were inconsistent with the stability of the dynasty and of the Empire itself. In foreign affairs he balanced warmth toward Britain with coolness toward Italy and France. His sympathies were with the czar as a bulwark against revolution but he was an uncompromising enemy of Serbian nationalism. His visit to Sarajevo in Bosnia on the anniversary of the end of the medieval independence of Serbia was as a sworn enemy of the Serbian cause. His assassination on 28 June 1914 brought that conflict to a head, and destroyed everything for which Franz Ferdinand had worked throughout his life.

◄ The heir apparent of the Austro-Hungarian Empire, Archduke Franz Ferdinand, and his wife Sophia Chotek with their three children – the first orphans of the 1914–18 war.

In the late 19th and early 20th century no one had worked out a stable solution to the problems posed by the growth of the German Empire, problems both economic and political. When the German Empire was formed in 1871, its industrial revolution was well under way. Forty years later it was an economic and political power of the first order. But this was not enough; prodigious industrial growth had not been accompanied by a commensurate expansion in its sphere of influence in world affairs. There was thus an imbalance between the distribution of the economic and international political power of European states.

By 1900 Germany's leaders and many influential political groups refused to tolerate this situation indefinitely. It also was an important source of the growing antagonism between Germany and Britain in the prewar period as well as a key to German policy in the July 1914 crisis itself.

This is the context in which to place three sets of critical events that weigh heavily in the accounts of those who emphasize German responsibility for the war. The first is a plan fostered by Admiral Alfred von Tirpitz to strengthen the German high seas fleet to a level that would enable it to challenge British naval supremacy. The second is the increasing strength of the German army, underwritten by two smaller army bills in 1911 and 1912 and a third large one in 1913. The third is the evidence of belligerence and the acceptance of the likelihood of war among Germany's military elite at a "war council" summoned by Kaiser Wilhelm II on 8 December 1912. There is controversy over the importance of this last event in the road to war. Fischer places great weight on it; others do not. But in fairness to all opinions, the issues involved will be presented and then assessed.

▲ Otto von Bismarck, architect of the German Empire founded in 1871. After he resigned as chancellor in 1890, lesser men failed to control the system of power relations which in large part had been Bismarck's legacy.

Theobald von Bethmann-Hollweg 1856–1921

Descended from prosperous Frankfurt bankers, Bethmann-Hollweg became chancellor of Germany in 1909. He was only moderately successful in mediating between competing factions in domestic policy in the prewar period, but more adroit in convincing the German nation that it was fighting a defensive war in 1914. He adopted a fatalistic pose in the war crisis, but played a crucial part in presenting the military with the best possible political conditions for the waging of war. He tried to float several peace initiatives during the war, but the German high command never let them get out of hand. By 1917 he had lost the support of all political groups, and his dismissal was demanded by Hindenburg and Ludendorff. The Kaiser concurred and he retired in July 1917.

▲ The Krupp family dynasty created an industrial empire based on the production of steel and armaments. Founded in the early 19th century, the Krupp works employed 10,000 men in the 1860s, and owned coal and iron mines. In 1902 the firm acquired the "Germania" shipbuilding yards in Kiel, and provided steel plate for the German navy. During the war, it produced artillery, including "Big Bertha", the heavy gun that bombarded Paris.

◀▼ The German fleet created under Admiral Alfred von Tirpitz (left) was intended to deter any of Germany's rivals from going to war with it. The fleet was, therefore, a monumental failure.

The Rise of Germany

On the eve of World War I the German Empire was the youngest as well as the strongest of the great European powers. Its creator was Otto von Bismarck, chief minister of Prussia from 1862, whose foreign policy culminated in a double triumph: Prussia's victory over France in the war of 1870–71 and the proclamation of the king of Prussia as emperor or Kaiser of a united Germany (1871). Twenty-five German states came together to form the new *Reich*, which was designed as a federation; but Prussia was easily the largest and most powerful of the states.

Between 1870 and 1914 Germany underwent a rapid industrial revolution and its population soared to almost 65 million. As early as the 1880s its iron and steel industries were challenging Britain's, and new chemical and electrical industries were growing. Under Bismarck's guidance the state intervened to protect and encourage German industries, and set up a system of technical education that gave Germans a deserved reputation for workmanship and expertise.

The two faces of Prussian paternalism were in evidence during Bismarck's regime. He made protracted and ultimately unsuccessful efforts to control the Catholic Church and, later, to suppress the socialists (social democrats); but he also introduced "state socialism" – old age pensions and schemes for sickness and accident insurance. They were bold steps for a conservative regime. Even so, by 1914 the social democrats were the largest single party in the Reichstag.

After 1871 Bismarck made security rather than expansion his objective. In particular he aimed to keep France diplomatically isolated so that it would be in no position to fight a war to avenge the defeat of 1870–71 and recover the lost provinces of Alsace and Lorraine. Bismarck chose Austria-Hungary as Germany's principal ally (1879); later (1882) Italy was brought in to form the Triple Alliance. But Bismarck also cultivated Russia, seeking to smooth over Russo–Austrian differences and maintain a "Three Emperors' League" based on a common conservatism. German relations with Britain were more uncertain, since in the 1880s Germany began to take part in "the scramble for Africa", acquiring an empire there and in the Pacific. Ironically, in colonial affairs Bismarck and his successors found themselves collaborating with the French in opposition to Britain.

Significant changes followed the accession of Wilhelm II as German emperor in 1888. Wilful and impulsive, the Kaiser forced Bismarck to resign (1890) and took a prominent role in policy-making; he also made frequent statements that offended public opinion in other countries and reinforced the impression that Germany was an aggressive, warlike power. Russia became steadily alienated from Germany; and the great program of German naval building inaugurated in 1898 was seen as a threat by Britain. Inept German diplomacy was largely responsible for the formation of a French-Russian-British "Triple Entente", which intensified German fears of "encirclement". The decision to go to war was in part taken to end that encirclement and bring Germany the geopolitical power it deserved.

Wilhelm II 1859–1941

Wilhelm II ascended to the Hohenzollern throne in 1888. The young Kaiser had had a liberal education, as well as the requisite years of discipline in the regiment of guards and among the Prussian officer corps in Potsdam. He shared with them the view that Germany's place in world affairs required a strengthened military and naval arm, and an authoritarian regime to run domestic affairs. The strength of his personality and emotional temperament made it inevitable that he would find it difficult to work with Otto von Bismarck, the architect of his power and prestige. In dismissing Bismarck in 1890, Wilhelm opened the field to politicians who could not control the international system Bismarck had created. The "war council" called by the Kaiser with his military advisers in December 1912 shows that he was not averse to a general European war; his attitude in the war crisis itself was more equivocal. His chief influence after 1914 was in his choice of the men who would run the war effort. Their failure required his abdication as a condition of the Armistice. He fled to Holland, and was interned there at Doorn.

The Tirpitz Plan, sketched out between 1898 and 1900, formed the basis of an ambitious program of shipbuilding in the subsequent decade and a half. Its aim was political: to provide the German Empire with a weapon to wrest its fair share of imperial power from the hands of the British. Precisely what territorial gains Tirpitz and his followers had in mind is unclear, but there is no doubt about their determination to increase Germany's armaments and thereby to provide the German Empire with greater leverage in world affairs.

According to this interpretation, the German high command precipitated countermeasures – in particular, the arms race between Britain and Germany – for which Tirpitz and his circle, backed by a large number of nonsocialist Germans, were primarily responsible. The British reacted by effectively joining the Franco-Russian military alliance in 1904, which was interpreted in Germany as an act of encirclement. Thus Germany was not forced into a defensive war but acted throughout the prewar period in an aggressive manner, intending to break out of the "containment" of her empire.

It has been argued that this set of political objectives was made explicit in an extraordinary meeting called by the Kaiser on 8 December 1912, in response to a conversation between the German ambassador in London and the British minister of war, Lord Haldane. Haldane was reported to have said that, in the event of war, his government would not tolerate a French military defeat by Germany and would not stand idly by if Austria-Hungary attacked Serbia. The Kaiser's response was to call a meeting of his military – but not his political – advisers. This meeting debated the merits of going to war then and there, which was apparently favored by the chief of the imperial general staff, Helmuth von Moltke. Instead, it was agreed to play a waiting game, as advocated by Tirpitz, and put off any decision for a further 18 months, until military and naval preparations would be completed, in particular the widening of the Kiel Canal which would enable Germany's biggest ships to move from the Baltic to the North Sea.

Eighteen months from December 1912 brings us to the summer of 1914. In the light of German ambitions, Fritz Fischer and his supporters have concluded that well before the war Germany deliberately set out on a collision course with Russia and France, and was thereafter preparing for a major war.

All it required was an auspicious opportunity to utilize its military power. That occasion was presented by the Sarajevo murders of 28 June 1914. Far from defusing the situation, the Kaiser and his advisors decided to exploit it as part of their own carefully constructed long-term military and political strategy. For these reasons they must bear primary responsibility for the outbreak of the 1914 war. The events between the war council of December 1912 and the summer of 1914 had merely made them all the more determined to use the July crisis as the golden opportunity to achieve a major breakthrough, by military means, to world power status.

The "calculated risk" interpretation

Fischer's interpretation has been challenged. One set of qualifications can be summarized under the heading of the "calculated risk". According to this argument a distinction must be made between German policy in early July, when it was a matter of providing political support for Austria-Hungary in its quarrel with Serbia, and German policy in late July and early August, when the Balkan crisis turned into the world war. Most historians agree with Fischer and his school about the last days of peace: at this point the German military pressed for war and resisted all suggestions that they might pull back from the brink. But in early July, Fischer's critics believe, the German strategy was indeed to pursue the conflict, but to *contain* it within the Balkans. Germany's hope was to give Austria the opportunity to punish Serbia swiftly and thereby to present Russia, Britain and France with a resolved problem, which they would not challenge by going to war for Serbia. Austria-Hungary and its ally Germany, finding themselves increasingly isolated and with their international position deteriorating, would have won a major diplomatic victory. The ramshackle Habsburg Empire would have been propped up.

This argument holds, therefore, that Germany's political and military leaders tried to play a dangerous – but calculated – game, which simply got out of hand. They miscalculated the responses of each of their potential adversaries abroad and underestimated the momentum toward a general war that the Balkan crisis provided. The war was not an outcome of long-term strategy; it was a monumental failure of foreign policy.

Fischer would be fundamentally skeptical of this interpretation. There is controversy too over whether the outlook of the German military elite differed from that of its political leadership. Fischer believes that it is impossible to distinguish between the two. But those who subscribe to the "calculated risk" school think otherwise. They reject any suggestion of a *concerted* design by the German military and political elite to precipitate a major European war. Instead they suggest that when, by 25 July, it became clear that the limited strategy had failed and the war crisis had got out of hand, the German chancellor, Theobald von Bethmann-Hollweg, was defeated by the German military who now pushed for a major war. He saw it as his purpose to provide Germany with the best possible political conditions in which to wage war. This *required* that Russian mobilization should be seen to be the cause of German mobilization, and that consequently Germany's decision to go to war should be considered a *defensive* one. Such an argument was, he believed, essential to ensure the support of the mass of the German population – including the large socialist party – for the decision to go to war.

In the light of all the documentation available today, we can dismiss the claim that Germany was pushed by Russia into a defensive war in 1914. But this is not to say – as Fischer and his camp argue – that there is a clear and long-term line in German foreign policy leading to a general

► The signatures of Palmerston for Britain and Bülow for Germany on the 1839 Treaty guaranteeing Belgian independence were visible proof for British propaganda and public alike that the war against Germany was a just one.

▼ ► Europe's civil war in 1914–18 was also a war within European royal families, which were related through marriage. The interlocking of European royalty in the late 19th century is captured in this photograph which includes Wilhelm II and Nicholas II (numbers 2 and 3 in the key) in the family party surrounding Queen Victoria of the UK (1) at Baden-Baden in Germany.

European war. The bywords of this interpretation of the war crisis are incompetence and mismanagement rather than deliberate design.

This second line of argument has been extended in recent years by what may be termed the "primacy of domestic politics" approach. The key to this view is that the men who made foreign policy were also acutely aware of the threat to the existing monarchical system posed by a growing socialist movement, especially (but not only) in Germany. Some leaders may therefore have felt that a victorious war would unify the nation and close the increasingly ominous gap between the classes. This provides further information as to why certain leaders were willing to take the calculated risk and, when pushed, to go to the brink of war and beyond.

As might be expected, this revised view provoked fresh controversy, with its critics arguing that it presents too simple and conspiratorial a vision of foreign policy as being no more than a diversionary tactic. Of course political leaders were conscious of domestic tensions and of the possible effect of their actions on them. But the links between foreign policy and domestic policy are rarely clear or direct.

Those who emphasize the domestic origins of foreign policy have provided a real service in broadening the study of the origins of the war from a purely diplomatic level. It is important to place foreign policy in a wider political framework and to look at its interaction with domestic affairs. The difficulty is in moving from a general background of events to the specific links between one sphere of politics and another: the domestic origins approach is a useful addition to other interpretations, not an alternative to them.

Collective guilt

One way of interpreting the different schools of thought on the origins of World War I is to see them as asking different kinds of questions and therefore as emphasizing different kinds of evidence. Fischer's school uses primarily diplomatic and military evidence to trace the evolution of German imperialist ambitions. The "calculated risk" school exploits similar sources, but also explores questions of social history and class conflict. A third line of argument stresses the usefulness of understanding intellectual history and the climate of opinion in the analysis of both the war crisis of 1914 and the first phase of the conflict – the war of illusions. This approach has been pioneered by the British historian James Joll, who has pointed out the "unspoken assumptions" of both leaders and masses in 1914. Thus some scholars have moved beyond the field of German foreign policy to suggest that a more universal set of miscalculations and mistakes contributed to both the atmosphere in which the war crisis developed and its ultimate resolution in war. In this school of thought German belligerence is not excused, but rather it assumes an integral part in a wider European failure to keep the peace.

This interpretation rests upon a substantial body of evidence as to the pervasive unreality of perceptions, expectations and predictions that

▲ These wreath-layers are mourning the assassination of Jean Jaurès, the French socialist leader, on 31 July 1914 in Paris, a murder which robbed France and the international socialist movement, of their most eloquent leader. The voice of Jaurès was that of a moralist, denouncing capitalism as an outrage against human decency and fraternity. The founder-editor of the socialist newspaper *L'Humanité*, Jaurès spoke out fervently in a language which was both patriotic and internationalist. He was the author of a study of popular defense, *The New Army*, and the central figure in futile attempts to mobilize the socialist Second International against war in 1914.

Thus it comes that all nations attempting to live by conquest end by being themselves the victims of a military tyranny precisely similar to that which they hope to inflict; or, in other terms, that the attempt to impose by force of arms a disadvantageous commercial situation to the advantage of the conqueror ends in the conqueror's falling a victim to the very disadvantages from which he hoped by a process of spoilation to profit.

NORMAN ANGELL, 1910

characterized the judgment of *all* the major political leaders of the European powers and of public opinion, both during the growing crisis of 1912–14 and in the first six months of war.

Those who advance this argument accept that the growth of German power made international politics inherently unstable in the prewar period. But they assert that structures do not go to war; individual states do so on the advice of their leaders, who, in turn, are pushed on by nationalist and militaristic lobbies. Hence they base their view of the crisis on an analysis of how international affairs were perceived by key political figures in all the major powers of Europe.

Scholars who believe in collective responsibility for the outbreak of war stress the limitations of the argument (endorsed by the Versailles peace treaty) that Germany was exclusively to blame for the outbreak of war. They admit that German support for Austria was crucial in the escalation of hostilities described above. But the other actors in this drama, they assert, also bear a degree of responsibility for the growing tensions and ultimately the transformation of a Balkan conflict into a world war, largely because so many of the key decisions they made in 1914 were based on misperceptions, miscalculations and illusions as well as on power-politics and imperialism.

Illusions about war

Such illusions were of many kinds and were shared by many politicians and other people in all the warring nations. Of all the illusions of 1914, five stand out: first, the illusion that since war involved domestic risks, both political and economic, relatively unstable regimes would avoid it; second, the illusion of the fail-safe and rational character of diplomacy; third, the illusion that any war would not be long; fourth, the illusion that war could be controlled and limited; fifth, the illusion that war could be a means of rebirth and rejuvenation.

The Third Republic in France

By 1914 the French Third Republic had been in existence for 43 years – far longer than any previous system of government in France since the Revolution of 1789. For much of its history there had been bitter political strife; yet, against all odds, the Republic had survived. And as a result of its unexpected durability, France had been able to recover from the defeat by Prussia in 1870–71 and to become a great power again. By the standards of the period, republican France was an advanced democracy in which all adult males were entitled to vote. But no political party ever won a majority of seats in the chamber of deputies, so that each new government had to be based on a fragile coalition, and prime ministers rarely held office for more than a few months.

The Republic faced its greatest internal crisis over the Dreyfus affair, which began in 1894 with the conviction for treason of a Jewish army officer. Attempts to prove Dreyfus innocent were frustrated by the army's general staff. Heightened by antisemitism, "the Affair" developed into a political confrontation between the parties committed to the Republic and the reactionary forces hostile to it – the army, the Church and the royalists. Dreyfus was eventually rehabilitated in 1906. It was a triumph for republicanism, but the Affair left bitter memories.

The early years of the 20th century brought new dissensions. Animosity between Church and State culminated in complete separation between the two. As gradual industrialization swelled the ranks of the working class, the Left became a force in French politics, and militant trade unionism challenged the established social order. But from about 1905 there was also a striking revival of right-wing and extreme nationalist feeling.

Meanwhile, French governments had worked since 1871 to improve the country's international standing. France followed the German example by introducing universal education and mass conscription. Frenchmen continued to resent the defeat of 1870 and the loss of Alsace-Lorraine to Germany, but dreams of a war of revenge faded as Germany forged ahead in industrial development and population. Partly in compensation, France turned to colonial expansion, mainly in Africa and Indo-China. In quest of security in Europe, France made an alliance with Russia (1894) and, formed an understanding, or "Entente", with the UK (1904).

In the last years of peace the French took a firmer line against Germany. Internal antagonisms persisted, however, and in 1913 a bill to extend military service to three years was fiercely resisted by the antimilitarist Left. But antimilitarism evaporated as soon as war was declared, and a united France prepared to face the enemy. In doing so, the population of France became fully Republican for the first time. The war had indeed created a political culture which was to last until 1940 and be reborn in 1944.

▶ The trial of Captain Dreyfus, 1894.

Raymond Poincaré 1850–1934

President of France throughout the 1914–18 war, Poincaré had a long and varied political career behind him. He served in various ministries in the 1890s, and became prime minister and minister of foreign affairs in 1912. During this period he introduced proportional representation and guided France through the Agadir crisis with Germany. The following year he was elected president, a post he held for seven years. In 1914 he learned of the Austrian ultimatum to Serbia while travelling home after a state visit to Russia. During the war he stood back while others ran the war. In the peace negotiations after the Armistice, Poincaré counted for little. He retired from the presidency in 1920, but reentered politics as a senator from the Department of the Meuse, where he had been born and raised. In January 1922 he once more became prime minister, and presided over the French occupation of the Ruhr, following Germany's failure to pay reparations. He formed three more coalition governments in the 1920s and died in 1934.

René Viviani 1863–1925

Algerian-born, Viviani was first elected as a socialist deputy for Paris in 1893. In 1906 he became minister of labor in Clemenceau's ministry, but created more of a stir by the clear enunciation of his nonreligious beliefs. By 1914 he had also served as minister of foreign affairs. In June 1914 he became premier. On the outbreak of war his oratory lifted the nation. He accompanied the government to Bordeaux in September 1914, and returned in December. In 1915 he made way as premier for Aristide Briand, and served as minister of justice. He shared the fate of all French politicians – with the exception of Clemenceau – of acting more as a figurehead than a formulator of policy during the war.

The first illusion was that a general European war would not break out since it was not worth the risk to the fragile political cohesion of several regimes. This belief may have prevented some politicians from acting to stop the spread of the conflict until it was too late. In economic terms, many people argued that the idea of war between the great powers was an absurdity, since no one in power stood the slightest chance of making any gain worth the required risk. Before the war, others had stated that a general European war had become an economic impossibility. Many of the world's bankers concurred; to them war would lead to international financial collapse and for Britain bankruptcy, as, in a way, it did. In 1911 the English author Norman Angell had published *The Great Illusion,* which argued that no one profited from war. In the midst of the war crisis Sir Edward Grey, British foreign secretary, predicted that bread queues would form in Britain by Christmas. To many people, then, a decision to go to war on a grand scale was economically irrational and out of the question.

Equally it seemed to make no political sense. The argument was raised that the so-called "Eastern Question" – what to do about the chronic instability of the region contested by Turkey, Austria and Russia – was a perennial political headache rather than a real threat to the peace of Europe; after all, numerous crises – in the Balkans and elsewhere – had come and gone in the two decades before 1914. Why should the assassination in Sarajevo lead to trouble when other explosive incidents had been defused? Furthermore, they pointed out that most of the crowned heads of Europe were related to each other and shared certain clearly conservative aspirations that could be compromised by war. Few monarchists needed a reminder that at the Stuttgart conference of 1907 the socialist parties affiliated to the Socialist International had committed themselves to taking all necessary steps to stop the outbreak of war. This would not rule out a general strike which could lead to revolution. Armed conflict therefore involved real internal risks for all European powers. In Germany the social democratic party, since 1912 the largest single party in the Reichstag (the German parliament), was committed to the eventual takeover of the state; who in his right mind would present them with the chance to achieve their ambition? The threat of industrial unrest was apparent in Italy in May 1914, when some of the worst strikes in history took place. Armies might be infected with dissent: who was rash enough to believe in the loyalty of the many nationalities who served in the armies of the Austro-Hungarian and Russian Empires? Some regimes were thought to be particularly vulnerable. After 1905 the Russian monarchy was regarded as particularly unstable.

In France and Britain it was doubted that there would be sufficient popular support for a decision to go to war. In France memories of the Dreyfus affair (1894–1906) were still very fresh. This controversy, over the false imprisonment of a Jewish officer on trumped-up charges of espionage, and the subsequent military cover-up had split the French nation. Supporters of the army and supporters of "justice and the people" had grown dangerously apart, at a time of growing socialist agitation. For many reasons, therefore, lists were prepared of troublemakers to be arrested in the event of war (known as the *Carnet B*). In Britain realistic doubts about the army's willingness to enforce Home Rule in Ireland (demonstrated in the so-called Curragh mutiny) posed questions about its general loyalty.

If this first set of opinions – that cautious people would avoid war because it was a Pandora's box – was clearly mistaken, then scholars who argue for collective responsibility for the outbreak of the 1914 war suggest that we must look elsewhere for the true reasons for the outbreak of war. Effectively they pose two questions. Why did all the Great Powers take the risk of war in the summer of 1914? And why, when their individual and collective bluff was called, did they actually go to war? Many clues, they note, may be found in other illusions of the men in power in 1914, as they operated against the background of years of nationalist and militarist agitation.

The Russian Empire

In 1914 Czar Nicholas II reigned over a vast, backward, multinational empire that stretched from Poland to the Caucasus, Central Asia and Siberia. Nicholas was an autocrat whose regime relied on a brutal if inefficient system of repression. Prison, exile and death were meted out to dissidents. Intense efforts were made to impose the Russian language and culture on all the czar's subjects, and from the 1880s, as opposition mounted, popular antisemitism was encouraged as a safety valve for discontent; widespread pogroms shocked the civilized world and persuaded hundreds of thousands of Russian Jews to emigrate, mainly to the USA. Inevitably, liberal-minded people everywhere looked on czarist Russia with distaste – yet the two most progressive great powers, France and the UK, made alliances with the czar.

The czar's subjects numbered about 150 million, of whom the overwhelming majority were peasants. Nevertheless, great changes were taking place in Russia. Industrialization had made rapid headway and there had been a dramatic increase in the reach of the railway network. Above all the growth of an industrial, urban working class transformed the political situation. Densely concentrated, badly paid and badly treated, it promised to become a highly effective force in the struggle against the autocracy. Trade unionism gathered strength and socialist ideas exercised a wide influence, even though most of the socialist leaders were imprisoned or living in exile abroad.

The autocracy remained unmoved until 1904–05, when Russian expansion in the Far East led to a war against the rising power of Japan. Humiliating reverses on land and sea discredited the regime, and "Bloody Sunday" – a massacre of peaceful demonstrators bound for the Winter Palace – dealt the czar's reputation as the "Little Father" of his people a blow from which it never recovered. Strikes, mutinies and disorders in town and country

paralyzed the government, and Nicholas had to grant a constitution and set up a "parliament", the Duma. However, these concessions enabled the czar to ride out and eventually destroy the 1905 Revolution: nothing survived but an emasculated Duma.

For a few years the autocracy seemed to be in the ascendant. But from 1912 strikes and disturbances became ever more frequent, while the rural order became destabilized by an ambitious attempt to create a new class of capitalist farmers. War came into this threatening situation when the long Balkan rivalry between Austria-Hungary and Russia, exacerbated by Russian disquiet at German influence in Turkey, produced a crisis that found neither side ready to back down. Yet Russia in 1914 was ill-prepared for war and industrially far behind its allies and enemies.

Military reversals in Galicia led to the entry of civilians, including representatives of the Duma, into the administration of the war economy. But the czar resisted calls for a coalition government, along British and French lines, to control munitions production and rally public support for the war. In September 1915 he prorogued the Duma and dismissed all liberal cabinet members in favor of coalition government. While the czar took up his post of commander in chief of his armies, the czarina commanded the court, filled with sycophants, charlatans, and religious fanatics, and stood in the path of any political reform, any hint of which was drowned out by a thunder of reactionary piety. Even the assassination of Rasputin did not deflect the czarina from placing every obstacle in the path of change. The meeting of the Duma was postponed again and again; when it was convened in February 1917, disturbances broke out in Petrograd, and soldiers refused to put them down. This was the beginning of the revolution which would put an end to the monarchy and to a war which brought Russia nothing but disaster.

The volatility of international politics

This is the place to consider the second illusion: that war could be avoided by traditional diplomatic gambits, which were based on rational and cool assessment of national interest. This illusion suffered from two flaws. The first was that the international political system in the years before 1914 was more volatile than anyone had realized. In the hands of a man like Otto von Bismarck, the founder and first chancellor of the German Empire, diplomacy was a game of chess played by a grandmaster. His aim had been to isolate France and never to allow Germany to be isolated from three of the Great Powers, with the support of only one other major nation. Since gaming images abound in studies of international relations, it may not be too fanciful to suggest that after Bismarck left the scene in 1890, world politics moved from the realm of chess to that of roulette or poker. The stakes were higher, the skill and intelligence of the players were less important than their nerve and their luck, and the outcome of events was far less predictable.

Any system of international affairs that relied on the skill of one major figure to keep it from falling apart was bound to collapse sooner or later. But the fact that it did so in 1914 is related to another feature of the war crisis, which is an area of much controversy. Some historians believe that the diplomats of 1914 saw perfectly well what they were doing. But others state that they failed to see until it was too late how dangerous a game they were playing. Furthermore – and this is the second flaw in the argument for "rational" diplomancy as a bulwark against war – they shared a tendency to miscalculate the intentions of both allies and adversaries. It is true, scholars in this tradition note, that some politicians in Vienna saw a short Balkan war as part of a wider scheme, and on 5 July Germany did offer its ally support for action against Serbia. But they also argue that, whatever was in the minds of the German military or of their political supporters, a general European war was not the objective of the diplomatic maneuvering of the major powers in 1914. That this happened anyway was because those in power did not adequately understand their adversaries' minds or likely responses.

This argument has already appeared in considering the approach of the "calculated risk" interpretation of the war crisis. But what the "collective guilt" school of thought suggests is that the failure of crisis management was general rather than specifically or primarily German. For example, there was insufficient appreciation in several European capitals of the dynamic potential of public opinion. As a result of the formation of a wide array of political groups working for imperial glory or increased armaments expenditure or the "mission" of the nation, the pressures on the international system had grown ominously in the prewar decades. Patriotic leagues were manipulated by politicians, but public opinion once aroused was difficult to ignore. It could be "turned on" – but not so easily "turned off". Consequently "rational" games in international politics had become more difficult to manage, as those in power in 1914 recognized belatedly.

The "collective guilt" school suggests a powerful image of international affairs: that of an outmoded but still intact roulette table at which a handful of old men staked empires and literally millions of lives. This indicates something of the character of the war crisis of 1914. But once the "game" was over, and war had begun, new illusions began to crowd out the old.

Belief in swift and decisive warfare

The third illusion was that any war would be short: in 1914 men went to war believing it would be over by Christmas. This illusion was a consequence of the military training of conscript armies in the prewar period. All had been versed in a war of movement which would lead to decisive victory. Something resembling this kind of warfare occurred in the east, but nothing of the kind occurred on the Western Front. Without a quick victory on the Western Front, the dream of a short war evaporated.

With it went the fourth illusion of the first months of war: that conflict was a kind of local

◄ The symbol of the corruption of the Romanov court was Gregory Rasputin, pictured here with a group of female admirers. His name means "the debauched one", and despite a poor background and no education, he managed to live up to it in the highest circles in the land. "Sin in order that you may obtain forgiveness" was Rasputin's message, proclaimed with a passion which converted lechery into a pietistic act. In 1907 he was presented at court, and made a deep impression on the czar and czarina, and became a power in church and court circles in the next decade. He was murdered in 1916 by his court enemies, but the empress built a chapel to his memory and worshiped at his grave.

◄ Nicholas II was the perfect illustration of the central defect of absolute monarchies: their tendency, through the accident of birth, to place men without the ability or the desire to lead in a position of authority they neither sought nor could spurn. The czar of Russia, shown here with his second daughter Tatiana, the young czarevitch (heir to the throne) Alexei, and Prince Nikita in 1916, was a shy and awkward man, who longed for the peace of family life which he would never know. His son Alexei was a hemophiliac, whose perilous situation turned the czar (and even more emphatically, the czarina) to the help of "holy men" like Rasputin. The czar's natural tendency was to look back to the remote and religious past for guidance in his attitude to contemporary developments. The temperaments of the czar and czarina thus presented reactionaries with a splendid weapon to foil reform. After revolution and abdication, Nicholas and his family were murdered by revolutionaries in July 1918.

surgery – painful, no doubt, to those at the cutting edge of war, but unlikely to disturb the health or life of the nation as a whole. Indeed there were many who argued precisely the opposite, along the lines of the fifth illusion: that war was a redemptive event, able to tear millions from their petty preoccupations, and give a new sense of direction to the nation.

In 1914 this did seem to have occurred. The so-called "subversives" on the French police lists could not be arrested in August 1914 because most had joined the army. The rhetoric of the Socialist International vanished in a puff of smoke, with socialist deputies in the German Reichstag voting for war credits. Protestant and Catholic Irishmen volunteered by the thousand.

But this remarkable moment of social solidarity was also partly an illusion. Class collaboration did not destroy class conflict in 1914. It masked it for a time, but only for a time, and when it returned it showed that perhaps the most profound illusion of the early days of the 1914–18 conflict was the belief in the unifying effects of war.

Toward a synthesis

One of the least satisfying aspects of the acrimonious debate over the war crisis of 1914 is that historians refuse to see that there are merits in all three interpretations. In a sense they must be combined to get a full sense of the causes of the war. Fischer is indisputably correct in asserting the imperialist ambitions of the German leadership in the prewar period. The "calculated risk" school is also justified in distinguishing the different phases of the war crisis. And the "collective guilt" argument presents powerful reasons to indict the leaders of other countries for a general failure to protect the peace of Europe. Perhaps the best way to fuse these arguments is to speak of levels of responsibility.

At the heart of the war crisis was the political and military leadership of Germany, and in its wake, that of Austria-Hungary. Given the structure of the German political system, the chancellor, Bethmann-Hollweg, was under great pressure from the military. He tried to appear to be a peacemaker while helping to create favorable conditions for a German declaration of war. What Bethmann-Hollweg did was to present Germany's case in the best possible light, as a defensive war not of its making. The fact that this is not corroborated by the documents that are now available means that primary responsibility for war must rest in Berlin and nowhere else.

Recently published research on all major European countries has established that the war was not planned nor fostered in any countries other than Germany and Austria-Hungary. Without German ambitions and without the joint German-Austrian handling of the July crisis, war would not have broken out.

But to argue that responsibility for the war crisis and war ends there is short-sighted and misleading, for it acquits the leaders of the other European countries of secondary responsibility for war. On the one hand, somebody had to pull the trigger. That was Germany. But on the other hand, its actions exposed the weaknesses and

confusions of both its allies and its adversaries. Their collective illusions about war may help to explain why greater and more effective efforts were not made to defuse the conflict.

The other European states must bear some responsibility for the war, first, because of their false and incomplete appreciation of the nature of international affairs in an age of imperialist designs and mass politics; and secondly, because of their fateful miscalculations of the likely responses of their adversaries to their own policy initiatives. If Germany may be said to have brought about World War I, it did so as part of a political community which collectively let the peace of Europe slip through its fingers.

Sir Edward Grey   1862–1933

Educated at Winchester and Oxford, Sir Edward Grey entered the House of Commons as a Liberal at the age of 23. he served as a junior minister in Liberal ministries in 1892–95, and became a foreign minister in 1905. His real test came in the war crisis of 1914. He saw immediately in the Austrian ultimatum to Serbia the potential for a general war, and tried various schemes of conciliation and mediation. All failed. What troubled his conscience in later years was whether he had made British policy sufficiently clear. The nagging doubt remained that caution and diplomatic language had been the wrong choice; bluntness and threats were the only way to derail the war party in Germany. Grey's education and temperament suited him to uphold the principles of honor and decency, exemplified by the defense of Belgium, but they did not enable him to prevent a war waged by more ruthless men. He resigned in 1916 due to failing eyesight. His departure from the foreign office after 11 years as foreign minister symbolized the end of an era, and perhaps the end of Liberalism itself.

The United Kingdom

◄ George V began the war as head of the House of Saxe-Coburg-Gotha, or the house of Hannover or Brunswick, and ended it as head of the House of Windsor. The severing of symbolic ties with German royalty was one way to support the war effort. Another was as confidant of General Haig, commander in chief of the British Expeditionary Force in France.

▲ After two elections in 1910, a Home Rule bill for Ireland was introduced by the ruling Liberal government. The bill was passed twice by the House of Commons and rejected by the House of Lords. In 1914 the Liberals introduced a compromise whereby the six provinces in the north of Ireland with a Protestant majority had the right to opt out of home rule for six years. The Home Rule bill passed for the third time on 26 May 1914, and under the Parliament Act of 1911 it was no longer subject to veto by the Lords. The measure became law on 18 September 1914, but its operation was suspended for the duration of the war. In fact it was a casualty of the war.

In 1914 the United Kingdom of Great Britain and Ireland appeared to be at the height of its power. A worldwide empire covered a fifth of the land surface of the globe. A vast network of imperial trade and comunications was sustained by a supremely powerful navy and merchant marine. Economically Britain continued to be highly productive, although its industrial structure was beginning to look a little old-fashioned by comparison with the dynamic economies of the USA and Germany. But its position in international trade was second to none; the City of London was the world's greatest money market; and Britain's prosperity seemed further assured by the immense volume of its investments abroad in both its imperial possessions and the USA.

Most Britons were proud of their institutions, including the "Mother of Parliaments" at Westminster, despite the fact that most men and all women were still without the right to vote. The two main parties were the Liberals and Conservatives, not yet seriously threatened by the Labour Party, which had been represented in Parliament only since 1906. By 1914 the Liberals had been in office for eight years; the period had been one of significant social reforms, including the introduction of old age pensions and, for some groups of workers, of national insurance against sickness and unemployment.

Yet early 20th-century Britain was beset by social conflict. In 1909 the House of Lords rejected Lloyd George's "People's Budget", mainly because it included a capital gains tax on landed property; after two bitter elections, the Lords were forced to consent to the Parliament Act of 1911, abolishing their absolute veto on legislation. Social unrest threatened for a time when an epidemic of strikes broke out in 1910–12, but ideas of direct union action to overthrow capitalism were never put to the test. By contrast, a determined suffragette campaign to win votes for women went over to often sensational militant action, and British society was shocked by the sight of respectable ladies being sent to prison and, when they went on hunger strike, forcibly fed.

The most serious problem concerned Ireland. Since 1885 the Liberals had been pledged to meet the demands of the majority of Irishmen by introducing a Home Rule Bill. This was fiercely opposed by the Conservatives, who encouraged the Protestant Ulstermen to arm and, if necessary, resist by force any attempt to incorporate them into a self-governing Ireland with a Catholic majority. In 1914, when the Home Rule Act finally reached the statute book, civil war in Ireland seemed possible. It even looked as if senior army officers might be unwilling to enforce the Act. But the war crisis buried the Act before it came into force.

In foreign affairs the UK had formed the "entente cordiale" with France in 1904 and had resolved many differences with Russia in 1907. By 1914 military and naval cooperation with France had become routine. The British fleet was concentrated in the Atlantic, leaving the French to guard the Mediterranean; and army reforms had created a highly trained force ready for service on the continent.

But in 1914 war was not seen as imminent. Relations with Germany were better than they had been for some time, and even after the Sarajevo assassinations the British foreign secretary, Sir Edward Grey, believed that the Austro–Serbian dispute could be settled by an international conference in London. The German invasion of Belgium ended British neutrality, and opened a war which, even in victory, impoverished the UK and marked the beginning of its decline to a second-rank power.

Herbert Henry Asquith 1852–1928

The son of a Yorkshire cloth manufacturer, H.H. Asquith moved south after his father's death and had a brilliant career at Oxford University. He was an accomplished barrister, who easily moved from the courtroom to the cabinet room. His first post was home secretary in W.E. Gladstone's government in 1892. In the following decade he championed first Liberal imperialism and then free trade. The latter issue brought the Liberals to power in 1906, and made Asquith chancellor of the exchequer. Two years later he succeeded Henry Campbell-Bannerman as prime minister. He presided over the most spectacular program of social reform in 20th-century British history.

His cabinet ran the war until May 1915, when, after serious problems of munitions supply and disputes over the Gallipoli invasion, he formed a coalition government. This arrangement undermined Asquith's position: he received all the criticism for mistakes and his chancellor of the exchequer, Lloyd George, all the credit for successes. In December 1916 Lloyd George ousted Asquith, who led the Liberal Party into the political wilderness.

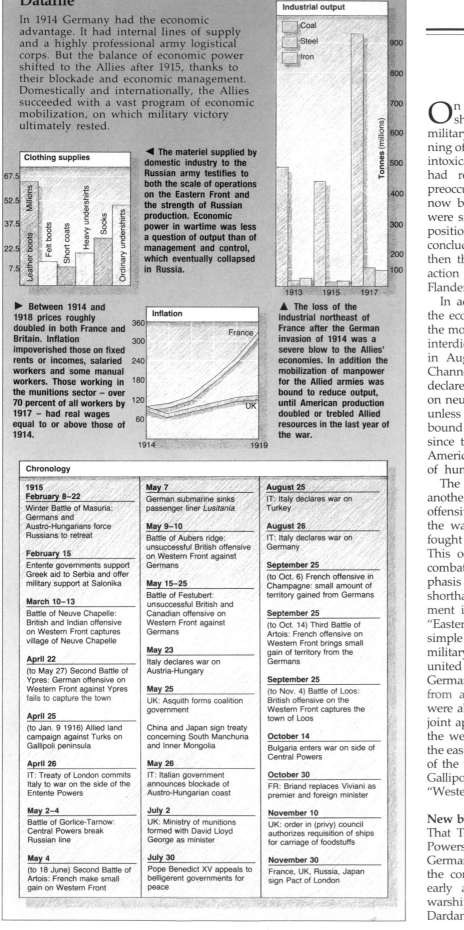

Datafile

In 1914 Germany had the economic advantage. It had internal lines of supply and a highly professional army logistical corps. But the balance of economic power shifted to the Allies after 1915, thanks to their blockade and economic management. Domestically and internationally, the Allies succeeded with a vast program of economic mobilization, on which military victory ultimately rested.

Clothing supplies

◀ The materiel supplied by domestic industry to the Russian army testifies to both the scale of operations on the Eastern Front and the strength of Russian production. Economic power in wartime was less a question of output than of management and control, which eventually collapsed in Russia.

▶ Between 1914 and 1918 prices roughly doubled in both France and Britain. Inflation impoverished those on fixed rents or incomes, salaried workers and some manual workers. Those working in the munitions sector – over 70 percent of all workers by 1917 – had real wages equal to or above those of 1914.

Inflation

Industrial output

▲ The loss of the industrial northeast of France after the German invasion of 1914 was a severe blow to the Allies' economies. In addition the mobilization of manpower for the Allied armies was bound to reduce output, until American production doubled or trebled Allied resources in the last year of the war.

Chronology

1915

February 8–22
Winter Battle of Masuria: Germans and Austro-Hungarians force Russians to retreat

February 15
Entente governments support Greek aid to Serbia and offer military support at Salonika

March 10–13
Battle of Neuve Chapelle: British and Indian offensive on Western Front captures village of Neuve Chapelle

April 22
(to May 27) Second Battle of Ypres: German offensive on Western Front against Ypres fails to capture the town

April 25
(to Jan. 9 1916) Allied land campaign against Turks on Gallipoli peninsula

April 26
IT: Treaty of London commits Italy to war on the side of the Entente Powers

May 2–4
Battle of Gorlice-Tarnow: Central Powers break Russian line

May 4
(to 18 June) Second Battle of Artois: French make small gain on Western Front

May 7
German submarine sinks passenger liner *Lusitania*

May 9–10
Battle of Aubers ridge: unsuccessful British offensive on Western Front against Germans

May 15–25
Battle of Festubert: unsuccessful British and Canadian offensive on Western Front against Germans

May 23
Italy declares war on Austria-Hungary

May 25
UK: Asquith forms coalition government

China and Japan sign treaty concerning South Manchuria and Inner Mongolia

May 26
IT: Italian government announces blockade of Austro-Hungarian coast

July 2
UK: Ministry of munitions formed with David Lloyd George as minister

July 30
Pope Benedict XV appeals to belligerent governments for peace

August 25
IT: Italy declares war on Turkey

August 26
IT: Italy declares war on Germany

September 25
(to Oct. 6) French offensive in Champagne: small amount of territory gained from Germans

September 25
(to Oct. 14) Third Battle of Artois: French offensive on Western Front brings small gain of territory from the Germans

September 25
(to Nov. 4) Battle of Loos: British offensive on the Western Front captures the town of Loos

October 14
Bulgaria enters war on side of Central Powers

October 30
FR: Briand replaces Viviani as premier and foreign minister

November 10
UK: order in (privy) council authorizes requisition of ships for carriage of foodstuffs

November 30
France, UK, Russia, Japan sign Pact of London

On the outbreak of hostilities the illusion of a short war was shared by most political and military leaders. Six months later, by the beginning of 1915, it began to dawn on all but those still intoxicated by their own propaganda that victory had receded over the horizon. The central preoccupation of those in authority on both sides now became what to do next. Their responses were similar. They tried to protect their political position both internationally and internally by concluding alliances or tacit agreements to strengthen the platform from which decisive military action could be launched, either in France and Flanders or on the Eastern Front.

In addition they further extended the war to the economic realm. This took many forms, but the most important was through blockade. Naval interdiction of supplies was a mutual act. Starting in August 1914, Germany mined the English Channel and within a few months the UK declared that consignments destined for Germany on neutral ships would be treated as contraband unless proven otherwise. Both measures were bound to raise the political stakes of the war, since they touched neutral – and in particular, American – shipping and ultimately took the lives of hundreds of noncombatants as well.

The geographic expansion of the war had another implication. The failure of the German offensive to achieve an early victory meant that the war would drag on, and that it would be fought on many fronts and in many countries. This occasioned a fierce political debate in all combatant countries over where the major emphasis on military action should be placed. The shorthand for this intense and protracted argument is to describe it as a difference between "Easterners" and "Westerners". This is much too simple a distinction. Both the political and the military leadership of the UK and France were united about the purpose of the war: to destroy German militarism and remove the German army from all of France and Belgium. The disputes were about how to achieve these aims. In 1915 a joint approach was tried: to keep up pressure in the west while launching a daring operation in the east to knock Germany's new ally, Turkey, out of the war. The failure of this campaign (on the Gallipoli Peninsula) gave the upper hand to the "Westerners" in future strategic debates.

New belligerents

That Turkey fought on the side of the Central Powers in World War I was one of the major German political triumphs of the early years of the conflict. Turkish inclinations were seen as early as 11 August 1914 when the German warships *Goeben* and *Breslau* passed through the Dardanelles, the Turkish straits between the

1915 STALEMATE AND STAGNATION

Aegean Sea and the Sea of Marmara, eluding British warships in the Mediterranean. The Turkish government officially purchased the cruisers to replace two that had been on order in British shipyards, but which had been commandeered by the British government on the outbreak of war, damaging Britain's standing in Istanbul.

This clear political sign of the attitude of the Turkish government was a worrying development. Numerous British diplomatic gestures were made to secure at least Turkish neutrality, but to no avail. Here was a major German diplomatic victory. In drawing Turkey into the Central Powers, Germany demonstrated that it could outbid Britain and spread the war to a point where British interests in the Middle East were threatened. Even more alarming for the Allies was the menace to the southern reaches of Russia. On 29 October the two cruisers shelled the Russian Black Sea ports of Odessa, Sevastopol and Theodosia. Russia declared war on Turkey three days later; Britain followed on 5 November.

With Turkey on the side of the Central Powers, the position of Bulgaria became of great strategic importance. Once again the bargaining for an alliance produced counteroffers aimed at satisfying Bulgarian territorial ambitions. What Bulgaria wanted was territory claimed or occupied by Serbia, Greece and Romania. This put Germany in an unassailable position. To satisfy Bulgaria the

The Ottoman Empire

In 1914 the Ottoman or Turkish Empire stretched from the Bulgarian and Russian coasts of the Black Sea to the Arabian peninsula as far south as present-day Bahrain on the Persian Gulf and South Yemen on the Red Sea. It was an Islamic sultanate. In the early 19th century Constantinople had controlled the Balkans, all of North Africa and the Middle East as far as Iran. A century later the centrifugal forces of nationalism and imperialism had stripped the Empire of substantial areas. Serbia, Albania, Bulgaria and Romania had all been Ottoman provinces, but by 1914 they were independent states. By then predatory imperial powers had taken indirect or direct control of all of North Africa and much of the Middle East. European bankers and merchants came by the thousands, and created the transportation networks and infrastructure necessary for linking this huge region to the European and world economies. The classic pattern of exchange of raw materials and primary products for finished European goods entered a new phase, and older hierarchical social structures began to give way to the rudiments of "modernity". The political echoes of these changes may be heard in the slogans of the "Young Turk" movement, many of whose members were liberals exiled in Europe, and who brought back to Turkey a new and strident nationalism. Their influence in the army grew, and lay behind the successful revolt of 1908 against the dictatorship of Sultan Abdul Hamid, who was deposed the following year. His brother Mohammed became Sultan but had no power. The Young Turk leader, Enver Pasha, became minister of war. He admired German military strength, and sponsored the appointment of Liman von Sanders as inspector general of the Turkish army. On 30 July 1914 Turkey concluded a treaty with Germany, and entered the war three months later, on the German side.

▶ **Territorial losses of the Ottoman Empire.**

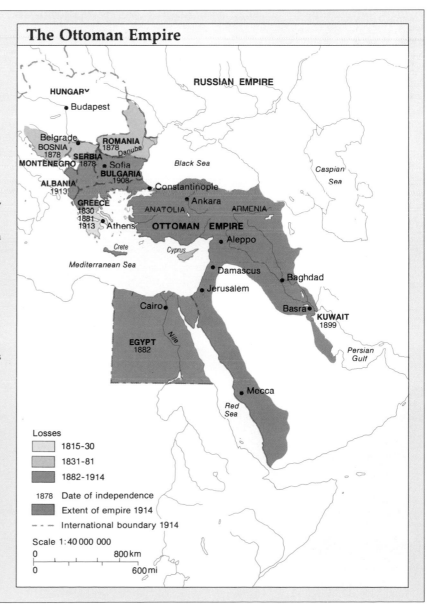

The Ottoman Empire

Losses

	1815-30
	1831-81
	1882-1914

1878 Date of independence

Extent of empire 1914

--- International boundary 1914

Scale 1:40 000 000

0   800 km

0   600 mi

Allies would have to promise to raid one set of countries which were either already on their side, or which were being courted to join the Allied cause, in order to obtain the assistance of another set. Allied diplomats were not above doing this: it was rather that their promises lacked credibility. Consequently in September 1915 Bulgaria concluded an alliance (planned in 1913) with Germany and Austria-Hungary, received substantial financial credits, and mobilized for war against Serbia. As a result Serbia appealed to Greece for assistance, to which it was entitled under a treaty of May 1913. This was given in the form of Greek secret approval (and public disapproval) for an Allied landing in Greece at Salonika, which was intended to provide assistance for Serbia. (It took place in October – see p. 76.)

The German coup of landing Bulgaria as an ally counterbalanced to some extent the intervention of Italy on the Allied side a few months earlier in 1915. Italy had been allied to Germany and Austria-Hungary before the war, but took the attack on Serbia as an excuse to declare neutrality. Now the shoe was on the other foot: what had hampered Allied approaches to Bulgaria now stymied German pleas to Italy, since Italian territorial ambitions (to acquire Italian-speaking areas of Austria) collided with Austrian interests. Under German pressure Austria-Hungary granted concessions, but not enough to satisfy the Italians, who pressed for more than any Austrian government could politically afford to make. The Germans pressed the Austrians for more, to which Vienna reluctantly and belatedly agreed.

The delay coincided with the growth of a popular movement within Italy to bring it into

the war on the side of the Allies. This brought together strange bedfellows: conservative nationalists and the king on the one hand, Futurist artists and socialists on the other. The Italian socialist Mussolini, who had originally opposed the war on socialist grounds, reversed his position within a few months and founded a newspaper, *Il Popolo d'Italia*, to put forward the interventionist case.

There is still some dispute about the extent to which all this was paid for by French subsidies; there is less argument about its effect. The campaign increased the pressure on the Italian government to jump off the tightrope of neutrality. It was prepared to do so, but of course only

◄ **Kaiser Wilhelm II** inspecting Bulgarian troops in the Serbian city of Nish, on the vital rail link between the Serbian capital of Belgrade and the Bulgarian capital of Sofia. Nish fell to the Bulgarians during combined operations with the German and Austrian armies on 5 November 1915.

◄ **The accession to the throne of Romania** in October 1914 of Ferdinand on the death of his uncle Carol – an ardent supporter of Austria – opened the way for Romanian entry into the war on the Allied side. This took place in August 1916 with disastrous results for Romania.

▼ **The German cruiser** *Breslau* in Constantinople harbor in August 1914. After eluding the British Royal Navy, the warship was purchased by the Turks.

Italy in 1915

Italy was not a great power in prewar Europe. Yet the rivalries between the true European great powers enabled Italy's leaders to fish in troubled waters, neglecting pressing problems at home in pursuit of an elusive and insubstantial greatness.

Like the German Empire, Italy was a recent arrival among European states. The Kingdom of Italy had been founded in 1860, uniting most of the peninsula. Its largely ineffective participation in the Austro-Prussian War of 1866 had gained her the Venetia, the last major province held by Austria. In 1870 the occupation of Rome, which became the capital, completed prewar Italy. The displaced ruler of Rome, the Pope, refused to accept his loss of political power or to recognize the new state. He became the voluntary "prisoner of the Vatican". For 20 years Catholics were forbidden to take part in Italian politics, and the breach between Church and State remained a serious difficulty in 1915.

The new Italy had an increasing population (36 million by 1914), but was economically backward and beset by problems such as widespread rural poverty and mass illiteracy. Against this background the parliamentary system functioned badly; political parties were poorly disciplined and engaged in the most unlikely alliances in order to gain power. Social reforms tended to be shelved or implemented with staggering inefficiency. Italian prime ministers generally occupied themselves with political intrigues or foreign affairs.

After 1870 many Italians hoped to claim *Italia irredenta* – "unredeemed Italy", territories with large Italian populations that were still under Austrian rule, notably Trentino in the north and the great Adriatic port of Trieste. But "irredentism" was not practical politics once Germany and Austria-Hungary had become allies, and Italy's leaders turned to colonial expansion. Italian designs on Tunis were frustrated by French action, and Franco-Italian hostility persisted into the mid-1890s. This was the principal reason for Italy's adhesion to the Triple Alliance of 1882, which brought it into partnership with Germany and Austria-Hungary.

Italian imperialism scored a modest success in 1885, when its outposts on the Red Sea were organized into the colony of Eritrea. But an Italian attempt to conquer Ethiopia turned into a disaster: the Italian army was crushed at the Battle of Adowa (1896) and Italy was forced to recognize Ethiopian independence. This unparalleled humiliation by a "native" people led to a suspension of Italian colonial ambitions, although Italian governments prepared for a takeover of Tripoli (present-day Libya), which was part of the Turkish Empire, by making a number of separate – and secret – agreements with each of the great powers. Finally, in 1911 Italy waged a successful war on Turkey; confronted with a looming Balkan War the Turks ceded Tripoli.

The Libyan war split the socialists and led to the expulsion of those who supported the government's African policy. The revolutionary left gained a majority at the 1912 party convention. Mussolini proclaimed the revolutionary line as editor of the party newspaper *Avanti*.

In 1914 Italy remained neutral, but the prime minister, Antonio Salandra, favored intervention, and during the winter of 1914–15 irredentist and interventionist sentiment gathered force. In effect, Italy sold itself to the highest bidder. In spite of intense German pressure, the Austrians yielded only slowly to Italian demands for the Trentino, Trieste and substantial territories in Dalmatia. By the time they agreed, it was too late. The Triple Entente had promised Italy everything it wanted, and in April 1915 it agreed to undertake hostilities against Austria-Hungary. Italians, like other peoples, entered the war in a patriotic haze.

Antonio Salandra   1853–1931

Salandra was an authoritarian conservative who presided over both Italy's decision to adopt a neutral stance in August 1914 and its decision to go to war ten months later in May 1915. He entered politics after training as a barrister and a career as a professor of public administration at the University of Rome. He adopted what in Italy were called "liberal" politics (for which in his case read conservative), served in several prewar cabinets, and became premier on Giovanni Giolitti's resignation in March 1914. The stormy days of the "Red week" of socialist and anarchist demonstrations and violence in May 1914 were the first major challenges he had to meet. The second was the war crisis of the summer. Salandra's initial line was a cautious one. Italy was an ally of Germany and Austria-Hungary, but Salandra wisely concluded that the quarrel with Serbia was not one which required Italian entry into the war on the side of the Central Powers. Over the following months, wisdom vanished and instead Italy conducted a diplomatic auction, promising its services in war to the highest bidder. The Allies won, and Salandra the neutralist became Salandra the war leader. He was forced to resign after military reversals in 1916. In the postwar years he smiled benignly on the aims of the Fascist movement.

for a price, specified in secret in the Treaty of London of 26 April 1915. At the end of the war Italy was to get what it wanted in the areas disputed with Austria, as well as financial reparations and chunks of German colonies in Africa. Four weeks after the secret treaty had been concluded, Italy declared war on Austria, and entered a disastrous phase of its history.

New allies

The way in which Italy entered the conflict reflected one of the most important political changes of the war: the eclipse of parliamentary power. The Treaty of London only came to light years later, when the Bolsheviks began to read the archives of the czar's foreign office and let foreign journalists into the secrets of Allied diplomacy. Similarly, Italian legislators only learned of their government's initial war policy in 1915 through a Swedish newspaperman's Russian sources.

Perhaps this kind of executive fiat is inevitable in wartime, when time is short and secrecy a necessity. But in all major combatant countries, the assumption of untrammeled power by the executive had two important results: it gave a small number of men virtually unheard-of powers, and it created new political alliances which would have been impossible before the war.

Wartime politics can be described as varying types and degrees of military dictatorship, supported by a wide range of civilian coalitions. In France, in the first three years of the war, dictatorship and coalition largely went hand in hand. Some attempts to revive parliamentary authority occurred from time to time, but it was only in 1918 that Georges Clemenceau reasserted the right of the prime minister to have the final say over military policy.

General Joseph Gallieni 1849–1916

Gallieni was military governor of Paris during the German advance on the capital in August and September 1914. He was a veteran of the Franco-Prussian war in which he had been wounded and taken prisoner. In 1914 he was a 65-year old professional soldier, recently retired, and a veteran colonial administrator. He was in line for the post of commander in chief of the armies, but deferred to Joffre on grounds of age and health. Gallieni energetically mobilized the Paris garrison and was the first to see the opportunity to counterattack the flank of the advancing German army. He played a significant part in launching the decisive French attack on the line of the Ourcq north of the Marne (6–10 September).

Recognition of his achievement followed when Briand brought him into the cabinet as minister of war. His military and administrative experience in the colonies gave his voice authority, which he used to defend Joffre and the high command. The crisis of Verdun showed the need for further reorganization of French command, but by then Gallieni had resigned on grounds of ill health. He died on 27 May 1916, was given a state funeral and the posthumous rank of marshal.

▲ The Serbian general staff, with the 71-year-old King Peter seated among his officers, crossing the River Drina in what is now Yugoslavia in late 1915. The ordeal of the Serbian army in the winter of 1915 was one of the tragedies of the war. General von Mackensen's joint Central Powers operation against Serbia began in October 1915 and successfully swept the Serbian army to the Albanian mountains in the west. They and the thousands of prisoners and refugees with them endured appalling conditions in the mountains of Albania. How many died before reaching the sea will never be known.

In the early months of the conflict the French government almost ceased to exist. It fled to Bordeaux to avoid the embarrassment of being trapped in Paris, as had happened in 1870–71, and granted Generals Gallieni and Joffre full authority to run the city of Paris and the war. But once the first crisis had passed, and the lines had stabilized on the Marne, an attempt was made to restore some semblance of civilian control. In December 1914 most ministers returned to Paris, but the important ministries of war, the navy and justice stayed in the south. At this stage there was little politicians could do to reassert their right to run the war. Instead they declared a political truce and supported the creation of a coalition government of all the talents to provide whatever the army decided it had to have.

This brought socialists into government early in the war. The most important of these was Albert Thomas, who in 1915 became undersecretary in charge of artillery and military equipment at the French ministry of war. Thomas was instrumental in giving the French trade union movement a chance to help run the war.

In the UK the same suspension of the normal political game occurred. The Liberal prime minister Herbert Asquith appointed Lord Kitchener as minister of war soon after hostilities began. At this stage his word was final, among both politicians and generals. Later in the war it was not so easy to tell who was running the war, but for a time it was Kitchener.

The British parliament passed the Defence of the Realm Act, or DORA as it was universally known, which gave the government powers to do what it liked during the war. Initially many prominent men were reluctant to accept the argument that Britain had a moral obligation to

Albert Thomas   1878–1932

Like his mentor Jean Jaurès, Thomas was an intellectual who espoused socialist internationalism and French patriotism. He was the quintessential reformist socialist, a leader of moderate opinion both within the French trade union movement and in the socialist party. The son of a baker, Thomas's family still managed to send him to the *Ecole Normale Supérieure* in Paris, the breeding ground for France's intellectual and political elite. His brilliance brought him to the attention of Jaurès. In 1904 Thomas became assistant editor on the new socialist newspaper, *L'Humanité*. In 1910 he was elected to the French chamber of deputies.

On the outbreak of war Thomas, now 36, adopted a patriotic stance and joined his regiment. He was soon recalled to organize the railways. In May 1915 he joined the French cabinet as under-secretary (and later minister) of munitions and served in successive administrations. In the accompanying photograph he is addressing workers at the opening of a canteen in the Citroën factory in Paris in 1917.

After the war he became the guiding force behind the International Labor Organization (ILO) of the League of Nations. This organization remains his most enduring memorial.

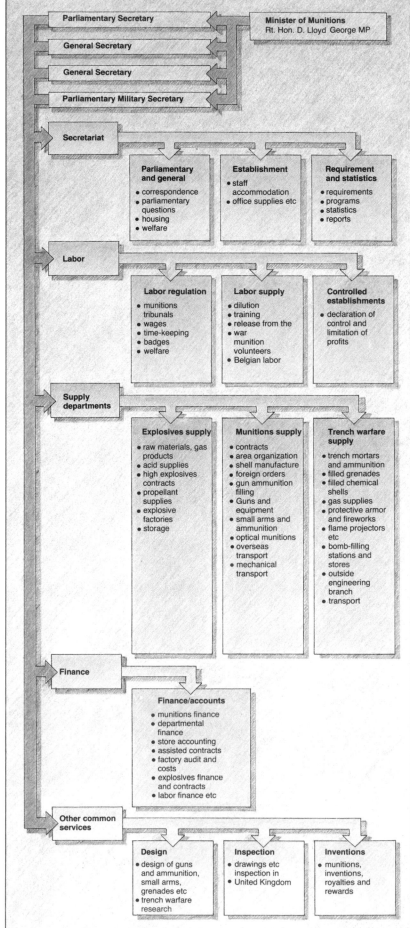

join in the conflict. Within the Liberal camp and in Labour Party circles individual voices were raised against intervention, but such doubts and anxieties did not inform a wider political movement against the war. A characteristic attitude was that of J.A. Pease, the Quaker president of the British Peace Society, who was also a cabinet minister. In August 1914 he wavered, he worried, but he did not resign. J. Ramsay MacDonald, a prominent Labour leader, gave up his chairmanship of the Parliamentary Labour Party, but he did not try to convince his colleagues to vote against war credits. Some artists and writers turned their backs emphatically against the war, but elsewhere unanimity reigned. The war had to be won. Even the Irish Nationalist Party – which participated in the Westminster parliament simply to legislate itself out of existence by bringing Home Rule to Ireland – did its bit for the war effort. The party encouraged its supporters to join up and thus reinforce claims for Home Rule, which was still to be won by constitutional means. The Liberal government had already sponsored legislation to this effect, but it had been shelved on account of the war.

Soon after the invasion of Belgium the British trade union movement declared its unequivocal support for the war. In the first months of the conflict so many workingmen joined up that supplies of essential war materiel were scarce. Something had to be done to rationalize labor. The result was the Treasury Agreement of 1915: the trade unions accepted restrictions for the duration of the war in return for recognition as a partner in the management of the war economy.

What they gave up were the right to strike and the restrictive practices that determined the skill composition of the labor force in any munitions factory. These concessions assured continuous production and the injection of workers into jobs previously only done by skilled men – in a word, dilution. In return they received recognition – no

Arthur Henderson 1863–1935

Henderson was the single most powerful Labour leader in wartime Britain. In 1914 he was aged 51 and was a member of parliament for a mining district in the Northeast of England as well as a veteran of the trade union movement. He believed in the rise of labor rather than in any specific socialist doctrine. In May 1915 Henderson became the first Labour member of parliament to sit in a British cabinet, as president of the board of education. In reality his role was as a trouble-shooter and mediator with organized labor. When Lloyd George came to power in 1916, Henderson served in his inner cabinet. After a visit Petrograd to convince Russia to stay in a war during which his own son had been killed, Henderson began to adopt a wider political vision. He spoke out for British attendance at a socialist meeting at Stockholm, and for his independence he was sacked from the cabinet. He returned to rebuild the Labour Party as a national party. In later years he served as a cabinet minister and won the Nobel Peace Prize for his work for disarmament.

Lord Kitchener of Khartoum 1850–1916

One of the best-known images of World War I is the British recruiting poster with Kitchener's face and pointing finger, calling on British men to join up (see p. 119). In 1914 Kitchener was Britain's most famous soldier and prime minister Asquith's natural choice as secretary of state for war. Kitchener had made his reputation in Britain's imperial wars from Egypt to South Africa and was aged 64 in 1914. He saw quickly that the war could last at least three years, an opinion contrary to the popular illusion of a short war. It was his decision to create a mass army of volunteers to bolster Britain's small standing army and territorial force. The popular response to his call was far beyond his (or anyone else's) expectations. One million men joined up voluntarily in 1914 alone. These men formed what became known as the "Kitchener armies". The first trained units were despatched to France in 1915, and formed the heart of the force which led the disastrous attacks on the Somme in July–November 1916.

Initially Kitchener ran the war virtually single-handed. He was closer to his French colleagues than to many British politicians, and helped to build up the necessary liaison to secure the Western Front. By mid-1915 the task of provisioning the armies was entrusted to the ministry of munitions, under Lloyd George. The inevitable political intrigues and maneuvers which the war bred hampered Kitchener's leadership on questions of strategy to the point that he considered resigning in late 1915. He stayed on, in part because he knew he was an indispensable symbol of the nation's will.

In June 1916 Kitchener embarked on a mission to Russia. He never reached his destination. He and all hands drowned when HMS *Hampshire* was sunk by a mine in the Atlantic Ocean.

◀ The cartoon from the English magazine *Punch* shows the British chancellor of the exchequer David Lloyd George harnessing capital and labor to produce the weapons needed to win the war. The cartoon appeared shortly after the Treasury Agreement of 1915, whereby trade unionists abrogated both restrictive practices and the right to strike in return for a recognized place in the management of the war economy. This they duly received, and participated at all levels of the new ministry of munitions, whose structure in August 1916 is sketched left. The ministry was staffed by civil servants and businessmen who put together a successful industrial empire efficient enough to keep the allied armies supplied for the next three years.

mean achievement at a time when strikes were often held to gain union recognition.

This arrangement was given legal force in the Munitions of War Act of July 1915. It also created a ministry of munitions to oversee war production. At its head was David Lloyd George, previously Liberal chancellor of the exchequer, who used his reputation as a man of "push and go" to improve both war production and his chances of becoming prime minister. By then the Liberal government had agreed to invite leaders of opposition parties into a coalition to run the war. Thus Arthur Henderson, a moderate trade unionist, became the first member of the Labour Party to sit in a British cabinet.

The coalition occurred in the light of the second major military crisis of the war: that of the Dardanelles (for which, see p. 82). The major political casualty of this disastrous episode was the first lord of the admiralty, Winston Churchill. He was replaced by the former Conservative prime minister, Arthur Balfour.

Political effects

In the UK and France the war's political effects were twofold: to displace power from elected leaders to generals, and to blur prewar political lines. In Germany and Austria-Hungary the situation was more stable, due to the accepted limits of parliamentary power. Legislators had the right to vote war credits – and then, to keep their doubts to themselves. This was, of course, the rule in Russia too.

But in Central and Eastern Europe the war brought about one fundamental political change, which in 1915 was still simmering under the surface. This was the divide within the international socialist movement between those who supported the war and those who, whatever their initial positions, were beginning to ask questions about its direction, its costs and even its justification.

Datafile

In the 1914–18 war German war production succeeded but the German war economy failed. This was because the key to victory was the maintenance of a balance between civilian and military needs. In Germany that balance was never struck, in part because of the Allied blockade and in part because of the way the war economy was run. The result was rampant inflation, a black market and the impoverishment of the population.

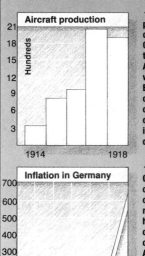

Aircraft production

(Hundreds)
21, 18, 15, 12, 9, 6, 3
1914 — 1918

Inflation in Germany

700, 600, 500, 400, 300, 200, 100
1914 — 1920

Industrial output

Coal | Iron | Steel

360, 300, 240, 180, 120, 60, 30
Tonnes (millions)
1913 1915 1917

◄ The German economy produced prodigious feats during the 1914–18 war. One was the expansion of the aircraft industry. The Albatros factory in Berlin was a typical example. Between 1914 and 1918 output of aircraft rose by over 600 percent and the quality of the machines improved equally dramatically.

◄ The official rise in German retail prices was only the tip of the iceberg of inflation. The black market provided perhaps half of the essential items of daily consumption for ordinary Germans by 1917. A realistic graph of price rises would show inflation in Germany in the last year of the war at perhaps 400 percent of 1914 figures.

▲ Until 1917 the Central Powers roughly matched or exceeded Allied levels of industrial output of coal, iron and steel. But from 1917 the disparity between the two camps grew wider. US output alone equalled that of the Central Powers in basic producers' goods, and US finance provided the foundation for the entire Allied war effort.

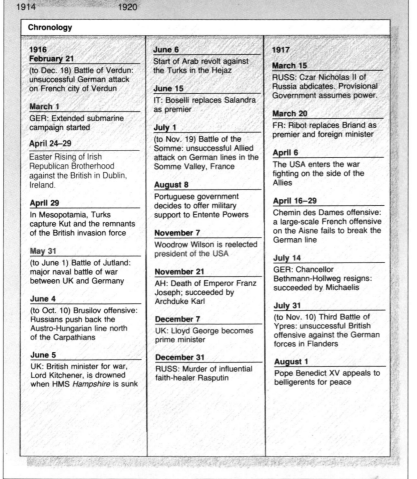

Chronology

1916

February 21
(to Dec. 18) Battle of Verdun: unsuccessful German attack on French city of Verdun

March 1
GER: Extended submarine campaign started

April 24–29
Easter Rising of Irish Republican Brotherhood against the British in Dublin, Ireland.

April 29
In Mesopotamia, Turks capture Kut and the remnants of the British invasion force

May 31
(to June 1) Battle of Jutland: major naval battle of war between UK and Germany

June 4
(to Oct. 10) Brusilov offensive: Russians push back the Austro-Hungarian line north of the Carpathians

June 5
UK: British minister for war, Lord Kitchener, is drowned when HMS *Hampshire* is sunk

June 6
Start of Arab revolt against the Turks in the Hejaz

June 15
IT: Boselli replaces Salandra as premier

July 1
(to Nov. 19) Battle of the Somme: unsuccessful Allied attack on German lines in the Somme Valley, France

August 8
Portuguese government decides to offer military support to Entente Powers

November 7
Woodrow Wilson is reelected president of the USA

November 21
AH: Death of Emperor Franz Joseph; succeeded by Archduke Karl

December 7
UK: Lloyd George becomes prime minister

December 31
RUSS: Murder of influential faith-healer Rasputin

1917

March 15
RUSS: Czar Nicholas II of Russia abdicates. Provisional Government assumes power.

March 20
FR: Ribot replaces Briand as premier and foreign minister

April 6
The USA enters the war fighting on the side of the Allies

April 16–29
Chemin des Dames offensive: a large-scale French offensive on the Aisne fails to break the German line

July 14
GER: Chancellor Bethmann-Hollweg resigns: succeeded by Michaelis

July 31
(to Nov. 10) Third Battle of Ypres: unsuccessful British offensive against the German forces in Flanders

August 1
Pope Benedict XV appeals to belligerents for peace

If 1915 was the time during World War I when the conflict was broadened to include new alliances both among the warring parties and within them, 1916 was the time when the war was deepened, invading every facet of economic, social and political life: when total war was born. In the Central Powers this happened later than in the Entente Powers, but the general tendency was the same on both sides.

For the state to become the center of virtually all social affairs involved major political risks, for it raised the stakes of the war considerably. A ruling elite that took over most of the key tasks of social organization, and demanded unprecedented sacrifices, could not afford to lose the war. Total war exposed the weaknesses of policies and politicians, and placed in the balance the very legitimacy of the regimes that waged it.

This is at least partly why the ferocity of the war increased as it went on. Furthermore the political stakes rose as the casualty lists lengthened, for the reason advanced in one of Abraham Lincoln's phrases, that the dead could not be seen to have died in vain.

But as the war killed literally millions of men, it both brought the men and women of nations and empires together and began to tear them apart. On the one hand, social bonds had been created in wartime that enabled the war to expand to unprecedented heights. In all countries labor and capital worked together. After a few months' work, recruits to the war factories were doing jobs that were supposed to require years of training. Furthermore, huge armies of a dozen nationalities had been forged in Austria-Hungary and in France, where alongside indigenous French forces stood Algerians and Senegalese as well as laborers brought from Vietnam and China, such as Ho Chi Minh and Zhou Enlai.

Shrill patriots, who had shouted down the few who dared to dissent in 1914, grew more and more shrill two years later. Everything for the nation; no sacrifice is too great for the state, they declared from Preston to Prague to Petrograd. The flag-wavers and chauvinists failed to see that the longer the war went on, the less likely it was that some of the combatant countries would carry the struggle through to a decisive conclusion.

That this should have been the case with Russia is not surprising, given the inherent instability of the regime. But it was also a truth that the rulers of Germany ignored, to their cost. The reason is simple. The deeper those in power dug, as it were, to lay the foundations of the war effort, the more they exposed the fissures which threatened to bring down the scaffolding on their heads. Those fissures were clearly visible in 1914, reflecting all the hatreds and animosities that made going to war such a risk in the first place.

1916–17 THE GREAT SLAUGHTER

By the end of 1916 they were visible again, and widened further, given the onset of war weariness and wartime shortages, presenting a real and growing threat to the authoritarian regimes that ran the war.

The political economy of total war

Economic warfare was an integral part of the war. As was noted earlier, blockade was used as an instrument of war from virtually the beginning of the conflict. It put a strain on both sides, and together with the ever-growing demand for munitions production, necessitated major adjustments in economic organization and management. These changes evolved everywhere in piecemeal fashion in 1915.

A year later, even greater efforts at industrial rationalization were required. The Allies' industrial strength was brought home forcibly to the Central Powers by the great battles of 1916 on the

As the war deepens, the state assumes the key tasks of social organization

In Germany military leaders assume command of the economy

Production increases but at considerable cost

In France and Britain the government controls supplies to industry

1916 sees protests against the war in Germany

Britain supports the Arab revolt agains the Turks

Germany supports an Irish insurrection against Britain

▶ Kaiser Wilhelm, flanked by Hindenburg (left) and Ludendorff (right).

▼ Albert Thomas and Lloyd George (left and right) with Haig and Joffre (center).

Western Front. Allied firepower, more than anything else, convinced Germany's military and industrial leaders that only by a massive effort of industrial mobilization could it win the war. In 1914 industrialists carried little weight in German politics. Two years later the situation was entirely different. Working closely with the high command, German industrialists planned a new approach to the war effort. This was known as the Hindenburg Plan.

To understand it we must look back at the early stages of the formation of the German war economy. Early in the war Walther Rathenau, head of the General Electric Company (*AEG*), went to Falkenhayn, then Prussian minister of war, and sketched out a plan for the organization of raw materials production. Consequently Rathenau became head of the *Kriegsrohstoffabteilung* (*KRA*), or war raw materials department, and produced results by setting up war corporations to handle problems of supply. Rathenau was one of many men of industry who helped harness the benefits of German science – in particular the Haber-Bosch process of nitrate synthesis – to the needs of war.

Given the Allied blockade and the consequent shortages of imported saltpeter, essential for the production of explosives for the army and navy, this contribution was of the highest importance to the German war effort.

As the war went on, though, it became apparent that scientific ingenuity alone would not win the war. Increasing criticism was directed by army and industry at the responsible agencies – the Prussian war ministry and the ministry of the interior – which had clearly been unable to provide adequate supplies of guns and butter. The outcome was a price spiral and, even more ominously, the emergence in the shadows of a black market on which virtually anything could be bought.

The quarrel was as much about political power as about economic policy. Its outcome was the creation of what some scholars term "the silent dictatorship" of the two most powerful men in Germany, Paul von Hindenburg, chief of the imperial staff of the German army, and Erich Ludendorff, first quartermaster general. According to one school of historians, in all important respects these two men – together with their allies in industry and politics – ran the German war effort between 1916 and 1918. Again this is an area of historical controversy: other scholars see German wartime politics and administration in much more complicated terms.

But all agree that the new leadership's solution to the supply problem was to give army and industry full control over the economy. An important aspect of the authority of the Prussian war ministry was vested in a new war office, run by General Groener, the man in charge of military railways in 1914. This created the framework for the working out of the Hindenburg Plan, derived from a letter the chief of staff wrote to the minister of war on 31 August 1916. Hindenburg demanded, among other things, a doubling of the output of machine guns and a trebling of the output of artillery by the spring of 1917.

This gigantic program was planned and run by industrialists. Any worries they may have had about state dominance in economic affairs were allayed by the fact that pricing and profit margins remained their responsibility. Labor too was given incentives to increase productivity: under the Auxiliary Service Law of 5 December 1916 a new framework of industrial bargaining was promulgated – no mean achievement in a country in which trade unions were regarded by many military men and industrialists with suspicion or contempt. Labor mobility was curtailed, but works councils were created to arbitrate disputes over permission to leave work.

This gives in outline what has been termed the "corporatist" solution to Germany's wartime economic difficulties. It left the management of the economy to particular interest groups – the large firms, working under the aegis of the army. The result was total chaos. Labor shortages remained chronic, in part due to the demand for more and more men for the Front. The big firms benefited from the scheme, at the expense of prewar competitors and of the state. War production did increase, and by 1918 Germany produced more ammunition than at any time during World War II. But profits soared, with the costs passed on to the army and then to the consumer, thus ensuring the acceleration of the inflationary spiral of the war years, as well as producing a subsistence crisis that undermined the regime itself.

The contrast with Germany's two most important adversaries, the UK and France, tells us much about why Germany lost the war. The French abjured a military solution to economic difficulties, and found a way to increase production without giving in to particular interest groups. It was the consortium system, created in

1916 under the leadership of Etienne Clémentel, the minister of commerce. This apparatus of controls grew out of the international character of the Allied war effort. Given the disastrous loss of men, materiel and industrial potential suffered by France in the first months of the war, there was no alternative to a growing reliance on British economic support. The British insisted upon the coordination of Allied supply policy, and set up international commissions to oversee wheat, coal, credit and shipping. This structure gave Britain virtual control of the essential supplies required by French industry.

What the Allies were forced to do on the international level, Clémentel succeeded in doing within the French economy. He used French dependence on Britain to justify his control of supply to individual firms, undermining their autonomy and room for maneuver. It worked. Through the consortium system the rapacity of individual firms was checked, and an essential balance was maintained: production and profits were secured without undue pressure on prices and thus on wages and living standards.

The same was true in the UK. Even though Lloyd George saw it as an imperative task to bring in the best business talent available to run the war economy, the edifice over which he presided as minister of munitions, and after December 1916 as prime minister, never became either a "business state" or the economic equivalent of the internal war of rapacious self-interest that evolved in Germany. Output of war materiel in the UK was assured within a framework which managed – not without difficulty – to place national interests above employers' interests.

It is therefore one of the paradoxes of the war that the most authoritarian war economy was probably the least efficient. This was because the waging of war – in economic matters as much as

Walther Rathenau 1867–1922

The son of an industrialist, Rathenau was one of the most powerful leaders of German industry before World War I. He was a man of philosophical as well as scientific and industrial interests. In 1899 he became director of *AEG*, the General Electric Company founded by his father. His managerial talent, scientific training, energy and vision made him an indispensable adviser to the German ministry of war in 1914. He created the war raw materials department (*KRA*), and helped ease the transition from a war of annihilation to a war of attrition. After the Armistice he was active in centrist politics, both within industry and in parliamentary affairs. In 1921–22, as minister of reconstruction and later as foreign minister, he helped to ease the burdens of reparations and to fashion a rapprochement with the Soviet Union, expressed in the Rapallo Treaty of 1922. He was a magnet for right-wing and antisemitic malice, and was assassinated on 24 June 1922.

Wilhelm Groener 1867–1939

Groener was a maverick among the German military: a highly efficient administrator with moderate political views. In 1914 he headed the railway section of the German general staff and was responsible for the timetabling of mobilization. His record of success made him the ideal choice as head of the new war office set up in 1916 to reorganize German industry. His fairness and honesty made him enemies among industrialists and the military, and he was fired in 1917. He then served on the Eastern Front, and succeeded Ludendorff as quartermaster general at the end of the war. He came to an understanding with Ebert that the army would support the new regime, and later served in various governments as minister of communications, defense, and the interior.

The *KRA* and German Industry

Germany had many disadvantages in the economic war. The Allied blockade made it impossible for Germany to secure an uninterrupted flow of essential raw materials. In 1915 Walther Rathenau, director of *AEG*, offered to help deal with the crisis of supply. His plea was for the establishment of the *Kriegsrohstoffabteilung* (*KRA*), or war raw materials department. This office set up war corporations to oversee supply to domestic industry. All raw materials were categorized as "emergency materials", and procurement strategies were fixed. A constant search for primary and secondary product substitutes was undertaken. Then priorities were set, by which different industrial claimants for supply were placed in order of importance to the war effort. By late 1915 over 100 war materials companies controlled supplies of basic commodities, with which German industry provided munitions of war. This system worked and provided a temporary solution to Germany's economic problems which, the longer the war dragged on, proved ultimately insurmountable.

◀ German barbed wire destined for the Western Front.

▲ One of the most prominent dissenters in Germany was Karl Liebknecht, shown here imprisoned, pushing a wheelbarrow while working in a munitions factory in occupied France in 1915. Prisoners of conscience in Britain included the prominent philosopher Bertrand Russell, who also lost his post at Trinity College, Cambridge. Only in Russia did antiwar sentiment become a popular force; in the west, pacifism was unable to shorten the war by one day.

in other spheres – is essentially a political matter. However much they juggled the bureaucratic forms, Germany's leaders never established effective political control over the war economy – neither in industry nor in agriculture. They therefore could not hope to balance the claims of competing sectors for scarce commodities. The result was a free-for-all, despite the strenuous efforts of the military authorities. As the American historian Gerald Feldman has demonstrated, under the pressure of industrial war the German state dissolved and competing interest groups grabbed what they could.

The worsening economic outlook at home is also the context in which to set Germany's increasingly aggressive campaign of submarine warfare, as well as the exploitation of both occupied Belgium and a new adversary, Romania, which entered the war on the Allies' side in August 1916 and was subdued six months later. But all of these compensatory steps were ultimately futile, since they could do little other than postpone the demise of a regime that collapsed from within.

Dissent and dissenters

On the evening of 1 May 1916 a small demonstration occurred in the center of Berlin. It was led by Karl Liebknecht, the son of one of the founders of the German social democratic party who had opposed Germany's war effort in 1870–71. In 1916 it took perhaps even more courage for his son to stand up within sight of passing soldiers, and shout "Down with the war! Down with the government!" The outcome was predictable. Liebknecht was arrested, charged with treason, and sentenced by a military court to two and a half years in jail, raised to four years and one month on appeal. But the affair led to the first major political strike of the war. On the day of the trial about 50,000 workers in over 40 Berlin munitions factories downed tools in solidarity with Liebknecht. Similar protests took place in other German towns.

None of this posed a direct threat to the war effort, but such vocal opposition signaled that the

It should have been understood that each new form of production or increase in industrial activity needs a starting period dependent on a whole series of requirements: availability of working space, machines, raw materials and so forth. This was constantly overlooked in the high command and stemming from this, the first sense of disappointment arose.... and so the Hindenburg Plan suffered from the suddenness with which it was issued like a bullet from the barrel, and this at a time when food shortages were growing at a catastrophic rate following the poor harvest of 1916.

WILHELM GROENER

days of the social truce were over. This was the precondition for the reemergence of the international socialist movement, which had unceremoniously collapsed in 1914.

Several attempts had been made to revive it in the ensuing months. Two international conferences of socialists opposed to the war were held in the Swiss hamlets of Zimmerwald in September 1915 and Kienthal in April 1916. There the Russian socialist Lenin met other socialists, whose views on the war and how to end it varied considerably. They agreed that this war was not their war, but few were prepared to accept Lenin's view that the old international movement was dead and that a new one, based on new principles, had to take its place.

In the course of 1916 other dissenters came to public prominence too. In Britain the introduction of compulsory military service created its share of political prisoners, men like the young socialist activists Clifford Allen and Fenner Brockway, who refused even alternative noncombative service which would free someone else to carry a gun. A conspicuous voice among the "No Conscription Fellowship" was the philosopher Bertrand Russell, who helped defend war resisters facing military tribunals, and as a result, later in the war, found that his lectureship at Trinity College, Cambridge, would not be renewed. He also spent a brief period in prison for suggesting in print that American troops would more likely be used to intimidate British workers than attack German soldiers.

It was easier for a government to tolerate dissent when it came from a soldier, which accounts for the extraordinary success of one of the most powerful novels of the war, Henri Barbusse's *Under Fire*, which won the French Goncourt literary prize in 1916 and subsequently became a bestseller. It is a mystery how this book got past the censors, for it broadcast all kinds of subversive ideas. On the eve of his own death, one of the most attractive figures in the book, a young French officer, tells the narrator that only one name will emerge with any honor at the end of the war: the name of Liebknecht. In a final scene, mud-encrusted soldiers on both sides cry out that the war is a crime, which those who had fought it would never allow to happen again. Strong words for 1916, and an indication that the certainties of the war's early days were gone.

Further afield other cracks appeared in both opposition camps. In the spring of 1916 an Arab revolt against Turkish rule began, and was carefully nurtured by the British. But subversion was a game both sides could play. The Germans took a keen interest in Irish nationalism, and helped provide the means for an insurrection in Dublin against British rule planned for Easter 1916. The rising was a military disaster, but a political victory. The rebels were easily overpowered, but the execution of their leaders turned them into martyrs.

Repression in the aftermath of the Easter Rising did no good to the efforts of the British to bring the USA into the war. The Irish vote mattered in American urban politics; and the Irish revolt occurred in the run-up to the 1916 election, fought by both major candidates (Woodrow Wilson for the Democrats and Charles Evans Hughes for the Republicans) on a ticket pledging them to stay out of the war.

▼ Etienne Clémentel, French minister of commerce, succeeded in converting the economic weakness of France into a domestic political weapon. The UK controlled French imports; hence the careful distribution of supply in France was a key to economic survival. Clémentel's consortium system succeeded in subordinating the interests of individual firms to the needs of the economy as a whole.

David Lloyd George 1863–1945

David Lloyd George was the son of a schoolmaster turned farmer, and grew up in impoverished circumstances in North Wales. He trained as a solicitor and entered parliament as a Liberal in 1890. He built a reputation as a fiery orator, and staunchly opposed British policy in the Anglo-Boer War (1899–1902). In 1906 he became president of the board of trade, and from 1908–1914 he served as chancellor of the exchequer. In these years he piloted through parliament a series of bills which laid the foundation of the welfare state. To pay for them, he incurred the wrath of the propertied classes and the Conservative Party. The House of Lords rejected his Finance Bill. Two general elections followed, leaving Lloyd George and the Liberals in power, determined to restrict the veto power of the House of Lords. This they did through the Parliament Act of 1911. During the war Lloyd George served as minister of munitions (1915–16) and then as prime minister (1916–18). He conducted a long and ultimately unsuccessful guerrilla campaign against Haig and the general staff to wrest from them control of war policy. He was more successful in domestic affairs. He brought men from outside politics to run the home front, and symbolized British determination to see the war through. He was reelected prime minister in 1918 and served until 1922.

World War I and Ireland

The "Irish question" has been a perennial headache in British politics. It is more accurately called the "British problem", since the occupation of Catholic Ireland in the 17th century first by Presbyterian settlers from Scotland and then by Oliver Cromwell's armies, never succeeded in merging the political cultures of Britain and Ireland. In the years following the potato famine of 1846, which reduced the population of Ireland by 2 million within five years, separatist and nationalist movements grew. In 1858 the Irish Republican Brotherhood was founded. In 1870 the Home Rule Association was created to work for self-government for Ireland. Irish members of parliament, led by Charles Stewart Parnell, fought for home rule and assistance to the rural poor.

The Liberal-dominated House of Commons passed a Home Rule bill in 1893, but it was blocked by the House of Lords. In 1900 a new party, Sinn Fein ("Ourselves Alone"), was founded, and tapped a surge of Irish nationalism among a new generation of militants. When the Liberals once more passed a Home Rule bill in 1912, it could no longer be vetoed by the Lords. Protestants then insisted on the exclusion of the six northern counties with a Protestant majority, and on armed resistance. German arms were landed at Larne for the Protestant "Ulster

volunteers", and a number of British officers stated that they would not enforce Home Rule. Catholics formed the "Irish volunteers", and shots were fired when troops attempted to block their arms shipments.

Civil war seemed likely, when in 1914 the world war overtook it. Catholic leaders joined Protestants in rallying to the cause. Over 200,000 Irishmen volunteered, with the full support of the Irish Nationalist Party. Irish nationalism, though, grew as the war went on.

A small group of nationalists in the Irish Republican Brotherhood decided to seize the moment and fight for independence. Their plan to smuggle in German arms went hopelessly wrong on 21 April 1916, two days before their planned insurrection. The mobilization order was cancelled, but 2,000 men took over the Central Post Office and other key buildings in Dublin anyway. The rebels had no hope of victory, and after a week of fighting, they surrendered. The leaders were executed, shocking Irish opinion and boosting Sinn Fein support. Their "martyrdom" inspired the Irish Republican Army in its nasty guerrilla war against British troops and Irish "collaborators", which was partially resolved in 1921 by the creation of the Irish Free State, without the six counties of Ulster.

▲ The burnt-out shell of the central Post Office in Dublin announced the end of the "Easter Rising" of 1916. This seizure of key points in Dublin by lightly-armed members of the Irish Republican Brotherhood had no hope of military success. The insurgents were outnumbered and probably under few illusions about their chances of sparking off a general uprising. But their quixotic action succeeded politically, when the British decided to execute the leaders of the uprising. Their martyrdom fuelled Irish resistance to continued British occupation, which ended in the south of Ireland in 1922. The six northern provinces of "Ulster" remain British to this day.

Datafile

The entry of the United States into the war and the two Russian revolutions of 1917 changed the character of World War I. Initially American involvement strengthened the Allies' claim to be fighting a war for democratic principles. In military terms, these parallel developments presented both a serious threat to and a fundamental reinforcement of the Allied position. With Russia out of the war from December 1917, the question was how rapidly could American military power be brought to bear on the Central Powers. In political terms, these changes were momentous. What had begun as a war between Europe's great multinational and imperial powers threatened to turn into a revolutionary war. Wilson and Lenin thought in terms very different from those of the men of 1914. In 1918 each offered a different vision of the future. When it became clear in 1918 that the German cause was lost, the question became which vision would guide the future of Europe and the world?

▼ **Wilson's 14 points had three foundations: self-determination of peoples, free trade, and the desirability of a League of Nations. The difficulty was that in recognizing nationalism, he undermined the second and the third propositions. Wilson's political failure arose from this dilemma.**

▶ **The Treaty of Brest-Litovsk exposed the full imperialist objectives of the German war effort. The Treaty created a system of satellite states between Germany and Russia, remarkably similar to that which the Soviet Union established after 1945. Had the Germans won the war in the west, a similar settlement was likely.**

The Treaty of Brest-Litovsk 3 March 1918

— Line of treaty
▨ RSFSR 1918
☐ Land lost 1914–18

1. Territories previously belonging to Russia west of the agreed line will no longer be subject to Russian sovereignty. Germany and Austria-Hungary will determine the future status of these regions in agreement with their populations.

2. Russia to demobilize its army and bring its warships to port; mines to be removed from the Black Sea.

3. Russia to conclude peace with the Ukrainian People's Republic and recognize the treaty of 9 February 1918 between the Republic and the Central Powers.

4. Estonia and Livonia to be cleared of Russian troops and occupied by a German police force until national institutions can ensure their security. Finland to be cleared of Russian troops and ships.

5. The contracting parties renounce compensation for war expenses and war losses.

6. Independence of Persia and Afghanistan to be maintained.

President Wilson's 14 Points

1. Open covenants of peace, openly arrived at

2. Freedom of navigation upon the seas in peace or war

3. The removal of all economic barriers and the establishment of an equality of trade conditions among all nations

4. Adequate safeguards given and taken that national armaments will be reduced to the lowest point consistent with domestic safety

5. A free, open-minded and impartial adjustment of all colonial claims, based on the principle that the interests of the populations concerned have equal weight with the equitable claims of the government whose title is to be determined

6. The evacuation of all Russian territory

7. Belgium must be evacuated and restored

8. All French territory should be freed and the invaded portions restored, and the loss of Alsace-Lorraine in 1871 righted

9. Readjustment of the frontiers of Italy should be effected along clearly recognizable lines of nationality

10. The peoples of Austria-Hungary should be accorded the freest opportunity of autonomous development

11. Rumania, Serbia and Montenegro should be evacuated; occupied territory restored; and the relations of the several Balkan states to one another determined by friendly counsel along lines of allegiance and nationality

12. The Turkish portions of the Ottoman empire should be assured secure sovereignty, but the other nationalities now under Turkish rule should be assured an undoubted security of life and unmolested opportunity of autonomous development

13. An independent Polish state should be erected, including territories inhabited by indisputably Polish populations, which should be assured a free and secure access to the sea

14. A general association of nations must be formed under specific covenants for the purpose of affording mutual guarantees of political independence and territorial integrity to great and small states alike.

Chronology

1917

August 6
Kerensky appointed prime minister of Russia

September 3
Germans capture Riga on the Baltic coast

November 7
Bolshevik socialists in Russia overthrow the provisional government

November 16
FR: Clemenceau becomes premier and minister for war

December 3
The Bolshevik government in Russia signs an armistice with Germany

December 6
Finland declares independence from Russia

December 7
USA: Declares war on Austro-Hungarian Empire

1918
January 8
US president Woodrow Wilson publishes his 14 points as a basis for peace

March 3
Russia signs the Treaty of Brest-Litovsk

March 21
The Germans launch their Spring Offensive on the Western Front and push back the Allied forces

April 14
Foch appointed commander in chief of Allied forces (except for Belgian army)

May
(to Oct. 1919) Allied forces intervene in the Russian civil war

May 7
The Central Powers and Rumania sign the Peace of Bucharest

July 16
RUSS: Ex-czar Nicholas II and family murdered

July 18
(to Nov. 10) Allied counteroffensive on the Western Front: German forces are pushed back toward the German border

September 30
The Allies and Bulgaria conclude an armistice

October 3–4
The German government offers peace based on President Wilson's 14 points

GER: Max von Baden replaces Hertling as chancellor

October 4
British and Arab forces occupy Damascus

October 14
Turkey sends note to Wilson proposing an armistice

October 16
AH: Government declares AH as federal state based on nationalities (except for kingdom of Hungary)

October 27
AH/IT: Austro-Hungarian government asks Italian government for an armistice

October 28
German sailors mutiny at Kiel

November 3
Austria–Hungary sues for peace with the Allies

November 4–5
Antiwar and pro-Bolshevik risings in Germany

November 7
GER: A republic is proclaimed in Bavaria

November 9
Kaiser Wilhelm II abdicates

November 11
The Allies and Germany sign the Armistice: fighting ends on the Western Front at 11 a.m.

1917–18 REVOLUTION AND PEACE

- The German U-boat campaign brings America into the war
- Strikes, riots and mutiny topple Russia's imperial regime
- The new Russian government fails on both military and diplomatic fronts
- Bolsheviks seize power and take Russia out of the war
- Germany launches another western offensive
- But under the strain of counterattacks the German army retreats

▼ "Wake Up America Day" parade in New York, 19 April 1917.

Within a few months of his victory in the presidential election of 1916, Woodrow Wilson brought the USA into the war. That he could do so with his country behind him was almost certainly due to the impact of unrestricted submarine campaign waged by Germany from 1 February 1917.

Even before that date, German–American relations had been damaged by the interception by British naval intelligence of a message from the German foreign secretary Arthur Zimmermann – to Heinrich von Eckhardt, the German minister in Mexico. The message (now known as the Zimmermann Telegram) spoke of two matters: the need to offer Mexico an alliance with Germany in the event that the United States would go to war, and the possibility of German assistance for Mexico "to regain by conquest its lost territories in Texas, Arizona, and New Mexico". The cable, dated 17 January 1917, was intercepted by British naval intelligence and was passed on to President Wilson on 24 February. He was furious, and a week later released the text to the press. Astoundingly, Zimmermann confirmed its authenticity and thereby undermined the noninterventionist argument completely.

Long before this episode, though, Germany and the United States were on a collision course, so to speak, over the sinking of neutral ships or of ships with neutrals aboard, like the British liner *Lusitania,* on which over 100 Americans died when she went down on 7 May 1915. American protests brought some German assurances that it would not adopt a sink-without-warning policy.

But the assurances were worthless, as the German sinking of the British steamship *Sussex* showed on 24 March 1916. This time Wilson issued an ultimatum to Germany and again Germany appeared to back off.

But only for a brief interval. By early 1917 it was the hope in Berlin that Britain – cut off at sea and with an increasingly exhausted French ally in tow – would sue for peace. The submarine campaign was thus an effort to restrict the flow of essential supplies to the UK and force it to its knees. It was a disastrous gamble. Not only did it fail to throttle the UK's war effort, it also provided Wilson with the pretext for war he needed. The United States declared war on Germany on 6 April 1917.

This was an outcome that Bethmann-Hollweg, the German chancellor, had tried to forestall. His own views on the U-boat campaign were not unequivocal, but his strictures were ignored by the military, who believed that the United States was already effectively on the side of the Allies. Bethmann-Hollweg had antagonized the military even more by his advocacy of the reform of the Prussian franchise. Ludendorff and Hindenburg were so incensed that they hurried to Berlin and threatened to resign if these "radical" measures were adopted. The Kaiser consulted the crown prince, well known for his reactionary views. More remarkably the crown prince consulted a number of political leaders. This was an unprecedented step, which yielded a surprisingly broad consensus against the chancellor. On 14 July 1917, in face of opposition from all sides, Bethmann-Hollweg resigned, and was replaced by the Prussian food controller, Georg Michaelis, a figure who dutifully carried out the orders of the ruling military junta.

Five days later the Reichstag passed a resolution calling for a negotiated peace on the basis of no annexations. This measure reflected the political mood in Germany after most people had come to see that the U-boat campaign would not bring about a decisive victory. But the Reichstag peace resolution was a dead letter from the start. This was partly due to the vague wording, which could be (and was) interpreted to mean everything and nothing at the same time. But it was also because the very notion of giving up territory after three years of war was completely unacceptable to the German high command and its political suporters.

Similarly stillborn was a papal peace initiative launched in August 1917. This attempt at mediation ran aground over the question of the future of Belgium. Whatever the Reichstag had said, the high command of the German army was simply not prepared to agree to the unconditional restoration of the prewar situation. And without such assurances, there was no hope of finding a basis for a negotiated settlement between the Entente and Central Powers.

Later in the summer of 1917 and beyond, those conservative and reactionary elements opposed to a compromise peace rallied around a new political formation, the Fatherland Party. This grew into a mass organization of the right, and drew support from heavy industry, farmers' organizations, middle-class groups, and extreme nationalist

▼ The neutral stance of the Roman Catholic Church in the war offended patriotic communicants in several combatant countries, each convinced of the holy mission of their fighting men. Pope Benedict XV condemned both the sinking of the *Lusitania* and the blockade of Germany, and thereby outraged French Catholics in particular. The pope made a peace overture in 1917, but it got nowhere, since it suggested a return to the prewar situation which to the Allies was simply out of the question.

Russia in 1917

In 1917 the war in the Russian sector of the Eastern Front came to an end. The army at the front lost any belief in victory; the army in the rear joined rebellious masses no longer prepared to fight for the czar. When riots broke out in Petrograd on 8 March soldiers refused to put them down. On 15 March the Duma created a Provisional government, which persuaded the czar to abdicate. Alongside this new executive body, a series of workers' and soldiers' councils (soviets) were set up to defend the revolution. These groups appeared spontaneously in cities, towns and villages. Soldiers' councils abolished much of the degrading routine of military life; if officers wanted to keep their units intact, they worked with the soviets.

The Provisional government was destroyed by the war, which it refused to abandon. To continue the fight, it had to keep much of the old regime intact. The generals, the bankers, the industrialists were still there. But while bureaucratic power was held by the Provisional government, popular power – in particular among soldiers and urban workers – shifted to the Petrograd soviet. The new government effectively lost control of the peasantry and then of the army. The first was unavoidable. Peasants simply seized land and tried to survive the chaos of 1917. The second arose out of the impossibility of continuing the war.

The central problem was that Russia could not continue the war, but all political groups,

save the Bolsheviks, ruled out the idea of a separate peace. This was a recipe for political paralysis, visible in the countless mass demonstrations held daily on the streets of Moscow and Petrograd. A sense of these extraordinary days may be gained from Boris Pasternak's *Dr Zhivago*. The choice was between the Provisional government and its leader Kerensky, who upheld "revolutionary defensism", throwing the invader off the soil of the new regime, and "revolutionary defeatism", the conversion of war into class war and the overthrow of the Provisional government. This was the position of Lenin and his Bolshevik supporters, whose ideas were captured in two slogans: "All power to the soviets" and "Bread, peace, and land."

The moderates launched a peace offensive, aimed at European socialist movements, who could put pressure on Western governments to end the war. This policy got nowhere. Without peace, and without an army, which dissolved after the military defeats incurred during the Kerensky offensive of June and July 1917, the Provisional government simply held on. This presented the Bolsheviks with ideal conditions to increase their support. An attempt to suppress them in July failed. Equally unsuccessful was an abortive right-wing coup, led by General Kornilov. On 6 November 1917 the moment to strike had come. Bolshevik red guards captured the Winter Palace and other key points in Petrograd. Kerensky fled. The Bolshevik Revolution had begun.

◄ The Russian army sealed the fate of the Provisional government of Kerensky by its disintegration after the July 1917 offensive. Soldiers simply had had enough. They streamed home, and joined peace demonstrations in the major cities. Power slipped from the hands of the Kerensky regime into those of the Bolsheviks, the one political group unequivocally committed to ending Russian participation in the war.

▶ After an abortive counterrevolutionary coup led by the White Russian General Kornilov, the Bolsheviks secured majorities on the Soviet of Workers' and Soldiers' Deputies in Petrograd and Moscow. This prepared the way for the seizure of power on 7 November (25 October in the old calendar) 1917, by a revolutionary committee of the Petrograd Soviet. The Winter Palace – the seat of the government – was shelled by the cruiser *Aurora* and by guns at the Peter and Paul Fortress. Kerensky was forced to flee. The Second All Russian Congress of Soviets endorsed the coup and handed power to the Bolsheviks.

Aleksandr Fyodorovich Kerensky 1881–1970

Kerensky was born at Simbirsk and trained as a lawyer. He was a powerful orator and joined the Duma as a member of the labor group. He served as minister of justice in the first Provisional government of February 1917. Later on he became minister of war, and prime minister of the doomed regime. His commitment to carrying on the war, announced in powerful speeches, ensured his political failure. By July 1917 the middle ground on which he stood had crumbled. After the Bolshevik coup he fled Petrograd, and after failing to rally forces loyal to the regime, began a life of exile in the West. He died in 1971.

Lenin (Vladimir Ilyich Ulyanov) 1870–1924

In 1917 Lenin was a 44-year-old exile in Switzerland. After the February revolution he returned to Russia, with German assistance, and through his theoretical writings and daily leadership, prepared the ground for the Bolshevik revolution. He blocked moves toward an insurrection in July, and then led the seizure of power in November. In 1917–18 he took Russia out of the war, ratified peasant seizures of land and, with Trotsky, led the struggle against counterrevolutionary armies. Lenin was the only man in Russia with the political insight and iron determination both to seize power and to hold it. He died in 1924.

Leon Trotsky 1879–1940

Trotsky was raised in the Ukraine and took an active part in the 1905 revolution. In February 1917 he was a 38-year-old exile in America. He returned to Russia, joined the Bolsheviks and after the November revolution became people's commissar for war. He forged the Red Army and must be credited with having saved the revolution. After Lenin's death he lost the succession struggle to Stalin, was expelled from the party (1927), and resumed his earlier life as an émigré. He was murdered in Mexico in 1940 by one of Stalin's agents. A spell-binding orator, Trotsky embodied the spirit of the revolution before it was deformed by Stalinism.

associations. The party's program was unashamedly imperialistic, and advocated control of the Belgian and Dutch coasts and expansion into Russia and Turkey. Elements in the high command smiled benignly on this mad vision of Germany's future greatness. It was apparent, therefore, that the question of war aims further deepened the perilous social and political divisions within the Wilhelmine empire.

The Bolshevik road to peace

In the last year of the war, diplomacy moved both west and east. The Pope attempted to act as a middleman in diplomatic moves toward a compromise peace, but failed. Perhaps the high-minded Presbyterian in the White House could find a way to break the deadlock. Long before the United States entered the war, President Wilson had publicly pressed the belligerents for a declaration of war aims that could form the basis of a negotiated settlement. In January 1917 he had told the United States Senate of his commitment to "peace without victory". But initially his efforts were an insufficient force in and of themselves to get the combatants to consider realistically an alternative to the continuation of the war.

What concentrated their minds wonderfully was the first Russian revolution of March 1917. Strikes, riots and a general mutiny toppled the Russian imperial regime and a Provisional government was installed. But the new government, headed by Prince Lvov and later Aleksandr Kerensky, was committed to driving the German invaders off Russian land. This policy was termed "revolutionary defensism" – and ensured a collision with those who, like Lenin and his radical or Bolshevik followers, proclaimed the need to end the war, no matter what the cost.

The Germans were fully aware of the potentially disruptive effects of Bolshevik ideas on the course of the Russian war effort. They therefore had no difficulty in arranging passage for the exiled Lenin from Switzerland through the German and Austrian lines back to the Finland Station in Petrograd in April 1917.

Lenin proceeded to draw support to the Bolshevik position through his indictment of the war policy of the Provisional government. Many of these oppositional elements clustered around the councils of workers' and soldiers' deputies, or soviets. The most important such council sat in Petrograd, and in the chaotic conditions of early 1917 it assumed a position of power rivaling that of the Provisional government itself.

At this time the radical (or Bolshevik) wing of the Russian social democratic party did not have anything like a majority in the soviets, but the decision to continue the war ultimately gave it to them. The new Russian regime was trying to keep open both diplomatic and military options. It therefore looked favorably on attempts by the Petrograd soviet to convene an international conference of socialists at Stockholm in the summer of 1917. The hope was that delegates from both sides would reach agreement on the basis of a negotiated settlement, and then return to lobby their respective governments to find an end to the war.

◀ Trotsky signed an armistice on 5 December 1917 in Brest-Litovsk. But peace negotiations dragged on for three months, while Trotsky (seen here on the right, arriving at Brest-Litovsk) tried to avoid the harsh terms set by the Germans.

▶ The German response to the Bolshevik tactic of "No war, no peace" was simply to move forward on a broad front in the Ukraine. Here German troops enter Minsk.

▼ Red Army soldiers choosing delegates in Petrograd for the first post-revolutionary congress of soviets.

Even though delegations were formed from all European belligerents, the full conference never took place. The reason was that, to increase its standing with the Allies, the Russian government authorized an offensive. It opened on 1 July 1917, and soon turned into a fiasco. Consequently Britain and France saw little military advantage in supporting the Kerensky government politically, by going along with the Stockholm idea. The French government withheld passports from its delegates, British seamen refused to transport the British delegation and so the initiative sank, along with the chances of survival of those still advocating "revolutionary defensism".

A few months later, in November, Lenin and the Bolsheviks seized power, and proceeded to act on their commitment to end the war. The price was the humiliating Treaty of Brest-Litovsk,

signed on 3 March 1918, giving Germany a huge satellite empire in the east. But Lenin (and the Germans who had organized his return to Russia) judged correctly that bad as these terms were most Russians preferred them to the continuation of the war.

This "betrayal" of the Allied cause, not Bolshevik Marxism (which the Western leaders did not understand anyway), led Britain and France to sponsor the domestic enemies of the new regime. In 1918–19 British, French and American troops arrived in Russia, to try to hold down German troops and prevent their acquisition of Allied supplies, and then, if possible, to topple the regime. This intervention was half-hearted and futile. It did not possess the strength to influence Russian events one way or the other, and it betrayed a phenomenal ignorance of Russian conditions. The only outcome of Allied intervention was to create in the new regime a suspicion of Western motives which to some extent exists to this day.

Peace or revolution

German victory on the Eastern Front presented the Allies with the specter of increased military pressure in the west producing a decisive German thrust in France and Flanders before the American army could take the field. This is *almost* what happened, following the last German gamble of the war, the offensive launched on 21 March 1918. Within a few days the Germans had achieved what had eluded everyone else since 1914: a dislodgement of the enemy and an advance of about 65km (40mi). Further gains were made south of Ypres in April, and in Champagne in late May, and as far as the Marne on 30 May, at a point only 60km (37mi) from Paris.

But, though it was unclear at the time, that was the end of the offensive. The German army had staged a remarkable coup, but like every other major offensive of the war on the Western Front it could not produce a *decisive* breakthrough. The German army did not have the means to exploit its initial successes and rout the French or British armies completely. Faced with considerable logistical difficulties, and with few reserves on which to call, the German army could not stop the Allied counterattacks of August 1918.

Ludendorff later wrote that the "black day" of the German army was 8 August 1918. On the ground Canadian, Australian and British troops succeeded in pushing the Germans back from Amiens. In fact little in these developments was earth-shattering. Much more ominous than the outcome of this particular engagement were reports reaching the German high command of demoralization among their troops, leading to mass surrenders. This is what gave the 8th of August its real significance. It is not that the German army collapsed; it is rather that, from that moment, it ceased to believe it could achieve victory. Ludendorff was presented with increasing and undeniable evidence of a soldiers' strike among his men in the late summer and early autumn of 1918. After four years of believing their own claims of invincibility and propaganda about a pending victory, the recognition that they could not win came suddenly and bitterly to the German army.

This collapse of military morale was rapidly conveyed to the home front, which by the summer of 1918, had its own reasons for believing that the game was up. In March 1918 the nation had united once again, and great hopes had been placed on the one final push needed for victory. But when this proved chimerical, disillusionment spread like wildfire. Shortages of essential supplies became intolerable, and the situation was made worse by the onset of the worst epidemic of influenza the world had ever seen.

In military terms the disintegration of the Eastern Front and the loss of Bulgaria in September – which stripped Germany of essential petroleum reserves – were probably the last straws. The German high command simply could not carry on for more than a few weeks with what had become an increasingly mechanized war. Under the circumstances Ludendorff bitterly recognized that an outright victory had eluded him, and that the only alternatives to a military collapse in the west and an Allied invasion of Bohemia and southern Germany were an armistice and a negotiated peace. To seek an end to hostilities was also imperative for another, domestic, reason: it was to Ludendorff the only alternative to chaos – by which he meant the spread of revolution.

It is therefore ironic that Ludendorff turned to Woodrow Wilson as the man who could save Germany from catastrophe, both military and political. Ludendorff knew that Wilson would not deal with the old regime. Consequently he and his allies proceeded to hand over to his arch enemies in the Reichstag the political power the high command had exercised with such disastrous results over the previous two years.

In October 1918 the political scene was transformed. With the blessings of the high command, a major set of constitutional reforms was implemented. These steps virtually introduced parliamentary government, as a means of saving the Hohenzollern monarchy and of forestalling more radical developments. A new government under Prince Max of Baden was formed on 1 October, supported by a party political majority in the

Georges Benjamin Clemenceau 1841–1929

The son of a Vendée physician, Clemenceau received a medical education, and then entered political life. He was mayor of Montmartre at the time of the Paris commune. In the 1870s he became the leader of the radical party. He championed Zola and Dreyfus in his newspaper *L'Aurore*, and became minister of the interior in 1906, and premier from 1906 to 1909. His second ministry was during the war, when in 1917, at the age of 76, he became premier and minister of war, and reasserted parliamentary control over military affairs. He served until 1920, and died nine years later.

The Armistice of 11 November

The collapse of the Central Powers began on the Eastern Front. In September 1918 a major Allied offensive broke the German-Bulgarian line. On 30 September the Bulgarian government signed an armistice at Salonika. This convinced the German high command to force the government to enter into negotiations for an immediate general armistice, understood by Hindenburg and Ludendorff as creating a breathing space for regrouping their forces rather than as surrender. On 3 October Prince Max von Baden sent a note to President Wilson asking him to arrange an armistice. This was an admission of defeat, on which there was no going back. In the next three weeks the Allies pressed their offensive in bitter fighting on the Western Front, but the German line, in full retreat, did not break. Worse news for the Germans came from the Italian Front, where the Austro-Hungarian army was split into two in an Italian drive towards Vittorio Veneto. On 3 November Austria-Hungary capitulated. This followed by a few days the surrender of Turkey, on 30 October, after they had suffered a major defeat at the hands of British forces under Allenby. By early November, Germany was stripped of oil supplies, had run out of allies, men and essential materiel, faced revolution at home, and an Allied invasion of Germany from the south and east. The only option was to sue for peace. On 6 November a German armistice commission, led by the centrist deputy Mathias Erzberger, met General Foch in a railway carriage in Compiègne. They negotiated an armistice to come into effect at 11am on 11 November, to last 30 days. It was periodically renewed. The terms agreed were the immediate German evacuation of occupied territory behind the Western Front, the renunciation of the Treaty of Brest-Litovsk, the withdrawal of German troops in the east, and the surrender of certain war materiel, including 10 battleships, 6 cruisers, 8 light cruisers, 50 destroyers and 160 submarines. The U-boat fleet sailed into Harwich on 20 November. France was evacuated by the German army on 18 November; the Germans finally left Belgium eight days later. An Allied occupation of Germany began on 1 December. The naval blockade continued, to prevent any renewal of hostilities.

▶ **Foch and German delegates outside Foch's carriage.**

Reichstag. Within two days the new regime sent a note to President Wilson asking him personally "to take steps for the restoration of peace". This note and later exchanges were published, and made it apparent that the price of peace was to be high. The negotiations dragged on, and given the publicity that surrounded them, they contributed to a sense of despair and confusion in the population at large as to why the war was continuing.

The collapse of the Austro-Hungarian Empire in October 1918 placed in unmistakably high relief the hopelessness of the German cause. Consequently the pressure to conclude a peace at virtually any price grew apace. The process of political reform was accelerated simply to bring

about an armistice. This helps account for the fact that on the same day, 26 October, Ludendorff resigned as quartermaster general, and the Reichstag completed its deliberations on the shape of a future parliamentary government. Ludendorff's replacement was Groener.

Thus the decision to end the war and to accept political reform – the "revolution from above" was taken by the German high command and their allies well before the outbreak of widespread revolutionary activity among workers and sailors from 28 October – "the revolution from below".

What in the eyes of the masses seemed to make peace all the more urgent was the treasonous activities of the admirals. Concerned to secure a future for the navy in postwar Germany, they ordered a sortie of the battle fleet for a heroic do-or-die encounter with the more powerful Royal Navy. They did so in the knowledge that this was bound to discredit the armistice negotiations of their political superiors. But the "honor" of the navy, as they understood it, was more important to them than an end to the war or the lives of the men they led. The sailors, learning of the suicide mission, took a different view and disobeyed orders. This time mutiny merged with revolution; the sailors had won the day. Demonstrations broke out, first in the port cities and then in other urban centers. By 7–8 November the situation had got completely out of hand. The "revolution from below" was underway.

Prince Max announced the abdication of the Kaiser before the latter had given his consent. His generals persuaded the monarch that he had no choice but to go; they arranged for him to slip across the Dutch border near his headquarters at Spa in Belgium. Prince Max also resigned, and the Hohenzollern monarchy simply collapsed. Power was lying in the streets of Berlin, as it did in other capitals of Central Europe.

On 11 November 1918 the Armistice was signed. In Germany the old order had put an end to the military conflict and had managed to transfer responsibility for the mess they had created to the new democratic regime. At last the politicians' war was over.

We know, too, that the object of the war is attained; the object upon which all free men had set their hearts; and attained with a sweeping completeness which even now we do not realize. Armed imperialism such as the men conceived who were but yesterday the masters of Germany is at an end, its illicit ambitions engulfed in black disaster. Who will now seek to revive it?

WOODROW WILSON
11 NOVEMBER 1918

Thomas Woodrow Wilson 1856–1924

The son of a Presbyterian minister from Virginia, Wilson was an academic, a moralist and a Democratic politician. In 1910 he was elected governor of New Jersey, and two years later, president of the United States. He was reelected in 1916, in the midst of a war toward which he had maintained a neutral stance. Wilson tried to act as an honest broker between the sides, but gradually saw war with Germany as inevitable, given German unrestricted submarine warfare and approaches to Mexico. He led his country into war in April 1917. After the Armistice he played a central part in the creation of the League of Nations. The rejection of its covenant by the US senate was the worst reversal of Wilson's career. He was not reelected in 1920, and died four years later.

THE
GENERALS'
WAR

Datafile

The first phase of the war was fought according to preordained plans. The French launched Plan XVII eastward toward Alsace, Lorraine and the Rhine, in part to achieve a lightning victory and invade Germany itself, and in part to aid their Russian allies, whose mobilization was bound to be a protracted affair. The Germans unfolded with clockwork precision the opening phases of the Schlieffen Plan, under which one million German troops invaded Belgium and Luxembourg, before wheeling south into France itself. The result was a bloodbath. Plan XVII played directly into German hands. The weight of French forces moved east, thereby exposing their forces to the north of Paris to the brunt of the German advance. Fortunately for the French, reinforcements moved west by railroad and north by any form of transport available, including the Parisian taxi fleet, and stopped the Germans on the River Marne. The failure of the Schlieffen Plan created a "race to the sea", the indecisive outcome of which fixed the military stalemate of the Western Front.

The parallel Russian advance into East Prussia resulted in a crushing German victory, on a scale similar to that inflicted on the French in 1870–71. Between 26 and 30 August a carefully executed redeployment of German troops took the Russians by surprise, at Tannenberg. The Russian Second Army under Samsonov was annihilated. Over 100,000 prisoners were taken, and Samsonov committed suicide. Two new heroes of German military history emerged: Erich Ludendorff and Paul von Hindenburg.

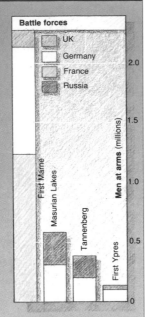

Battle forces

- UK
- Germany
- France
- Russia

Men at arms (millions): 2.0, 1.5, 1.0, 0.5, 0

First Marne · Masurian Lakes · Tannenberg · First Ypres

▲ The Battle of the Marne dwarfed the other major encounters of the first year of the war. The weight of combat on the Western Front as a whole was greater still, in that it included the French thrust eastward in Plan XVII. At this stage, the British part in the war was minor. It grew rapidly, bolstered by significant imperial forces.

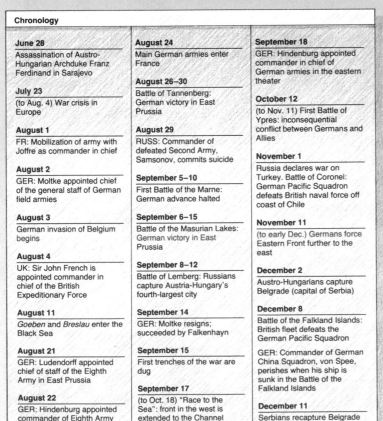

Chronology

June 28	**August 24**	**September 18**
Assassination of Austro-Hungarian Archduke Franz Ferdinand in Sarajevo	Main German armies enter France	GER: Hindenburg appointed commander in chief of German armies in the eastern theater
July 23	**August 26–30**	
(to Aug. 4) War crisis in Europe	Battle of Tannenberg: German victory in East Prussia	**October 12**
		(to Nov. 11) First Battle of Ypres: inconsequential conflict between Germans and Allies
August 1	**August 29**	
FR: Mobilization of army with Joffre as commander in chief	RUSS: Commander of defeated Second Army, Samsonov, commits suicide	**November 1**
		Russia declares war on Turkey. Battle of Coronel: German Pacific Squadron defeats British naval force off coast of Chile
August 2	**September 5–10**	
GER: Moltke appointed chief of the general staff of German field armies	First Battle of the Marne: German advance halted	
		November 11
August 3	**September 6–15**	(to early Dec.) Germans force Eastern Front further to the east
German invasion of Belgium begins	Battle of the Masurian Lakes: German victory in East Prussia	
		December 2
August 4	**September 8–12**	Austro-Hungarians capture Belgrade (capital of Serbia)
UK: Sir John French is appointed commander in chief of the British Expeditionary Force	Battle of Lemberg: Russians capture Austria-Hungary's fourth-largest city	
		December 8
August 11	**September 14**	Battle of the Falkland Islands: British fleet defeats the German Pacific Squadron
Goeben and Breslau enter the Black Sea	GER: Moltke resigns; succeeded by Falkenhayn	
		GER: Commander of German China Squadron, von Spee, perishes when his ship is sunk in the Battle of the Falkland Islands
August 21	**September 15**	
GER: Ludendorff appointed chief of staff of the Eighth Army in East Prussia	First trenches of the war are dug	
August 22	**September 17**	**December 11**
GER: Hindenburg appointed commander of Eighth Army	(to Oct. 18) "Race to the Sea": front in the west is extended to the Channel coast	Serbians recapture Belgrade

---

In warfare, according to the Prussian theorist Karl von Clausewitz (1780–1831), everything is simple, and the simplest things are infinitely complicated. The way World War I was fought in its first phase demonstrates the disturbing truth of these words. The vision of those who planned for war in 1914 was in some respects remarkable, but what they had not taken into account was another of Clausewitz's ideas. That is the concept of "friction", the tendency for plans to come unstuck, for things to go awry, for the unexpected to govern events.

Successful command in World War I was not the ability to execute great preconceived programs, to meet rigid timetables and to adhere to a set pattern of given objectives. It was rather the art of living with confusion and uncertainty, and accepting the limitations of even the best technology of the day. In this context the war fought by

Prewar Military Planning

Military planners before 1914 were set the task of finding ways to respond to potential threats to national interests. The instability of the international system provided many such threats. The existence of plans, however, increased political tension and contributed to the outbreak of war itself. In prewar Western Europe three plans caused problems. The first was for the enhancement of German naval strength, devised by Admiral Alfred von Tirpitz (see pp.30–31). The second was the French Plan XVII for the reversal of its humiliating defeat by Prussia in the war of 1870–71, which gave birth to the German Empire and stripped France of Alsace and Lorraine. The third was the German Schlieffen Plan, to break out of the "encirclement" of Germany, faced with the prospect of a two-front war against France and Russia. Each plan led Europe toward war, but when war came, each plan did not produce the anticipated outcome. The result was an unforeseen protracted and bloody war.

Count Alfred von Schlieffen   1833–1913

Schlieffen was a military strategist of genius. From his experience in the Franco-Prussian War (1870–71) and his interest in military theory and history he was able, as chief of the German imperial general staff (1891–1906), to conceive a daring plan for fighting a war on two fronts, the so-called Schlieffen Plan. Its aim was the annihilation of the French army before Russian mobilization was completed. Although he died before his plan could be tested in the field, he left his successor, Moltke, with a clear strategy wedded to an effective logistical support system. But Moltke weakened the crucial right wing and failed to take Paris in 1914. Whether or not Schlieffen's original plan could have succeeded is a controversial question.

1914 THE WAR OF ILLUSIONS

the generals was littered with disasters, arising from limitations of imagination and materiel. Those who succeeded did so through improvisation, not planning.

From the Schlieffen Plan to the Marne

These points were epitomized by the first major campaign of the war, that of the German army in Belgium and France in August–September 1914. The war planned by the German general staff was in line with the strategic objective of knocking France out of the conflict before Russia would conquer Eastern Germany. It accepted the risks of an early Russian move westward and a French attack on Alsace and Lorraine, in order to unleash five armies – three-quarters of the entire German army in a gigantic westward sweep across Belgium and Luxembourg, followed by a wheel south into France. The whole operation was to

take precisely 42 days. This was the "Schlieffen Plan", the German army's gamble to win the war in one fell swoop. It was devised between 1897 and 1905 by Alfred von Schlieffen, head of the German general staff (1891–1906), was modified in the next few years, and then finally put into operation by his successor, General Helmuth von Moltke, in August 1914.

German mobilization was underway by 1 August 1914. Between 1 and 3 August the German Fourth Army occupied Luxembourg; the following day, just as Schlieffen had planned, forward units advanced into Belgium. The forts surrounding Liège held up the progress of the Second Army, but the city surrendered on 16 August, after an 11-day siege.

The French army, under General Joffre, was unaware of its enemy's true intentions. In any event the French had their own preconceived set

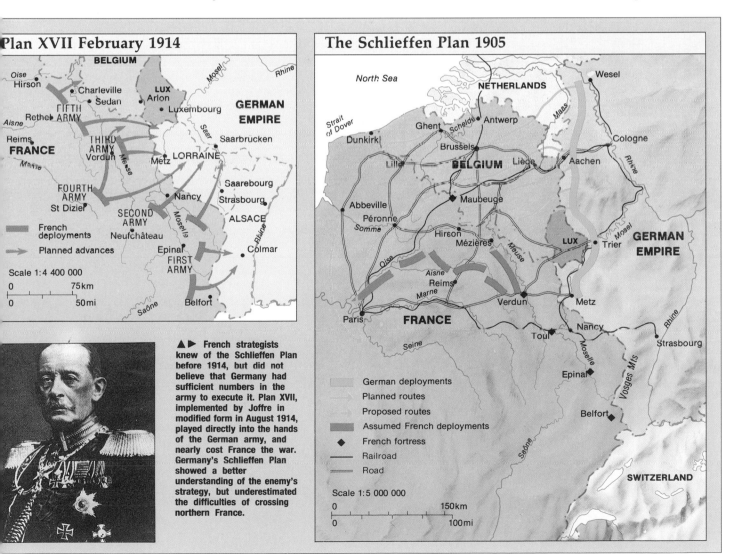

Plan XVII February 1914

BELGIUM
Oise
Hirson
Charleville
Sedan
LUX
Arlon
Luxembourg
GERMAN
EMPIRE
FIFTH ARMY
Rethel
Aisne
Reims
THIRD ARMY
Verdun
Saarbrucken
Metz
LORRAINE
FRANCE
Marne
FOURTH ARMY
St Dizier
Nancy
Saarebourg
Strasbourg
SECOND ARMY
Neufchâteau
ALSACE
Epinal
FIRST ARMY
Colmar
Belfort
Saône

French deployments

Planned advances

Scale 1:4 400 000

0   75km
0   50mi

▲ ▶ French strategists knew of the Schlieffen Plan before 1914, but did not believe that Germany had sufficient numbers in the army to execute it. Plan XVII, implemented by Joffre in modified form in August 1914, played directly into the hands of the German army, and nearly cost France the war. Germany's Schlieffen Plan showed a better understanding of the enemy's strategy, but underestimated the difficulties of crossing northern France.

The Schlieffen Plan 1905

North Sea
NETHERLANDS
Wesel
Strait of Dover
Ghent
Schelde
Antwerp
Dunkirk
Brussels
Cologne
Lille
BELGIUM
Liège
Aachen
Rhine
Abbeville
Maubeuge
Péronne
Somme
Hirson
Mézières
Oise
Meuse
LUX
Trier
GERMAN EMPIRE
Aisne
Reims
Marne
Verdun
Metz
Paris
FRANCE
Nancy
Toul
Strasbourg
Seine
Moselle
Epinal
Vosges Mts
Belfort
Saône
SWITZERLAND

German deployments

Planned routes

Proposed routes

Assumed French deployments

◆ French fortress

Railroad

Road

Scale 1:5 000 000

0   150km
0   100mi

Helmuth von Moltke 1848–1916

Sixty-six years old in 1914 and in failing health, Moltke (chief of the imperial general staff since 1906) had to translate Schlieffen's plans into action. Faced with war on two fronts, he followed Schlieffen's principles of containing the Russian army with minimum forces in the east and outflanking the French in the west. Unfortunately he had modified Schlieffen's original plan by withdrawing six divisions from the west to strengthen the eastern forces. He was blamed for the German defeat at the First Battle of the Marne and relieved of his post.

Joseph Jacques Joffre 1852–1931

A veteran of the defense of Paris in 1870 and numerous colonial skirmishes, Joffre in the summer of 1914 was one of France's most experienced soldiers. At 63 he was commander in chief of the French army and led the resistance to the German invasion. He checked the German advance at the First Battle of the Marne. After the indecisive "race to the sea" and onset of trench warfare he became more a symbolic figure than a decisive leader. The Battle of Verdun gave the politicians the opportunity to ease him out. He played no further part in the war.

Sir John French 1852–1925

When Britain entered the war in August 1914 French was chosen to command the British Expeditionary Force, at the age of 66. A veteran cavalry officer, he retained command of the British army on the Western Front until the end of 1915. His departure was provoked by the fruitless struggles at Ypres and elsewhere, culminating in the Battle of Loos when British losses far outweighed those of the Germans for no gain. Like other cavalry men, he was puzzled by the nature of the war of 1914–15.

of operations to put into effect: Plan XVII. This was an eastward thrust into the provinces of Alsace and Lorraine (which had been occupied by Germany in the Franco-Prussian war of 1870). Such a move was precisely what the Germans wanted the French to do, since it weakened the French lines at the point at which they intended to strike, in the north. The implementation of Plan XVII (in an amended form) was a complete and bloody failure. The Germans repulsed repeated French attacks in the east between 10 and 28 August, while opening the key phase of their campaign in the west.

Five armies participated in the German invasion as a whole, but the most important was the First, under Alexander von Kluck. His forces (an army initially of 320,000 men) were on the outer edge of the German arc and would therefore cover the most ground of any unit. His men crossed into Belgium on 16 August, and entered Brussels four days later. The German armies then headed south, and by 29 August, in successful operations at Mons, Le Cateau and Charleroi, they had forced heavily outnumbered troops of the British Expeditionary Force (Britain's contribution to the defense of Belgium and France, commanded by Sir John French) and the French army to retreat southward.

Retreat is one of the most dangerous military maneuvers: the fact that it was accomplished at all was one of the wonders of the war. The new Allied line formed in early September just south of the Marne, and swept from the city of Meaux above Paris to Verdun on the River Meuse, 260km (160mi) away.

Along the River Marne, between 5 and 10 September, Allied counterattacks, known as the First Battle of the Marne, stopped the larger German armies, forced them to regroup north of the river, and destroyed the Schlieffen Plan. World War I was born.

► German reserve units and reinforcements assembling in the old market square of Mechelen (or Malines), about 25km (15mi) north of Brussels, in August 1914. Belgian armed resistance was unable to do more than slow down the Germans; the city of Liège fell only on 16 August after stiff resistance. The capital was taken on 20 August. German troops lived off the land and took severe measures against Belgians accused of resisting the German advance. The result was a panic among civilians, leading to an exodus of one million Belgian refugees.

The German Invasion of Belgium and France 1914

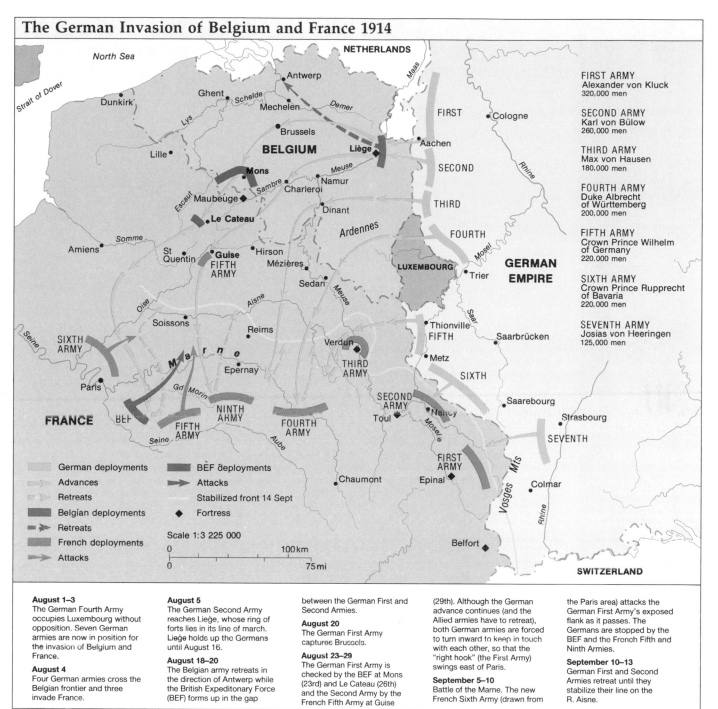

FIRST ARMY
Alexander von Kluck
320,000 men

SECOND ARMY
Karl von Bülow
260,000 men

THIRD ARMY
Max von Hausen
180,000 men

FOURTH ARMY
Duke Albrecht
of Württemberg
200,000 men

FIFTH ARMY
Crown Prince Wilhelm
of Germany
220,000 men

SIXTH ARMY
Crown Prince Rupprecht
of Bavaria
220,000 men

SEVENTH ARMY
Josias von Heeringen
125,000 men

German deployments
Advances
Retreats
Belgian deployments
Retreats
French deployments
Attacks

BEF deployments
Attacks
Stabilized front 14 Sept
Fortress

Scale 1:3 225 000
0   100 km
0   75 mi

August 1–3
The German Fourth Army occupies Luxembourg without opposition. Seven German armies are now in position for the invasion of Belgium and France.

August 4
Four German armies cross the Belgian frontier and three invade France.

August 5
The German Second Army reaches Liège, whose ring of forts lies in its line of march. Liège holds up the Germans until August 16.

August 18–20
The Belgian army retreats in the direction of Antwerp while the British Expeditonary Force (BEF) forms up in the gap between the German First and Second Armies.

August 20
The German First Army captures Brussels.

August 23–29
The German First Army is checked by the BEF at Mons (23rd) and Le Cateau (26th) and the Second Army by the French Fifth Army at Guise

(29th). Although the German advance continues (and the Allied armies have to retreat), both German armies are forced to turn inward to keep in touch with each other, so that the "right hook" (the First Army) swings east of Paris.

September 5–10
Battle of the Marne. The new French Sixth Army (drawn from the Paris area) attacks the German First Army's exposed flank as it passes. The Germans are stopped by the BEF and the French Fifth and Ninth Armies.

September 10–13
German First and Second Armies retreat until they stabilize their line on the R. Aisne.

Assessment of the Schlieffen Plan

Whether or not the Schlieffen Plan could have succeeded is one of the most hotly debated topics in military history. Critics of Moltke's tactics usually concentrate on the fact that his right wing (initially on the northern side) was not eight times stronger than his left wing, as stipulated by Schlieffen, but only three times stronger. They also question the wisdom of the decision to move north and east of Paris rather than south and west in an enveloping assault on the city, and point to the creation of a 48km (30mi) gap between the German First and Second Armies as a fatal mistake, leading to defeat on the Marne.

But these might-have-beens ignore three fundamental problems which doomed the Schlieffen Plan from the start. The first concerns human

endurance; the second, logistical difficulties; the third, communications problems. The plan failed to take account of the limitations of the individual soldier and of the system which supplied and directed him.

First, the men of the German First Army had to cover 30–40km (20–25mi) per day. Is it a surprise that by early September many units were simply exhausted, and that others had been reduced to 50 percent of their original strength? Secondly, their lines of supply were so extended that, even had they won the Battle of the Marne, they almost certainly could have gone no further. Thirdly, the speed of the operation outpaced the communications system between the Front and the high command, situated in Luxembourg, 240km (150mi) away. Thus Moltke could not obtain

▲ Schlieffen's idea was that the sleeve of the last German soldier on the right flank would almost brush the English Channel in an arcing movement west and then south through Belgium and France. Moltke's reality (above) was only slightly less breathtaking. The First Army (under Alexander von Kluck) had to march, fight and march again in a 350km (220mi) line extending from Aachen to Brussels to Le Cateau to the River Marne. That it was stopped there is not surprising; the troops had reached the limits of human endurance.

▲ German troops on the Eastern Front in 1914. "Eastern fronts" would be a more accurate description of the 1,000km (625mi) field of operations formed by the Germans and Austro-Hungarians on one side and the Russians and Serbians on the other. The Germans occupied the northern reaches of the "front" on the Baltic Sea near the present-day boundaries of Poland and Lithuania. The Austro-Hungarians were engaged in Eastern Galicia and in Serbia, in what is today Yugoslavia. This line included every conceivable kind of terrain, from marshland to forest to mountains, which gave to the Eastern Front its fluidity and varied character.

enough information to direct the campaign. In fact the crucial decision of 9 September to withdraw the German right flank from its original route to the River Aisne was taken not by Moltke but by First and Second Army staff officers and Lt-Col. Richard Hentsch, sent by his commander to find out what was going on. The fog of war had simply obscured the battlefield from the people at the top who needed to know. More than just human error was involved in the collapse of the Germans' grand design of winning the war in its first months and repeating their spectacular successes of 1870–71. The German army had tried to do the impossible.

Tannenberg

An even more spectacular example of an offensive that went wrong was the initial Russian move west in August and September 1914. The calculated risk of the Schlieffen Plan was that it offered Russia the chance to attack Germany in the east.

Alexander Samsonov 1859–1914

In 1914 Samsonov, a 55-year-old veteran of the Russo-Japanese War of 1904–05, was named as commander of the Second Army. It was ill-equipped and poorly trained and fell to the German Eighth Army in the Battle of Tannenberg. The German success was due in part to the failure of the Russian First Army to assist the Second, but no person was solely responsible for the debacle. However, after the defeat Samsonov shot himself, thereby providing an object of blame for Russian officials.

This challenge was accepted, and in the initial stages of the operation, between 17 and 22 August, two Russian armies advanced into East Prussia, one under Paul Rennenkampf in the north and the other under Alexander Samsonov further south. This led the commander of the German Eighth Army, Max von Prittwitz, to contemplate a general retreat to the River Vistula.

The thought of retreat convinced Moltke that Prittwitz had to go. He was sacked and replaced by the two men who later came to run the entire German war effort: Paul von Hindenburg, an elderly retired general (he was 67 years old), and Erich Ludendorff, a 49-year-old officer who had distinguished himself at the battle of Liège on 8 August, and who really directed military operations under Hindenburg's supervision. The reputation of these two men was made by the terrible defeat they inflicted on the Russian army at the end of August 1914 in the Battle of Tannenberg (southeast of Danzig). At Tannenberg a defensive force outwitted and outfought an offensive force superior to it in size. (It was therefore a closer parallel to the Battle of the Marne than the Germans were prepared to admit.)

It would be more accurate to give the credit for the victory not to Hindenburg and Ludendorff, but to a little-known staff officer, Max Hoffmann, who had already planned the master stroke well before Prittwitz's dismissal. This entailed negating the greater manpower of the combined Russian armies (totaling 21 infantry divisions as against 11 for the Germans) by withdrawing the forces facing the Russian first Army, under Rennenkampf, and sending them south to confront Samsonov's Second Army.

Paul von Hindenburg 1847–1934

In late August 1914 Hindenburg, a retired 66-year-old Prussian career soldier, was recalled to command the German Eighth Army. Success on the Eastern Front from 1914–16 made him a national hero and the natural choice in August 1916 to succeed Falkenhayn as chief of staff. He ended the war of attrition at Verdun and withdrew the army to the more defensive Hindenburg line. In 1918 he and Ludendorff launched a massive offensive on the Western Front. Its failure led to the Armistice. He was called again from retirement in 1926 to become president of Germany. One of his last acts was the appointment of Hitler as chancellor in 1933.

Erich Ludendorff 1856–1937

A brilliant tactician, Ludendorff was appointed quartermaster general of the German Second Army in the mobilization of July 1914. In the opening invasion of Belgium he played a decisive role in the taking of Liège. His reward was to be made quartermaster general to Hindenburg. Their partnership lasted to 1918. He was a key figure in the militarization of the German economy and the prosecution of unrestricted submarine warfare. After the war he became a leader of anti-Jewish, anticommunist and anti-Jesuit agitation.

► The early stages of the war on the Eastern Front went badly for the Central Powers. In August the Austro-Hungarian invasion of Serbia was repulsed. A few weeks later the Russians took Lemberg and forced the Austro-Hungarians to evacuate eastern Galicia. The German army also suffered similar reverses. The Russian First Army advanced into East Prussia and on 20 August defeated the German Eighth Army under Prittwitz in the Battle of Gumbinnen. This set the stage for the Battle of Tannenberg between 26 and 30 August, which resulted in the greatest German victory of the war.

In our new Headquarters at Allenstein I entered the church, close by the old castle of the Teutonic Knights, while divine service was being held. As the clergyman uttered his closing words all those present, young soldiers as well as elderly "Landsturm", sank to their knees under the overwhelming impression of their experiences. It was a worthy curtain to their heroic achievements.

PAUL VON HINDENBURG

East Prussian Battles 1914

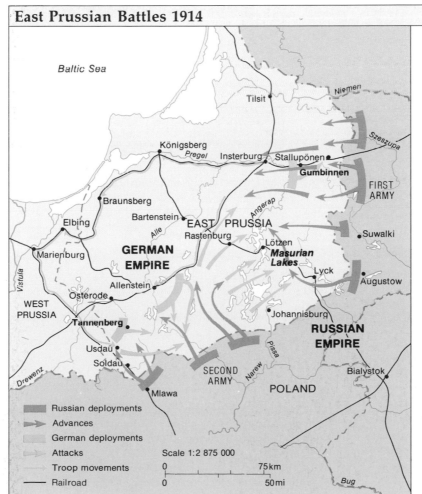

Baltic Sea

Tilsit · Niemen · Königsberg · Pregel · Insterburg · Stallupönen · Gumbinnen · Szeszupa · FIRST ARMY · Braunsberg · Bartenstein · Angerap · EAST PRUSSIA · Elbing · Alle · Rastenburg · Suwalki · Marienburg · Lötzen · Masurian Lakes · GERMAN EMPIRE · Vistula · Allenstein · Lyck · Augustow · Osterode · WEST PRUSSIA · Tannenberg · Johannisburg · RUSSIAN EMPIRE · Usdau · Soldau · Drewenz · Pissa · SECOND ARMY · Narew · Bialystok · Mlawa · POLAND · Bug

Russian deployments
Advances
German deployments
Attacks — Scale 1:2 875 000
Troop movements — 0 ... 75 km
Railroad — 0 ... 50 mi

August 17
The Russian First Army advances into East Prussia.

August 20
Battle of Gumbinnen. Nine divisions from the German Eighth Army attack the advancing Russian First Army but are beaten off. The German commander, Max von Prittwitz, informed that the Russian Second Army has crossed the border in the south, decides to abandon the defense of East Prussia and is promptly sacked.

August 23
New German commanders, Hindenburg and Ludendorff, arrive at Marienburg (HQ of German Eighth Army) and endorse Max Hoffmann's plan to denude the Front opposite the Russian First Army and concentrate on the Russian Second Army. German troops are moved south by rail. The Russians assume that the Germans are retreating.

August 26–30
Battle of Tannenberg. The Russian Second Army, pushing forward on orders to cut off "retreating" Germans in East Prussia, is smashed by the German Eighth Army.

August 31
(to Sept. 4) The Germans rapidly move troops northeast to face the Russian First Army.

September 5–9
Battle of the Masurian Lakes. Advancing German forces cause rapid Russian retreat from German territory.

The War in the Balkans

The conflict which began as a Serbo-Austrian dispute in 1914 enveloped the entire Balkan region within two years. This brought to the surface all the rival ethnic, religious and national tensions which had existed for generations. The Allied and Central Powers tried desperately to manipulate these tensions in their favor. They shared the honors. Bulgaria entered the war in October 1915 on the German side; Romania, on the Allied side in August 1916. With Bulgaria as an enemy, the Allies landed two divisions at Salonika in Greece. They could hardly help the besieged Serbians, whose position deteriorated rapidly. The day after the Allied landing in Greece (5 Oct. 1915), General von Mackensen led a major Austro-German offensive against Serbia, which was totally defeated. The remnants of its army were forced on a long winter retreat through Albania to the sea. The survivors were shipped to Corfu, which had been specially occupied by the French. While none of the campaigns in this theater was decisive, they took a toll in lives proportionately greater than that on the Western Front.

◀ Retreating Serbian cavalry cross the R. Drina.

War in the Balkans 1914–18

1914

August 12–21
Austria-Hungary invades Serbia, expecting to crush the defenders easily. The invasion is a complete failure.

September 6–28
Both Austria-Hungary and Serbia launch attacks against the other. Neither can gain the upper hand and trench warfare begins.

November 6
(to Dec. 15) Austro-Hungarian forces capture Belgrade but are then beaten back.

1915

October 5
French and British troops begin disembarking at Salonika in neutral Greece to aid Serbia.

October 6
Bulgaria enters the war on the side of the Central Powers. Serbia now faces invasion from three sides.

October 7
(to Nov. 20) Stiffened by the presence of German troops a further Austro-Hungarian invasion of Serbia makes progress. The Serbian army is forced to retreat southwest while Bulgarian troops move to contain the Allied force at Salonika.

November 21
The Serbian army begins a fighting withdrawal to the sea through Albania.

1916

January 8–17
The Austro-Hungarians attack Montenegro and knock it out

of the war. The Serbian army is evacuated by sea from Durazzo and Valona and taken to Corfu. After being reequipped it is despatched to Salonika.

August 17
(to Sept. 11) Aware that the Romanians wish to join the Allied side (Romania enters the war on August 27), the Bulgarians attempt to reduce the Salonika enclave.

September 12
(to Dec. 11) The French, British and Serbians counterattack from Salonika and retake some lost ground but cannot aid the hapless Romanians, who are crushed by a combined German, Austro-Hungarian and Bulgarian onslaught.

1917

April 24
(to May 22) Battle of Doiran. The Allies attack Salonika but suffer heavy casualties for few gains.

June 27
Greece enters the war on the side of the Allies.

1918

September 14–29
A renewed Allied offensive from Salonika causes the Bulgarian army to crumple. For the first time the Allies begin to make gains.

September 29
Bulgaria agrees to an armistice.

November 3
Austria-Hungary agrees to an armistice.

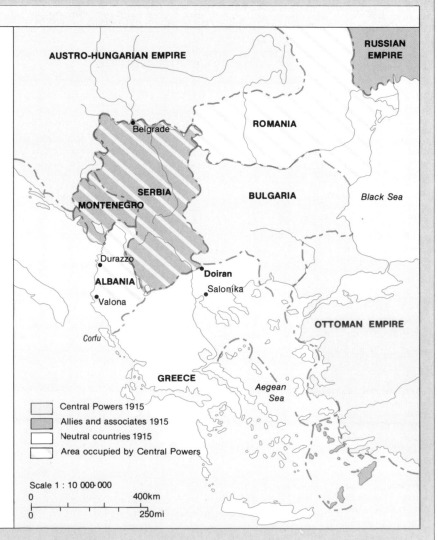

Central Powers 1915
Allies and associates 1915
Neutral countries 1915
Area occupied by Central Powers

Scale 1 : 10 000 000
0 — 400km
0 — 250mi

Between 26 and 30 August Ludendorff sprang his (and Hoffmann's) trap, into which Samsonov's army fell with ease. Everything went wrong for the Russians. Their supply system had collapsed, so the infantry were half-starved and also worn out by their long march. Because officers were unable to decode messages, the signals corps was reduced to sending uncoded signals which were easily intercepted by the Germans who thus knew both the intentions and position of their enemy.

In contrast the Russian high command had no idea what the Germans were up to until it was too late to prevent it. Samsonov believed that the Germans were retreating, and steadily advanced toward the whole German army. Rennenkampf was totally baffled by the elusiveness of the enemy, who seemed to have vanished in front of his eyes. Similarly Zhilinski, military commander of the entire northwestern sector of Russia, had at least six divisions of support troops, but never brought them into action.

The outcome was catastrophic for the Russians. Samsonov's army was destroyed and he committed suicide. The Germans captured over 100,000 men and 500 guns. Within two weeks, after a series of engagements known as the Battle of the Masurian Lakes, Rennenkampf's army was also forced back across the border.

The situation elsewhere in the east was more confused. Austrian forces went on a "punitive expedition" against Serbia in mid-August. They took Belgrade, but were pushed out again and suffered heavy losses, perhaps as many as 200,000 men. The Austrians also lost the Battle of Lemberg of 8–12 September to a group of Russian armies, which occupied large parts of Galicia (a Polish-Ukrainian-Jewish province of Austria-Hungary). Indecisive but bloody fighting between the Central Powers and Russia continued in Poland for the rest of the year, leaving the outcome of the war in the east as uncertain as that in the west.

The end of 1914 on land

By Christmas 1914 a rough balance of forces had formed in the west which was to last for years. After the Battle of the Marne, each side attempted to outflank the other to the north, but both sides lost the "race to the sea", and reached the coast without outflanking the other. Particularly bloody fighting took place around Ypres, which was held with difficulty by British and French forces.

After four months of war no decision was in sight. The German strategic plan was in ruins, but German armies had occupied most of Belgium and much of the most heavily industrialized parts of France. The costs of 1914's military operations were staggering. Casualty lists already stretched into millions, and all the armies could show for the losses was stalemate. The effort to break this is the story of the rest of the war.

The initial phase of the naval war

The early phases of the naval war were on a much smaller scale but covered a much wider area than the land conflicts. Still, the trajectory of the war at sea in 1914 paralleled the war on land: initial

action followed by stalemate. Soon after the outbreak of the war, the German cruisers *Goeben* and *Breslau* escaped the Royal Navy in the Mediterranean and wound up in Turkey (3–11 August). Three weeks later, at Heligoland Bight in the North Sea, the British took revenge. A small squadron of British warships managed to sink four German ships and to inflict 1,200 casualties on the German navy. There were British losses too, and perhaps alarmingly, a British submarine had come within an ace of sinking the British light cruiser *Southampton*.

Soon thereafter German submarines began to pose a threat to Allied ships. On 22 September one U-boat managed to torpedo three British cruisers in the North Sea. This kind of warfare became increasingly important as the conflict dragged on. On 27 October a German mine accounted for the battleship HMS *Audacious* off the Irish coast, but both the British public and the German navy were unaware of the loss.

Further afield the fortunes of war were also shared. On 1 November 1914 Admiral von Spee's German "China Squadron" sank two British cruisers at Coronel, off the west coast of South America. But von Spee then made the mistake of deciding to raid Port Stanley in the Falkland Islands, 600km (375mi) off the east coast of Argentina, before returning to the North Atlantic. On 8 December 1914 the Germans ran into the battlecruisers *Inflexible* and *Invincible* which had arrived, with other support ships, the day before. The German squadron was destroyed; only one ship escaped, and that too was sunk a few months later.

In December 1914 the German navy shelled the northeast coast of England. A month later British ships inflicted serious losses on the German navy in the North Sea, at Dogger Bank. These events made the headlines, but the more significant part of the naval war lay elsewhere: in the crucial, if unspectacular, art of blockade.

▲ In 1914 the German East Asian fleet (above), under Admiral von Spee, stationed in Klauchow in China, avoided an Anglo-Japanese naval force, and sailed across the Pacific to the Mariana Islands; to German Somoa; and to Easter Island. There the German squadron was joined by cruisers stationed off the West Indies and the California coast. They moved to Coronel off Chile, where two pursuing British ships were sunk. Proceeding to the Atlantic, von Spee decided to attack the Falkland Islands, a British base. There he met a superior force: four of his ships were sunk, and he and 1,800 of his men were killed.

Samsonov said repeatedly that the disgrace of such a defeat was more than he could bear. "The Emperor trusted me. How can I face him after such a disaster?" He went aside and his staff heard a shot. They searched for his body without success, but all are convinced that he shot himself. The Chief of Staff and other officers managed to reach Russian territory, having covered forty miles on foot...

SIR ALFRED KNOX

SURFACE NAVAL WARFARE

In the century before World War I naval warfare was revolutionized: the wooden sailing ship armed with broadside batteries of smoothbore cannon firing solid shot over relatively short ranges was replaced by the armored metal steamship, equipped with rifled guns capable of hurling large explosive projectiles over distances of 16km (10mi) or more. In the decade before the war all the major powers and most of their smaller imitators poured massive resources into the construction of modern "dreadnought" battleships (named for the first ship of this type, the United Kingdom's HMS *Dreadnought*).

After the opening few months of the war, during which there were small naval battles in distant waters, the focus of the surface naval war moved to European waters. In both the North Sea and the Mediterranean, larger Allied fleets maintained a distant blockade of enemy naval bases, while in both the Black Sea and the Baltic the Russian navy, still not fully recovered from its heavy losses in the Russo-Japanese war (1904–05), was easily contained by smaller German and Turkish forces.

The Battle of Jutland, fought at the end of May 1916, was the only full-scale fleet action of the war. Otherwise the huge European battlefleets fought only a handful of skirmishes and suffered few serious losses in the process. The generally low level of fighting was the product, first, of the numerical inferiority of the Central Powers and, second, of the disinclination of all combatants to risk the loss of irreplaceable capital ships.

Jutland itself proved a disappointment to both the British and the Germans. The Germans failed to isolate and destroy a small detachment of the British fleet, and in the end only extracted their own fleet from a disastrous engagement with a superior force by the narrowest of margins. The British not only failed to destroy the enemy which they had waited to catch away from his base for almost two years, but also suffered the more serious capital ship losses in the process. Overall, however, Jutland was a strategic victory for the British Royal Navy simply because it did not alter a situation already heavily balanced in its favor.

In the 1916–18 period the continuing pre-eminence of Allied shipbuilding programs and the eventual arrival of part of the US battlefleet in European waters accentuated the numerical inferiority of the Central Powers. Neither surface nor submarine action ever released the Central Powers from the constricting effects of Allied blockade. While historical debate still rages as to the impact of the blockade on the German war effort, the simple fact remains that Germany was unable to restore valuable economic links with the wider world that had been severed in 1914 by British naval supriority. The failure of German naval expansion was underlined with symbolic finality at the end of the war when the German fleet was first interned in the British naval base at Scapa Flow and then scuttled by its own crews to prevent its being divided among the victors.

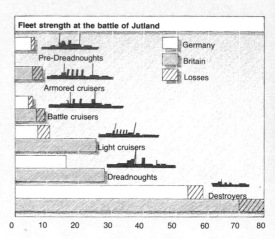

► The British fleet entered the Battle of Jutland with a profound numerical superiority over Germany's high seas fleet. German pre-Dreadnought ships and Britain's armored cruisers were obsolete vessels of limited fighting power, but in the case of both major fleet units (Dreadnoughts and battlecruisers) and their ancillary screens (light cruisers and destroyers), the British enjoyed an advantage in numbers which allowed the Germans little hope of victory. German success could have resulted only from isolating part of the British fleet.

The Battle of Jutland 1916

► The Battle of Jutland was fought on 31 May and 1 June 1916, the British grand fleet having sailed to intercept a German sortie detected by radio intercepts. A confused series of encounters began in the afternoon with a clash between the rival battlecruiser forces in which the outnumbered Germans destroyed two enemy vessels while drawing the remainder south toward their own main body. British forces then turned north in the face of superior numbers, bringing the Germans into contact with the full might of the grand fleet's Dreadnought squadrons. Although the British lost a third battlecruiser, they inflicted a severe mauling on leading elements of the German high seas fleet. The Germans eventually managed to extricate themselves and escape south in the night, losing a battlecruiser and pre-Dreadnought in the retreat.

► The German Kaiser inspecting a naval dockyard. The German command placed a high priority on fleet construction, but failed to grasp the limitations and difficulties of their naval policy, and gradually lost faith in the battlefleet when it proved incapable of breaking British naval superiority in the North Sea.

▼ The sinking of the armored cruiser *Blücher* at the Battle of Dogger Bank on 23 January 1915. Her early loss pushed the German naval high command toward a policy of extreme caution.

▼ Repair work in progress to Q Turret of HMS *Lion* after Jutland. British battlecruisers proved vulnerable to shell damage to their lightly protected turrets and magazines. In this case only the gun crew was lost, but when a ship blew up about 1,000 men could be killed.

▼ Elements of the German fleet at sea in 1910. At this stage the naval-building race with Britain was beginning to gather momentum with the introduction of the new Dreadnought battleships and battlecruisers. Although Germany entered the war with a powerful and impressive fleet, its failure as an instrument of strategic policy was all but predetermined by Britain's superiority.

Datafile

Military action on the Western Front in the second year of the war left the stalemate intact. Attempts were made on both land and sea to find a way around the concentration of forces in France and Flanders. Both sides launched naval blockades, and the Allies tried to knock Turkey out of the war by an invasion of Gallipoli, launched in April 1915. Eight months later the Allies admitted defeat and withdrew from the Turkish coast.

▼ In late August 1914 German ships began to mine the English Channel. The British Royal Navy declared the entire North Sea to be a military area, and initiated a parallel blockade of Germany. Allied shipping losses were more spectacular, but the Allied blockade of Germany was more effective in the long run.

▶ Over one million troops were engaged in the Gallipoli campaign of 1915. At the same time as the Allies were being pinned down in untenable positions on the Turkish coast, a combined German/Austrian breakthrough took place at Gorlice, in Poland, where the Russian line was breached and most of Poland was lost.

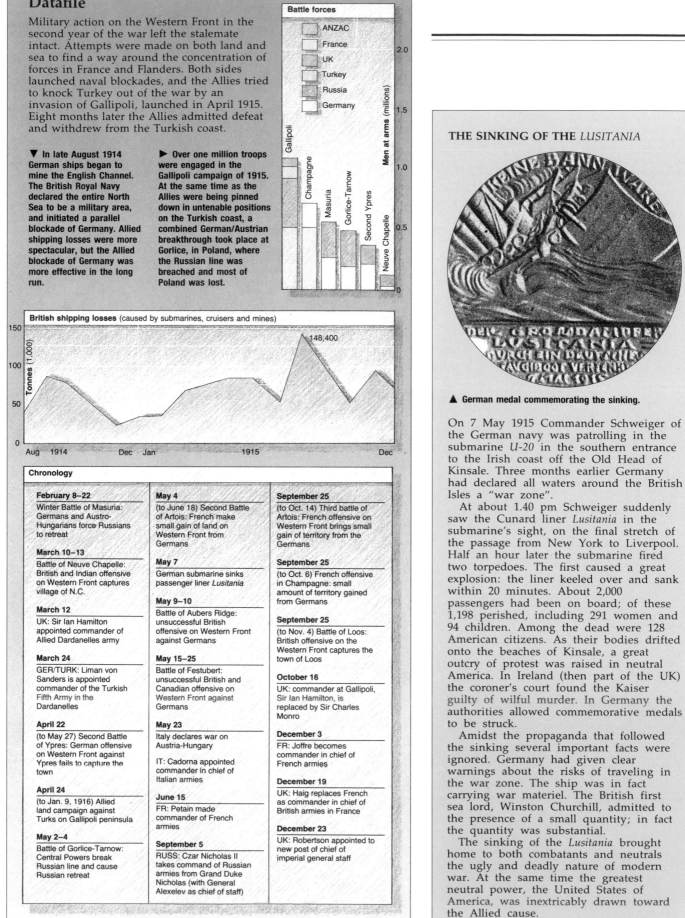

Battle forces

ANZAC / France / UK / Turkey / Russia / Germany

Men at arms (millions): 2.0, 1.5, 1.0, 0.5, 0

Gallipoli, Champagne, Masuria, Gorlice-Tarnow, Second Ypres, Neuve Chapelle

British shipping losses (caused by submarines, cruisers and mines)

Tonnes (1,000): 150, 100, 50, 0

148,400

Aug 1914 — Dec — Jan — 1915 — Dec

Chronology

February 8–22
Winter Battle of Masuria: Germans and Austro-Hungarians force Russians to retreat

March 10–13
Battle of Neuve Chapelle: British and Indian offensive on Western Front captures village of N.C.

March 12
UK: Sir Ian Hamilton appointed commander of Allied Dardanelles army

March 24
GER/TURK: Liman von Sanders is appointed commander of the Turkish Fifth Army in the Dardanelles

April 22
(to May 27) Second Battle of Ypres: German offensive on Western Front against Ypres fails to capture the town

April 24
(to Jan. 9, 1916) Allied land campaign against Turks on Gallipoli peninsula

May 2–4
Battle of Gorlice-Tarnow: Central Powers break Russian line and cause Russian retreat

May 4
(to June 18) Second Battle of Artois: French make small gain of land on Western Front from Germans

May 7
German submarine sinks passenger liner Lusitania

May 9–10
Battle of Aubers Ridge: unsuccessful British offensive on Western Front against Germans

May 15–25
Battle of Festubert: unsuccessful British and Canadian offensive on Western Front against Germans

May 23
Italy declares war on Austria-Hungary

IT: Cadorna appointed commander in chief of Italian armies

June 15
FR: Petain made commander of French armies

September 5
RUSS: Czar Nicholas II takes command of Russian armies from Grand Duke Nicholas (with General Alexelev as chief of staff)

September 25
(to Oct. 14) Third battle of Artois: French offensive on Western Front brings small gain of territory from the Germans

September 25
(to Oct. 6) French offensive in Champagne: small amount of territory gained from Germans

September 25
(to Nov. 4) Battle of Loos: British offensive on the Western Front captures the town of Loos

October 16
UK: commander at Gallipoli, Sir Ian Hamilton, is replaced by Sir Charles Monro

December 3
FR: Joffre becomes commander in chief of French armies

December 19
UK: Haig replaces French as commander in chief of British armies in France

December 23
UK: Robertson appointed to new post of chief of imperial general staff

---

THE SINKING OF THE *LUSITANIA*

▲ German medal commemorating the sinking.

On 7 May 1915 Commander Schweiger of the German navy was patrolling in the submarine *U-20* in the southern entrance to the Irish coast off the Old Head of Kinsale. Three months earlier Germany had declared all waters around the British Isles a "war zone".

At about 1.40 pm Schweiger suddenly saw the Cunard liner *Lusitania* in the submarine's sight, on the final stretch of the passage from New York to Liverpool. Half an hour later the submarine fired two torpedoes. The first caused a great explosion: the liner keeled over and sank within 20 minutes. About 2,000 passengers had been on board; of these 1,198 perished, including 291 women and 94 children. Among the dead were 128 American citizens. As their bodies drifted onto the beaches of Kinsale, a great outcry of protest was raised in neutral America. In Ireland (then part of the UK) the coroner's court found the Kaiser guilty of wilful murder. In Germany the authorities allowed commemorative medals to be struck.

Amidst the propaganda that followed the sinking several important facts were ignored. Germany had given clear warnings about the risks of traveling in the war zone. The ship was in fact carrying war materiel. The British first sea lord, Winston Churchill, admitted to the presence of a small quantity; in fact the quantity was substantial.

The sinking of the *Lusitania* brought home to both combatants and neutrals the ugly and deadly nature of modern war. At the same time the greatest neutral power, the United States of America, was inextricably drawn toward the Allied cause.

1915 STALEMATE AND STAGNATION

Britain imposes a naval blockade

Germany retaliates with unrestricted U-boat warfare

Britain seeks to knock out Turkey by landing at Gallipoli

Military failure leads to changes in the high commands

But the murderous cult of the offensive is maintained

In World War I there were two blockades: Germany's effort to cut the British lines of supply and Britain's attempt to cut the German ones. They developed together. Immediately on the outbreak of war, British ships began to patrol the North Sea, English Channel and Mediterranean, to prevent vessels reaching or leaving the ports of the Central Powers. In retaliation German Ships began to lay mines along the English coast. A major problem for both sides was posed by the presence of ships from neutral countries in blockaded waters. On 29 October 1914 a British order in council declared that neutral ships had to prove that their consignments were not destined for Germany. On 3 November the British declared the entire North Sea to be a military area. The Germans took this step to be a declaration of unrestricted economic warfare. They announced that from 4 February 1915 submarine warfare would begin against the UK. Three weeks later

Britain issued a "reprisal order", authorizing the seizure of cargo heading to or from Germany.

The German action threatened traffic across the Atlantic, so the American response was crucial. President Wilson laid down the doctrine of "strict accountability", placing the responsibility for any loss of American lives on Germany. When the British liner *Lusitania* – a passenger liner sailing from New York to Liverpool that was almost certainly also carrying munitions – was sunk on 7 May 1915, with the loss of 1,198 people, including 128 Americans, this disaster put Germany in the dock. On 19 August three Americans perished in the sinking of the liner *Arabic* south of Ireland, thereby increasing hostility to the Central Powers. The Germans were forced to give assurances that henceforth no ships would be sunk without warning and without adequate provision for rescuing noncombatants. "Henceforth" lasted for about a year.

▼ **Naval blockades. In the enforcement of blockades both sides broke the international regulations strictly determined by the London conference of 1909.**

Naval Blockades 1914–19

1914

August 4
British ships establish patrols in the Mediterranean (in cooperation with the French), the North Sea and the English Channel to prevent the passage of shipping to or from the Central Powers.

1915

February 4
The Germans, unwilling to challenge Allied superiority on the surface, establish a submarine blockade and declare any vessel in the seas around the UK a legitimate target.

May 7
The German submarine *U-20* torpedoes the passenger liner *Lusitania* without warning. Among the victims are 128 Americans.

May 23
Italy enters the war on the side of the Allies and joins Allied Mediterranean patrols.

August 19
The German submarine *U-24* torpedoes the passenger liner *Arabic* without warning. Among the dead are three Americans.

August 30
In response to American protests the Germans prohibit the sinking of passenger vessels without warning.

September 18
To reduce further the danger to American shipping the Germans withdraw their U-boats from the English Channel and western approaches.

1916

March 13
Germany loosens its U-boat restrictions to allow captains to sink British vessels in home waters without warning, if they do not appear to be passenger ships.

March 24
German U-boat *UB-29* torpedoes the passenger ship *Sussex* without warning, causing the loss of more American lives.

April 20
The USA threatens to break off diplomatic relations with Germany.

April 24
German U-boats are instructed not to sink vessels without warning.

1917

February 1
Germany again declares unrestricted submarine warfare.

February 3
The USA severs relations with Germany.

April 6
The USA enters the war on the side of the Allies.

April 30
British prime minister Lloyd George insists that the British admiralty experiments with convoys for merchant shipping. They prove a great success and enable the Allies to survive the German blockade. The Allied blockade continues until 1919.

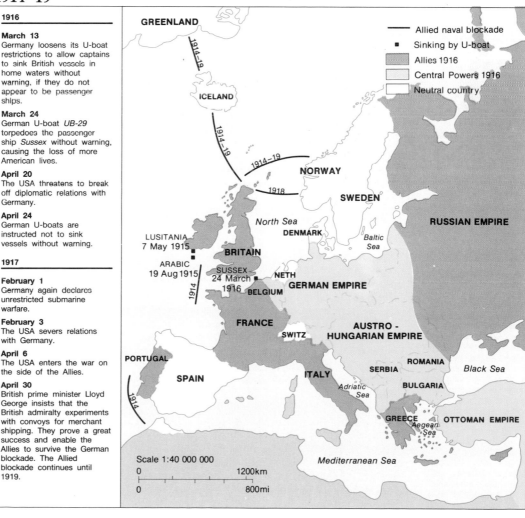

GREENLAND

—— Allied naval blockade

■ Sinking by U-boat

░ Allies 1916

Central Powers 1916

Neutral country

ICELAND

1914–19

NORWAY

1918

SWEDEN

North Sea

DENMARK

Baltic Sea

RUSSIAN EMPIRE

LUSITANIA 7 May 1915

BRITAIN

ARABIC 19 Aug 1915

SUSSEX 24 March 1916

NETH

GERMAN EMPIRE

BELGIUM

FRANCE

SWITZ

AUSTRO-HUNGARIAN EMPIRE

PORTUGAL

SPAIN

ITALY

SERBIA

ROMANIA

Black Sea

Adriatic Sea

BULGARIA

GREECE

Aegean Sea

OTTOMAN EMPIRE

Mediterranean Sea

Scale 1:40 000 000

0 ————— 1200km

0 ————— 800mi

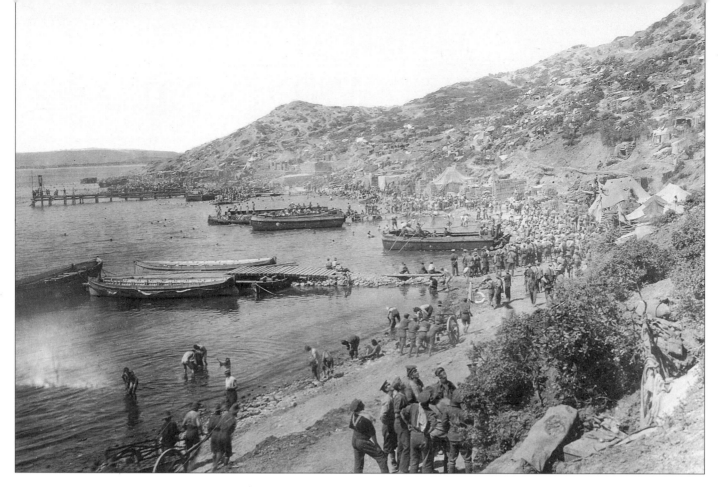

Gallipoli

Europe ends at Gallipoli, the Turkish peninsula at the tip of the Dardanelles straits which lead from the Aegean to the Sea of Marmara. This was the setting for one of the worst disasters suffered by the Allies in World War I.

The idea of knocking Turkey out of the war by naval action was first presented formally by the British first lord of the admiralty, Winston Churchill, to the British war council in late November 1914. In its initial form the plan was for a naval force to attack the straits to open a route to Constantinople. Despite reservations from several quarters, this was duly approved in January 1915.

The first stage of operations was a series of Allied naval bombardments beginning on 19 February. Minesweeping followed along the 60km (37mi) length of the straits, a stretch of water which narrowed from about 4km (2.5mi) across to a little over 1km (0.6mi). Had this been effective the campaign might have succeeded. But the hazard of mines was not eliminated. On 18 March the second phase of operations began. Allied ships again bombarded Turkish positions, but three battleships – two British and one French – were sunk by mines and three others were severely damaged. The effort to force the straits was suspended.

Instead, as a third phase of the operation, a land expedition was mounted. It put ashore, on 25 April, but by this time Turkish defenses had been strengthened. Some initial Allied gains were squandered, and the combined force of British, French, Australian and New Zealand troops found themselves pinned down between the sea and hills held by the Turks. Turkish defenses

▲ An Anzac soldier at Gallipoli. The Australian Imperial Force was the product of Maj.-Gen. Sir W.T. Bridges, inspector-general of Australian forces in 1914. Bridges commanded the Australian contingent at Gallipoli, and died as a result of wounds received there. His major achievement was to retain the national distinctiveness of Australian units, whose sacrifices helped create Australian national identity. The AIF was trained in Australia and then sent not to England as planned, but to Egypt and then to Gallipoli. Anzac units later served with distinction in Palestine and in France. Out of a home population of about 5 million, 330,000 Australian troops served during the war; of these men, 59,000 were killed. New Zealand lost 17,000 men out of 220,000. Total Anzac casualties – 62 percent of those who served – were the highest of all units from the Anglo-Saxon world.

Sir Ian Hamilton 1853–1947

Ian Hamilton enjoyed a long and successful military career before 1914. He had served in the Anglo-Boer War (1899–1902), and was appointed commander in chief of Mediterranean forces in 1910, aged 57. He was the obvious choice as commander for the Gallipoli campaign in 1915. It began inauspiciously: the British navy failed to force the Dardanelles straits. In the subsequent land campaign he failed to obtain his objectives, thanks to accomplished Turkish defense and poor Allied tactics. But in spite of appalling loss of life, Hamilton's communiques remained optimistic. His command ended after journalists leaked the truth about the scale of the Dardanelles disaster. Hamilton never again held a senior military position.

Otto Liman von Sanders 1855–1929

A Prussian career soldier, von Sanders was sent to Turkey in 1913 as leader of the German military mission. Its presence was a visible sign of Turkey's alignment with the Central Powers. Russian protests prevented von Sanders from taking command of the Turkish First Army, but he became "inspector" of Turkish forces and worked to increase the efficiency of Turkish military organization. In January 1914 von Sanders was made a commander of Turkish forces in the Caucasus. His real test came when appointed commander of the Turkish Fifth Army in Gallipoli in 1915. There he successfully opposed British, Anzac, and French attacks. Subsequently he saw action as Turkish commander in Palestine.

◀ Turkish troops fought on fronts extending over 1000km (625mi) during the war. The campaign in which they inflicted the most serious defeat was at Gallipoli, where an Anglo-French invasion was blunted. The landings at Anzac Cove (left) on 25 April 1915 were poorly planned. The Anzacs were put ashore at the wrong place: on a narrow beachfront bordered by sheer cliffs. They secured a tenuous foothold, and were then told to dig in. The Turks held the high ground, and once more demonstrated the ascendency of the defensive. The date of the landing is marked in Australia as one of national heroism; in Turkey, as one of national pride.

▶ The idea of the Gallipoli campaign was to reestablish direct lines of supply and communication between Russia and its Western allies by taking Constantinople and knocking Turkey out of the war. But the underlying Allied motive was to find a way around the stalemate on the Western Front. The failure of the Gallipoli campaign ensured the continuation of the war of attrition in France and Flanders.

Gallipoli 1915–16

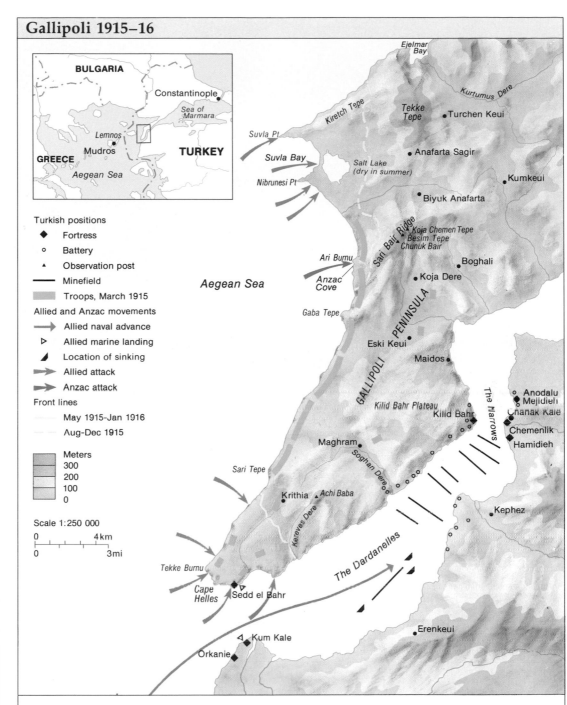

Turkish positions
◆ Fortress
○ Battery
▲ Observation post
— Minefield
▨ Troops, March 1915

Allied and Anzac movements
→ Allied naval advance
▷ Allied marine landing
◢ Location of sinking
➤ Allied attack
➤ Anzac attack

Front lines
—— May 1915–Jan 1916
---- Aug–Dec 1915

Meters
300
200
100
0

Scale 1:250 000

0 — 4km
0 — 3mi

1914
November 3
British and French (Allied) forces make an ill-considered bombardment of Dardanelles forts, which focuses Turkish attention on the area

1915
February 19
Allied ships bombard Turkish forts at the entrance to the Dardanelles.

February 25
After a period of poor weather the Allied ships resume their bombardment. Small groups of marines land with impunity on the Turkish mainland on demolition missions, but Turkish strength is growing.

March 4
An attempt to repeat February's landings meets strong resistance and fails.

March 18
Attempts to push ships through the Dardanelles end in failure, with three capital ships sunk and a fourth crippled by mines. The Turks have practically no heavy ammunition left now, but unaware of this, the Allies conclude that a substantial invasion will be necessary to clear the straits.

March 24
The new commander of the Turkish Fifth Army, Liman von Sanders, deploys his six divisions to block any landings.

April 25
Allied troops land at Cape Helles and Australians and New Zealanders at Anzac Cove. Neither force pushes far inland.

May 1–8
Turkish attacks and Allied counterattacks result in minor gains for the Allies.

May 19
The Turks attack the Anzac forces but fail to dislodge the defenders.

June 21
(to July 5) French and British forces attack separately from the Helles front line, but cannot break out.

July 12–13
French and British forces attack jointly at the Helles front with no more success. The French are now finished as an offensive force.

August 6–7
The overall Allied commander, Sir Ian Hamilton, launches a new three-pronged assault. While the existing two enclaves renew their attacks, a third is created by landing fresh troops at Suvla Bay. The Helles and Anzac attacks fail to make any gains, and the Suvla force becomes bogged down just like the others.

August 10
Forces landed at Anzac and Suvla join in line but cannot push the front forward.

October 16
Sir Ian Hamilton is relieved of his post.

October 28
Hamilton's replacement, Sir Charles Monro, arrives from the Western Front.

October 31
Monro recommends evacuation as the best option.

December 8–20
Forces at Suvla and Anzac are quietly reduced in size. The Turks only become aware of this after the last parties have withdrawn safely.

December 28
(to Jan. 9 1916) The Helles force is withdrawn safely.

▲ Austrian staff officers studying maps in Galicia in 1915, during which the Central Powers pushed back the Russian army from virtually all of present-day Poland. On 2 May a joint German-Austrian advance was launched in Galicia, and made progress on a wide front. By the end of June 1915 Russia had lost all of Galicia and Bukovina. Worse was to come later in the summer. In July a second joint offensive was opened. Warsaw fell to the Germans on 4 August; Brest-Litovsk fell on 25 August, and the city of Vilna, in Lithuania, was captured in September.

Military Communications

With the massive increase in the size of armies in World War I, the problem of communication between the various headquarters and the front lines became acute. This was especially the case because orders had to go through several layers of command, and therefore time became a critical factor – it was not possible for a headquarters to issue orders and expect a divisional attack to take place the next day. Moreover, communication tended to flow in one direction: from headquarters to the front. This was often made worse by the reluctance of senior commanders to accept that events were not going the way they envisioned, and thus information from the front was frequently ignored or altered to fit preconceptions.

A final difficulty was the actual technical means of communication transmission. Thus, while telephone land line was readily available between higher headquarters, once the front line was approached, telephone lines were often cut by shell fire or run over by tanks. After an offensive commenced, it was extremely difficult to stay in touch with advancing units. In this case, resort had to be made to traditional methods of communication such as pigeons, runners, or flares. Later, methods were supplemented or replaced by technical means such as power buzzers and wireless, as well as by aerial observation.

As an example of how communications worked in an army, it will be useful to look at the British Expeditionary Force (BEF). Assuming that General Haig and his general headquarters (GHQ) were putting into action the strategies decided upon in London (which was sometimes not the case), then Haig would outline his ideas for operations to the army commander concerned, who would draw up plans. These would be criticized by Haig and his staff, but Haig's training led him to leave tactical conduct of operations up to the army commander.

Relevant orders would then be passed through many levels of command. Thus the army commander often left corps HQ to solve the tactical problems presented by GHQ, while corps in turn would ask for ideas from their division and brigade staffs and attempt to coordinate them before sending them on to the battalion level, which then passed them on to lower levels, where their relevance was not always apparent. In addition, such was the length of the chain of command and the rigid centralization of the system that it was very hard to achieve changes from below, even at the level of division appealing to corps. This rigidity was partly due to the great difficulty of altering an exceedingly complex set of orders integrating different arms such as infantry, artillery, cavalry, air and the tank corps. Thus before the Somme offensive, one corps HQ issued a 76-page scheme for the attack, while there was a 365-page supplement for the divisional level.

Communication difficulties occurred therefore partly because of the huge size of armies, partly because technology was insufficient to the task and partly because prewar ideas were not appropriate to the needs of modern war.

▶ A German soldier with field-telephone equipment.

under the command of the German general Liman von Sanders, were ably manned, which greatly surprised the Allies. Among the men who distinguished themselves on the Turkish side was a young colonel, Mustapha Kemal, who was later to be president of Turkey and known as Atatürk.

A landing of fresh troops on 6 August made little difference, except to the casualty lists. These grew ominously in the summer heat. The conditions under which Allied soldiers were forced to operate were intolerable, but it took until November for the Allied high command to admit total failure. The survivors of the operation were evacuated in December 1915 and early January 1916. They left behind approximately 200,000 dead comrades.

The cult of the offensive

Gallipoli was but one in a series of disasters which marked the first year of World War I. It is remarkable that a catalog of defeats on both sides did not cause a change of heart about the way the war should be fought. It is true that some heads rolled on both sides. In Germany Moltke gave way to Erich von Falkenhayn as chief of the general staff. On the French side General Sarrail, a bit too popular for the comfort of his superiors, was sent to Salonika to command the French "Army of the East". In Britain Winston Churchill resigned as first lord of the admiralty after

Sir William Robertson 1860–1933

Robertson was the only man ever to enter the British army as a private and rise to the rank of field marshal. He joined in 1877 and gained a commission 11 years later. Service in the British Empire followed. After active service in the British Expeditionary Force in 1914–15 Robertson was recalled and at age 55 appointed chief of the imperial general staff. His central task was to act as middleman between the cabinet and the army. He maintained that the war would be won or lost on the Western Front and convinced the British cabinet to concentrate resources on France. Controversies over the management of manpower in 1917 made him enemies. He was removed from his post in February 1918.

Gallipoli, and Kitchener's powers as minister of war were much reduced by the appointment of General Sir William Robertson as chief of the imperial general staff. He formed a powerful partnership with Sir Douglas Haig, who replaced Sir John French as commander in chief of the British Expeditionary Force in France.

The change in personnel on the Allied side obscured an underlying continuity in purpose. After a year of combat on many fronts, the cult of the offensive was still in the ascendant. The British and French high commands were still wedded to the idea that the war would be won by offensive operations in France. The entry of Italy on the Allied side on 23 May 1915 made no difference to these calculations. Reversals on the Eastern Front seemed to justify increased aggression in the west.

On the German side General Erich Falkenhayn also subscribed to the concept of what the French called *la guerre à l'outrance* – war to the bitter end. But on the Western Front he was prepared to wage this by attrition rather than annihilation.

His adversaries took the lead in launching attacks in 1915. In January and February the focus of French action was Champagne; in May and June, and again in September, Artois. The British made a successful attack on the village of Neuve Chapelle (10–13 March). They actually broke through the German lines, but could not capitalize on their gains. Similarly at Loos in late September, initial British gains turned into stalemate. As always happened, the attackers' losses were staggering; the defenders' less severe.

Falkenhayn was content to let the Allies destroy their men against his lines in the west. In the east he had to contend with his own side, in particular with Hindenburg and Ludendorff, whose aggressive posture certainly paid off against the Russians and the Serbs. On 2 May 1915 the Russian front line was broken at Gorlice in Galicia, and a combined Austro-Hungarian and German force advanced 130km (80mi). Galicia and indeed most of Poland were abandoned by Russia. An equally severe defeat was suffered by the Serbs, crushed in a combined autumn operation by German, Austro-Hungarian and Bulgarian troops. Still, such successes for the Central Powers did not bring the end of the war any closer. Victory was still to be won on the Western Front.

All those who criticize the dispositions of a general ought first to study military history, unless they have themselves taken part in a war in a position of command. I should like to see people compelled to conduct a battle themselves. They would be overwhelmed by the greatness of their task, and when they realized the obscurity of the position, and the exacting nature of the enormous demands made on them, they would doubtless be more modest. Only the Head of Government, the Statesman, who has decided for war, and that with a clear conscience, shoulders the same or a bigger burden of responsibility than that of the Commander-in-Chief. In his case it is a question of one great decision only, but the Commander of an army is faced with decisions daily and hourly. He is continuously responsible for the welfare of many hundred-thousands of persons, even of nations.

ERICH LUDENDORFF

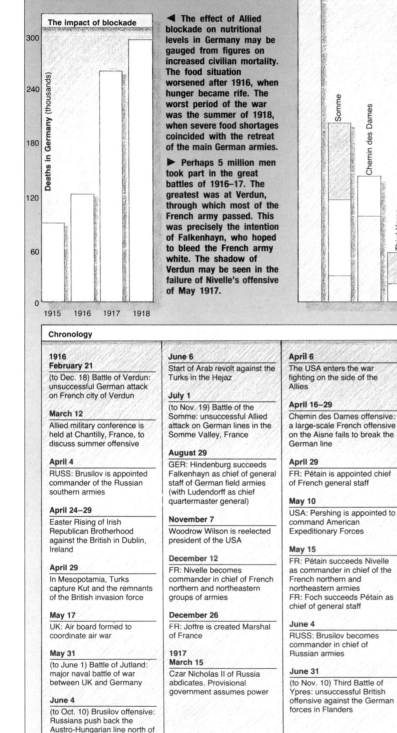

Datafile

The bloodiest battles of the war were fought in 1916–17. First, between February and November 1916, almost the entire French infantry fought to hold Verdun. In May 1917 the French army mutinied when a series of offensive operations pushed too far men whose bravery and patriotism had been demonstrated at Verdun. Second, the British army suffered the heaviest losses in its history at the Somme and Third Ypres.

The impact of blockade

Deaths in Germany (thousands)

1915 1916 1917 1918

Battle forces

UK
Germany
France

Men at arms (millions)

Verdun
Somme
Chemin des Dames
Third Ypres

◄ **The effect of Allied blockade on nutritional levels in Germany may be gauged from figures on increased civilian mortality. The food situation worsened after 1916, when hunger became rife. The worst period of the war was the summer of 1918, when severe food shortages coincided with the retreat of the main German armies.**

► **Perhaps 5 million men took part in the great battles of 1916–17. The greatest was at Verdun, through which most of the French army passed. This was precisely the intention of Falkenhayn, who hoped to bleed the French army white. The shadow of Verdun may be seen in the failure of Nivelle's offensive of May 1917.**

Chronology

1916
February 21
(to Dec. 18) Battle of Verdun: unsuccessful German attack on French city of Verdun

March 12
Allied military conference is held at Chantilly, France, to discuss summer offensive

April 4
RUSS: Brusilov is appointed commander of the Russian southern armies

April 24–29
Easter Rising of Irish Republican Brotherhood against the British in Dublin, Ireland

April 29
In Mesopotamia, Turks capture Kut and the remnants of the British invasion force

May 17
UK: Air board formed to coordinate air war

May 31
(to June 1) Battle of Jutland: major naval battle of war between UK and Germany

June 4
(to Oct. 10) Brusilov offensive: Russians push back the Austro-Hungarian line north of the Carpathians

June 6
Start of Arab revolt against the Turks in the Hejaz

July 1
(to Nov. 19) Battle of the Somme: unsuccessful Allied attack on German lines in the Somme Valley, France

August 29
GER: Hindenburg succeeds Falkenhayn as chief of general staff of German field armies (with Ludendorff as chief quartermaster general)

November 7
Woodrow Wilson is reelected president of the USA

December 12
FR: Nivelle becomes commander in chief of French northern and northeastern groups of armies

December 26
FR: Joffre is created Marshal of France

1917
March 15
Czar Nicholas II of Russia abdicates. Provisional government assumes power

April 6
The USA enters the war fighting on the side of the Allies

April 16–29
Chemin des Dames offensive: a large-scale French offensive on the Aisne fails to break the German line

April 29
FR: Pétain is appointed chief of French general staff

May 10
USA: Pershing is appointed to command American Expeditionary Forces

May 15
FR: Pétain succeeds Nivelle as commander in chief of the French northern and northeastern armies
FR: Foch succeeds Pétain as chief of general staff

June 4
RUSS: Brusilov becomes commander in chief of Russian armies

June 31
(to Nov. 10) Third Battle of Ypres: unsuccessful British offensive against the German forces in Flanders

---

In 1916 the chief of the German general staff, Erich von Falkenhayn, proposed to win the war in an indirect manner. By attacking the French salient at Verdun he intended not to make any major breakthrough, but rather to bleed the French army white. This was war of attrition with a vengeance, and it left a battlefield strewn with the corpses of over half a million men.

The clash at Verdun

Neither before nor since has there been such a bloody demonstration of the blindness of commanders, both political and military, as to the consequences of their actions. The French commander, Joffre, did not take very seriously the threat of a German assault on Verdun. Indeed, just before the attack was launched, its defenses were dismantled and reorganized. His response to those who worried about the depleted defenses was: "I ask only one thing, and this is that the Germans will attack me, and if they do attack me,

Erich von Falkenhayn 1861–1922

Fifty-three when war broke out, Falkenhayn was an experienced soldier who had been Prussian minister of war since 1913. After the German retreat in September 1914 he was chosen to replace the discredited Moltke. He rebuilt German strategy in the wake of the failure of the Schlieffen Plan. He believed that the war had to be won in the west, but after the failure of offensives at Ypres and elsewhere in 1915 he resorted to a policy of attrition to prevent the Allies from building up forces that could overwhelm his army. The high (or low) point of this policy was the massive German assault on Verdun in 1916. It succeeded in diverting French resources, but caused such losses of German troops that confidence in Falkenhayn faded. He was replaced by Hindenburg and Ludendorff.

Philippe Henri Pétain 1856–1951

Although he was a 58-year-old professional soldier in 1914, Pétain had never served outside France. Yet against the prevailing military consensus he had evolved his own views about the value of defensive strategy, a view that proved decisive once the war in France had become one of attrition. This strategy was tested to the limit at Verdun. In May 1917 he succeeded the discredited Nivelle as commander in chief of the French army and helped restore the morale of French troops. His "stinginess" with the lives of his men contrasted with earlier policy. He later earned the enmity of his country by presiding over France during the Nazi occupation. He was condemned to death in 1945, but the sentence was commuted by another veteran of Verdun, Charles de Gaulle.

1916–17 THE GREAT SLAUGHTER

that it will be at Verdun." Falkenhayn obliged.

On the first day of the assault, 21 February 1916, more than a million shells fell on French positions, clustered around a series of forts on both sides of the River Meuse. Fort Douaumont fell on 25 February. The next day, the town's defense was entrusted to the commander of the Second Army, Philippe Pétain.

The defense of Verdun was to become an emblem of French military might. To hold it turned into a symbol of the will of the entire French nation; in this way a powerful national myth was born. The city itself was of no great strategic importance, but its loss would have been politically catastrophic. For this reason the French prime minister, Aristide Briand, insisted on holding the town. "If you surrender Verdun," he told Joffre and his staff, "you will be cowards, cowards! And you needn't wait till then to hand in your resignation. If you abandon Verdun, I sack you all on the spot."

▼ Fort Douaumont, which dominated the countryside northeast of Verdun, seen in a German aerial photograph of 1916. The fort was stormed by the Germans in February, retaken by the French eight months later.

The French did not abandon Verdun but defended it at all costs: with a total of 259 of the 330 infantry regiments in the French army. This is precisely what Falkenhayn had hoped for. But once it had been started, the battle took on a momentum of its own.

The more the French resisted, the greater the importance the Germans attached to taking Verdun, and the battle gradually turned into a slaughterhouse for the German army as well. Throughout the spring the assaults and bombardments intensified. Flamethrowers and phosgene gas were used. By late spring and early summer, thirst added to the misery of both sides, particularly of the entrenched French defenders. Another symbol of resistance, Fort Vaux, fell to the Germans on 7 June.

Stories of fantastic courage multiplied, most of them true. Others were the stuff of myth. One such was the "trench of bayonets", near Fort Thiaumont, northeast of Verdun. Here the 3rd

The Battle of Verdun 1916

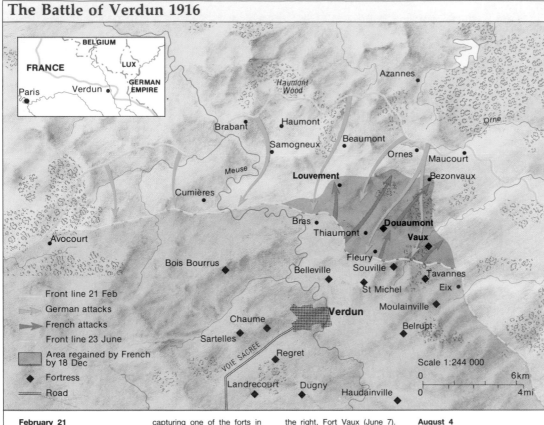

BELGIUM

FRANCE · LUX

GERMAN EMPIRE

Paris · Verdun

Azannes

Haumont Wood

Orne

Brabant · Haumont

Samogneux · Beaumont

Ornes · Maucourt

Meuse · Louvement · Bezonvaux

Cumières · Bras · Douaumont

Thiaumont · Vaux

Avocourt · Fleury

Bois Bourrus · Souville · Tavannes

Belleville · Eix

St Michel · Moulainville

Chaume · Verdun

Sartelles · Belrupt

VOIE SACRÉE · Regret

Landrecourt · Dugny · Haudainville

Scale 1:244 000

0 ——— 6km
0 ——— 4mi

Front line 21 Feb
German attacks
French attacks
Front line 23 June
Area regained by French by 18 Dec
◆ Fortress
—— Road

February 21
After mounting an artillery barrage, the Germans attack the French line in the area of Verdun.

February 22–29
The French fight fiercely to resist the German pressure, as Falkenhayn, chief of the German general staff had predicted. For him the Battle of Verdun is not about capturing ground but about killing Frenchmen. By maximizing artillery fire to keep his own losses down he will "bleed the French army white". His attack presses in the center of the salient surrounding Verdun,

capturing one of the forts in the city's defense ring – Fort Douaumont – on February 25.

March 6
(to April 9) Fresh German pressure on the northern flank squeezes the salient tighter.

April 20
The French make a local counterattack in the north but it is completely checked by the Germans.

May 3
(to June 23) The Germans continue to grind forward and capture Fort Douaumont's neighbor on

the right, Fort Vaux (June 7). By June 23 they hold a bulge stretching into the French defenses as far as Fleury. Because the French are constantly replacing chewed-up divisions with ones at full-strength, half the French army has now been affected by the fighting. But contrary to plan the German losses are also rising.

July 11
Following an unsuccessful attempt to absorb Fort Souville into the bulge, Falkenhayn orders his field commanders to hold their ground while he switches artillery to the Somme.

August 4
A French counterattack reduces the bulge and retakes Fleury.

October 24
(to Nov. 3) Nivelle's counteroffensive completely eliminates the German bulge and retakes Forts Douaumont (Oct. 24) and Vaux (Nov. 2).

December 15–18
Battle of Louvemont. The French force the Germans back further in the center, but the French abandon plans to regain more of the ground lost since February.

▲ **From February to July 1916 the Germans moved south toward Verdun, first on the right bank of the River Meuse, then on the left. At its height, the German attack had passed forts Douaumont, Vaux and Fleury, and stood 5km (3mi) from the city itself. From July the Germans went on the defensive. The battle of attrition went on for another six months, until the French had retaken virtually all terrain previously lost in the battle.**

▶ **A German photograph of an assault in progress near Verdun in the spring of 1916. These men were at least spared the appalling conditions of combat in the heat of the summer or in the freezing weeks early and late in the battle.**

▲ **There were three fortified French garrison cities on the Western Front: Dunkirk, Belfort, and Verdun. The last was 200km (125mi) east of Paris, but only 65km (40mi) from the German fortress of Metz. Verdun was defended by two rings of forts, on the left and right banks of the River Meuse. After the German advance was checked, the French line stabilized 10km (6mi) north of Verdun. The population of the city had shrunk from 15,000 to 3,000. During 1916 the city was severely damaged by artillery (above), but was rebuilt after the war. This was not the case in the surrounding countryside, where many small villages simply vanished.**

company of the 137th French Infantry Regiment
was wiped out in early June. After the battle, the
trench they had occupied was found to be completely covered in. Protruding from the earth at
regular intervals were 15 bayonets, beneath
which were the remains of the men in this unit.
The myth was that they had stayed at their posts
until they were buried alive; common sense suggests that they were buried by the men who
stormed their trench.

The Germans nearly broke the French lines on
23 June, but made no further progress thereafter.
They spent the next six months on the defensive,
repelling French counterattacks. In October and
November the French eliminated the bulge in the
center of the German line. Forts Douaumont and
Vaux were retaken on 24 October and 2 November, respectively. Among those distinguished
in combat at Verdun were Robert Nivelle, later to
command the ill-starred offensive of 1917, and the
young Charles de Gaulle. By mid-December the
battle was over. The French had held Verdun.

◄ For the French the key to
defending Verdun was the
problem of supply. Since the
Germans had cut out the
southern and western rail
links to the city, an alternative
had to be found. The only way
to keep roughly 20 divisions
provisioned was by motorized
transport, organized in a
constant stream of over 3,000
trucks per day on a minor
road south of Verdun to
Bar-le-Duc, 60km (38mi) to
the south. This lifeline to
Verdun took on the name of
the *Voie sacrée* or the sacred
path, the very name of which
points to the elevation of the
battle while it was still going
on into a national myth.

The Battle of the Somme

Just as the Battle of Verdun reached its climax, the Allies launched a major attack on the German lines further west, near the River Somme. On 1 July 1916, after a ferocious 5-day bombardment to level the German lines, 13 divisions of British troops and five of French assaulted German positions. But the bombardment had failed. The German positions were still intact, and no-man's-land, through which the British troops had to move, was a mass of craters and at points virtually impassable.

The combined infantry and artillery attack proceeded with clockwork precision. The artillery barrage, aimed at obstacles in front of the British troops, continued exactly as long as engineers believed was needed to destroy enemy emplacements, and then moved on to the next forward section of ground. Each infantry unit advanced in a straight line perpendicular to the Front.

Wave after wave of infantrymen left their trenches that brilliant, hot July morning, and were slaughtered by German machine-gunners. By the end of the first day, the British army had suffered 60,000 casualties, of whom one-third had been killed. This was the worst day of carnage suffered by any army during the war and the bloodiest day in the history of the British army.

The worst part of the story was that it continued in the same pattern, if not with the same intensity, for another six months. British and French casualties together exceeded 620,000; German casualties reached perhaps 450,000. Again the attackers suffered more than the defenders. The Somme was an Allied, and in particular a British, disaster.

The rigidity of the British plan was the source of its failure. Perhaps because Haig felt he could not trust an army of civilian volunteers to use their minds in battle, perhaps because he saw warfare as a large industrial operation, he presented his army with a plan which required no independent thought and tolerated no deviation from the timetable. Hence, when gains came unexpectedly, they were not followed up. This was warfare by the book; an attempt to control the uncertainties and confusions of battle by ignoring them. The results were meager enough:

▲ The meeting point of British and French forces on the Western Front was near the city of Amiens on the Somme. They faced a heavily defended German line which held the only high ground in a relatively flat terrain. The chalky subsoil presented ideal conditions for the construction of a honeycomb of deep trenches which protected German troops from artillery bombardment.

Sir Henry Seymour Rawlinson 1864–1925

Rawlinson's early military career was spent in India and South Africa. At the outbreak of war in 1914 he was 50 years old. As a field commander he fought at Antwerp, Ypres, Neuve Chapelle and Loos. He commanded the British Fourth Army at the Battle of the Somme, and operated within a rigid system of command largely responsible for the most disastrous failure in the history of the British army. The 18th and 30th Divisions, both under Rawlinson's command, did make progress at the beginning of the battle, but were forbidden to press ahead, since a further advance was not in the plan. Two years later his forces adopted different tactics and helped push the German army back from Amiens. In 1919 he directed the withdrawal of the British Expeditionary Force from Russia.

▲ ▶ The strategic aim of the Somme attack was to wear down the German reserves, which had frustrated any consolidation of Allied moves over the previous 18 months. This attrition, combined with the slaughter at Verdun, was (to Haig) the road to victory. The tactical aim of the battle was first to take the high ground between Albert and Bapaume, 20km (13mi) to the northeast, and then to drive north toward Arras, a further 25km (16mi) away.

▶ Plans for major offensives were made with meticulous care. Their effectiveness was compromised by poor communications, unreliable equipment, supply problems and clogged roads.

The Battle of the Somme 1916

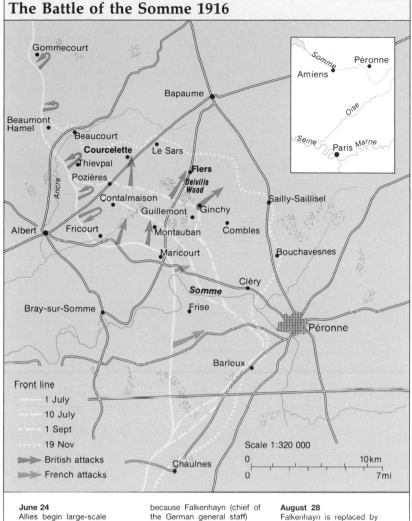

Gommecourt

Bapaume

Beaumont
Hamel

Beaucourt

Courcelette   Le Sars

Thievpal

Flers

Pozières
Delville
Wood

Contalmaison

Sailly-Saillisel

Guillemont   Ginchy

Albert   Fricourt

Montauban   Combles

Maricourt

Bouchavesnes

Somme   Cléry

Bray-sur-Somme   Frise

Péronne

Barleux

Front line

— 1 July
— 10 July
— 1 Sept
···· 19 Nov
➡ British attacks
➡ French attacks

Scale 1:320 000

0   10km
0   7mi

Chaulnes

Inset map:
Amiens   Péronne
Somme
Oise
Seine   Marne
Paris

June 24
Allies begin large-scale artillery bombardment.

July 1
British and French infantry divisions begin an assault on the German front line.

July 2–10
The French and the right wing of the British make some progress, but the British center and left are held in check. Casualties are enormous on both sides, because Falkenhayn (chief of the German general staff) refuses to give up ground to save lives.

July 11
Falkenhayn orders the Verdun attacks to stop, and transfers artillery from Verdun to the Somme.

July 12
(to Aug. 27) The Allied attacks continue, but the Germans bitterly contest each trench and immediately counterattack if one is lost.

August 28
Falkenhayn is replaced by Hindenburg and Ludendorff.

September 15–22
Battle of Flers-Courcelette. Further Allied attacks attempt to enlarge the meager gains of July and August, but German resistance is too strong.

September 25
(to Nov. 19) Battle of the Ancre. A final Allied effort again fails to achieve a breakthrough.

Planning the Somme

The Somme offensive emerged from the Allies' conference at Chantilly in December 1915, which hoped that a series of "wearing-out" operations and major offensives would bring Germany to sue for peace by the end of 1916. The German offensive at Verdun, which started in February 1916, eliminated the need for wearing-out operations and reduced the potential contribution of the French. So the main responsibility for the major offensive lay with the British and was assigned to the Fourth Army, commanded by Rawlinson. At this point, there developed a difference of opinion between the commander in chief, Haig, and Rawlinson. Rawlinson wanted a "bite and hold" type of offensive: the Fourth Army would make heavy use of artillery and the infantry would seize part of the German lines. The infantry would then consolidate and destroy the inevitable German counterattacks. The process would then be repeated and three lines of German defenses would be captured in about two weeks. This would theoretically reduce British casualties while inflicting heavy losses on the Germans. Haig believed that the infantry could break through the German defenses and then cavalry would exploit the success. Thus Haig saw infantry rather than artillery as the breakthrough force, and relied partly on a panic occurring in the German lines, partly on the speed of the advance, and partly on a short preliminary bombardment.

However, when Rawlinson submitted his plans for the offensive to Haig in April 1916, there developed a certain confusion as to which conception of the offensive was going to predominate – Rawlinson's "bite and hold" proposal or Haig's breakthrough idea. What eventually emerged was a mixed plan. Rawlinson was permitted a lengthy artillery bombardment and, in the south of the offensive, limited objectives. In the center and north of the offensive, the objectives of the infantry assault were much deeper, and the cavalry would stand by for the exploitation.

This mixed plan was perhaps slightly closer to Rawlinson's beliefs, and he felt confident (on the basis of experience in 1915) that the infantry would at least be able to capture the first line of German trenches, despite certain problems with the artillery preparation. On the opening day the main problem would be infantry consolidation *after* the capture of German trenches, in order to beat off the anticipated German counterattacks. It was for this reason that when the British infantry went over the top early on 1 July 1916 they were heavily burdened with material and supplies for consolidation, and were not ordered to run forward.

Thus the hopeful plans of the Chantilly conference eventually led to the Somme offensive on the Western Front. Ironically, if Haig had insisted on his breakthrough idea, instead of permitting the mixed plan to go ahead, it is possible that the initial rush would have been much more successful on that fateful morning.

approximately an 8km (5mi) gain at most, in an operation that cut the heart out of the Kitchener volunteer armies.

Chemin des Dames to Passchendaele

By the end of 1916 there was indisputable evidence that the tactic of frontal assault on the Western Front had failed. But, tragically, more major attacks were in train. Again some men at the top vanished, but their attitude to the war lived on. In Britain Lloyd George replaced Kitchener as secretary for war, who drowned when his ship the *Hampshire*, en route to Russia, hit a German mine and sank on 5 June 1916. Lloyd George loathed General Haig, but thought he lacked the political support to get rid of him. In Germany Hindenburg replaced Falkenhayn as chief of the general staff. But he adopted a similarly cautious policy, as shown in the German withdrawal to a new, more easily defended line (the Hindenburg line), east of Bapaume and north of Soissons, in March 1917. In France General Nivelle, the hero of Verdun, replaced Joffre as commander of the French army, but was even more fervently committed to *la guerre à l'outrance* (war to the bitter end).

This he demonstrated in his plans for a massive attack on well-fortified German positions in Champagne, north of Reims. The battle took the name of the "Chemin des Dames", after a road

Robert Georges Nivelle 1856–1924
After successfully commanding the French counterattack at Verdun, the 60-year-old Nivelle was given charge of the armies of the north and northeast. In 1917 he promised to break through the enemy lines. The "Nivelle offensive" of April 1917 was simple in its concept – after an artillery bombardment immense numbers of men would overwhelm the enemy – but murderous in its execution. Nivelle failed; the army mutinied; France's war effort faltered. He was replaced by the other hero of Verdun, Pétain, whose sympathetic handling of the crisis saved the army. Moved sideways into the French North African command, Nivelle played no further part in the war on the Western Front. He died in 1924.

overlooking the River Aisne. It began on 21 April 1917, and soon turned into the Somme all over again: perhaps 40,000 men were lost on the first day alone, with more bloody and futile attacks in the next six weeks.

The battle's failure was undeniable. Pétain replaced Nivelle and resolved to protect his men from similar folly. But by then it was too late. The Nivelle offensive in Champagne broke the French army as a fighting force. Mutinies broke out in 68 of the French army's 112 divisions.

▼ Nivelle's plan for the Chemin des Dames offensive (inset) envisaged an artillery barrage and a decisive breakthrough. As on the Somme, the barrage failed; the defenders held the initial French advance to a mere 500m (1600ft). Repeated French attacks were futile and their repetition, inhuman. The French army lost over 270,000 men and the will to fight this kind of war.

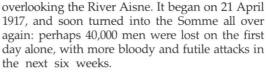

The Chemin des Dames Offensive 1917

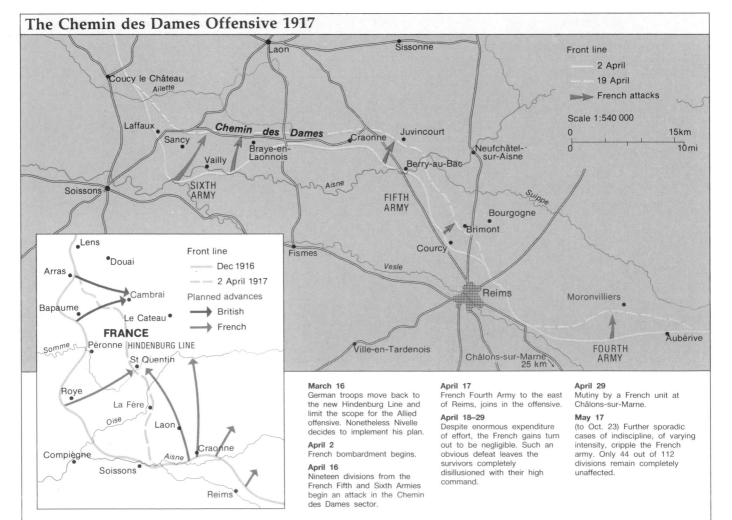

March 16
German troops move back to the new Hindenburg Line and limit the scope for the Allied offensive. Nonetheless Nivelle decides to implement his plan.

April 2
French bombardment begins.

April 16
Nineteen divisions from the French Fifth and Sixth Armies begin an attack in the Chemin des Dames sector.

April 17
French Fourth Army to the east of Reims, joins in the offensive.

April 18–29
Despite enormous expenditure of effort, the French gains turn out to be negligible. Such an obvious defeat leaves the survivors completely disillusioned with their high command.

April 29
Mutiny by a French unit at Châlons-sur-Marne.

May 17
(to Oct. 23) Further sporadic cases of indiscipline, of varying intensity, cripple the French army. Only 44 out of 112 divisions remain completely unaffected.

Provisioning Armies

Napoleon once remarked that armies march on their stomachs. When the European states put armies of millions into the field in World War I adequate provisioning became more crucial than ever before. In August 1914, for example, the ration strength of the (prewar) British regular army was 164,000 men and 27,500 animals: by November 1918 it stood at 5,363,352 men and 895,770 animals. Consequently prodigious amounts of food were required on a daily basis. Between 1914 and 1918 a total of 3,241,000 tons of foodstuffs, 5,438,602 tons of fodder and 5,253,538 tons of munitions were shipped from Britain to sustain the British forces in France and Flanders alone.

Not only were the quantities greater than ever before, the needs of the soldier had grown. During the American Civil War (1861–65) a soldier of the Union army consumed about 2kg (4.5lb) of supplies a day; his World War I counterpart in the American Expeditionary Forces required between 18 and 22kg (40–50lb). Requirements also increased irrespective of the size of armies: in 1914 a British infantry division of 17,000 men required 27 railroad wagon loads of supplies a day; the same division's daily requirements by 1916 filled 20 wagons with food and fodder and 30 wagons with other needs. Similarly a French division in 1918 was consuming more than a French army corps four years previously.

As a result the rear areas of armies came to resemble vast suburbs of depots. The British established major bases at locations such as Le Havre and Boulogne in France and Kantara in Egypt to receive foodstuffs requisitioned at home or purchased abroad. Fresh, frozen and preserved meat was imported from the United States, the Antipodes and Latin America; dairy products from the Netherlands; potatoes from Italy; and fish from Norway. Food was then sent to the Front by railway, internal waterways and motor transport. The latter became increasingly important – the British army's 80 motor vehicles of 1914 becoming 121,702 vehicles by 1918. At Verdun, too, it was motor transport that kept the French army supplied. During the defense of Verdun in 1916 one vehicle passed along the 60km (38mi) lifeline of the *Voie sacrée* between Bar-le-Duc and Verdun every 14 seconds. From advance depots, food would then be taken up to the Front on the backs of animals and men. Elsewhere methods might vary – in East Africa both sides used native porters.

Static trench warfare enabled armies to perfect lines of communication, but it must be remembered that difficulties multiplied in more mobile warfare. Armies might be reduced to foraging crops from the fields much as in the past, as the Germany army was compelled to do during its advance in France and Belgium in 1914 when marching columns simply outstripped the horse-drawn and motor transport vehicles that were endeavoring to bring supplies forward from distant railheads. Indeed, the architect of the original German invasion plan, von Schlieffen, had failed to appreciate fully the logistic difficulties of the enterprise, merely remarking that the troops would have to make "very great exertions". Thereafter generals could not ignore logistic considerations and the British army was well served by the expertise of such men as Lt-General Sir Travers Clarke, the BEF quartermaster-general.

▲ A mountain of stores destined for the British armies in France and Flanders piled up at Boulogne, one of the principal supply depots on the Channel coast. Large numbers of troops were required to handle supplies in such base areas while, from 1916 onward, the British army also employed some 193,500 native laborers drawn from China, India, South Africa, Egypt, the West Indies, Malta, Mauritius, Fiji and the Seychelles. There were similar native labor corps in Mesopotamia, East Africa, Egypt, Italy and at Salonika.

None of this deflected Haig from his chosen course of launching another massive attack on German lines, this time at Ypres in Belgium. There is some dispute as to his objective in this operation; he changed his own story several times in succeeding years. He might have been aiming at the German U-boat ports at Ostend, 50km (30mi) from Ypres; less ambitiously, he could have been trying to sever the rail link, roughly 15km (10mi) behind the Front, which supplied the German line; or attrition could have been the meaning of it all – the kind of attitude attributed, perhaps apocryphally, to the British commander Sir William Robertson, who is reported to have said that the war would end when there were two British soldiers and one German left in the field.

This last objective rings truest. Between 31 July and 10 November 1917 the British launched a series of attacks which are known as "Third Ypres", or more simply, Passchendaele, after an insignificant village 8km (5mi) east of Ypres which was finally taken in early November, and retaken by the Germans a few months later. The initial attack on German lines failed to achieve a breakthrough. In spite of this further attacks were ordered. Again casualties passed the 500,000 mark, for nothing. The British fought two battles: against the Germans and against the elements. The rain turned the battlefield into glutinous mud and destroyed any hope of a major advance. Again the only memorable feature of the operation was the resilience, the sheer persistence in the art of survival, of the men who fought.

Core and periphery: 1916–17

On one point Haig was right: the war would be won and lost on the Western Front. For this reason, even major military and naval operations in other theaters in 1916–17 were treated as of secondary significance. But it is wrong to draw a clear line between those generals who pressed for major campaigns on the Western Front and those who argued for initiatives elsewhere – so-called Westerners and Easterners. Both saw the war as a unity.

This was as true of Germany as it was of Britain and France. As perceived by its generals, the aims of Germany were to break the military threat to its vital interests posed in different ways by France, Russia and Britain. In 1914 this was to be done by a strategy of annihilation; later Falkenhayn adopted a strategy of attrition, to wear down enemy forces. But even when he was succeeded by Ludendorff and Hindenburg (in August 1916), and unrestricted submarine warfare was launched (in February 1917), the aim was the same: to defeat the more dangerous enemies in the west by military pressure in several theaters of operation.

Allied military leaders also accepted the need to see the war as a unity. Hence an attack in the east was both a way to outflank enemy strongpoints on the Western Front and to exploit British naval superiority. The argument was over how to distribute resources over many fronts. After the failure of the Gallipoli Campaign in 1915, though, a strategy of diverting men and materiel away

Sir Douglas Haig 1861–1928

When Haig sailed for France in August 1914 as head of the 1st army corps he was, at 53, one of the British army's most experienced generals. He returned in 1918 as a victor, but he was – and remains – one of the most controversial figures in British military history. In common with other leading soldiers in that conflict he failed to appreciate the changes that had occurred in military technology. His background was conventional enough: imperial and colonial wars culminating in the Anglo-Boer War of 1899–1902. His success in the field in 1914 and 1915 marked him out as the obvious successor to French as commander of the British Expeditionary Force. Yet as a cavalry man he had little knowledge of an infantry war and failed to see the passing of the cavalry into military history. His pursuit of impossible goals on the Somme and at Passchendaele cost the British dearly, and while he retained the affection of many, his name is still synonymous with an inhuman approach to command. Haig's answer to his critics was to say that he had fought one continuous battle in 1914–18 and had won it.

▶ The Third Battle of Ypres was a monumental exercise in futility. Just as on the Somme, overconfidence in artillery and underestimation of the difficulties imposed by the terrain yielded almost nothing for enormous costs. Ypres was a British salient overlooked by the German army on three sides. The prelude to the battle (known variously as Third Ypres or simply as Passchendaele) was the major British victory at Messines. On 7 June 1917, 19 mines were exploded under the German positions at Messines to the south of Ypres. This destroyed the German trenches, which were occupied and cleared by Irish, British and New Zealand troops. Six weeks later, the battle was joined.

Haig's aims (inset) are unclear: he may have intended to capture the railroad to Ostend or possibly to take Bruges and the U-boat base at Zeebrugge. On 16 July he launched a 10-day artillery bombardment, followed on 31 July by an advance on a 24km (15mi) front.

▼ Just as on the Somme, the very destruction unleashed during the battle ensured a British defeat. Heavy rains turned the battlefield into a quagmire, made worse by the obliteration of the Flemish drainage system. When the 2nd Canadian Division took the obliterated village of Passchendaele on 4 November, they reached an objective that had little military significance, but whose name has come to symbolize the appalling character of the war on the Western Front.

The Third Battle of Ypres 1917

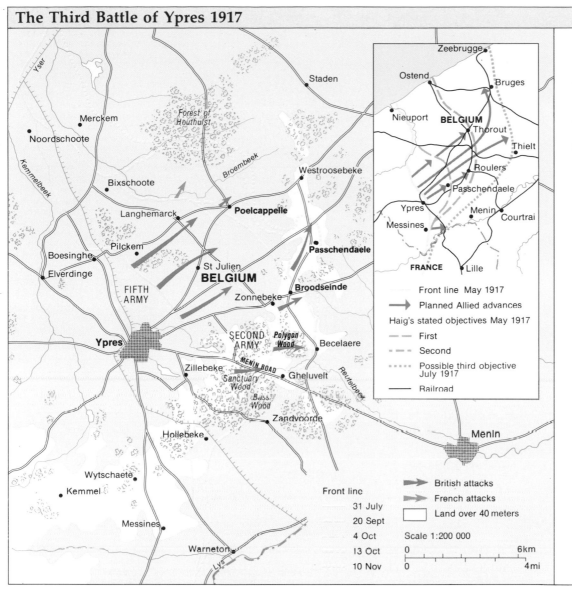

Front line May 1917
→ **Planned Allied advances**
Haig's stated objectives May 1917
– – – First
– – Second
········· Possible third objective July 1917
—— Railroad

Front line
31 July
20 Sept
4 Oct
13 Oct
10 Nov

➤ British attacks
➤ French attacks
☐ Land over 40 meters

Scale 1:200 000
0 ————————— 6km
0 ————————— 4mi

July 16
British artillery bombardment begins.

July 31
Despite poor conditions caused by bad weather, the British Second and Fifth Armies begin an infantry assault as planned.

August 1–18
The British find it impossible to achieve a breakthrough, but persist in their assaults.

September 20–25
Battle of the Menin Road. Haig, the British commander in chief, shifts the emphasis of the attack from General Sir Hubert Gough's Fifth Army, on the left, to General Sir Herbert Plumer's Second, on the right. Plumer adopts step-by-step tactics, and with the benefit of better weather achieves the objectives in this first step.

September 26
(to Oct. 3) Battle of Polygon Wood. Plumer's second step, is successful, so is his third, the Battle of Broodseinde (Oct. 4), but after that the weather begins to deteriorate again.

October 9
Battle of Poelcappelle. The main British attack and a subsidiary one to the north by the French gain little.

October 12
Battle of Passchendaele, which fails, and a halt is called until the conditions improve.

October 26
(to Nov. 10) Second Battle of Passchendaele. Spearheaded by the Canadians, the attack finally gains its objectives (including the village of Passchendaele). However, it comes nowhere near Haig's hope of a breakthrough.

The War against the Turks

Anti-Turkish Campaigns 1914–18

1914

December 22
(to Jan. 18, 1915) The Turks seize the initiative in the Caucasus and attack Russia, but the attack costs them far more casualties than they can afford and the initiative in this area swings back to the Russians for the rest of the war.

1915

February 3
Small Turkish and British detachments spar for control of the Suez Canal and a British force begins to advance up the River Tigris in Mesopotamia.

April 25
(to Jan. 8, 1916) Allied troops are landed at Gallipoli, drawing in Turkish divisions badly needed elsewhere. The Allied attack, however, is a complete failure in face of stiff Turkish resistance.

November 22
(to Dec. 4) Battle of Ctesiphon. The advance up the Tigris finds itself over-extended and the British force is pushed back to Kut-al-Amara.

December 5
The Turks lay siege to Kut.

1916

January 8
The Allies complete their withdrawal from Gallipoli.

January 10
(to April 18) In the Caucasus the Turkish Third Army is rolled back by the Russians, losing Erzerum (Feb. 16) and Trabzon (April 18).

April 29
In Mesopotamia, however, the Turks wipe out the British invasion force by finally capturing Kut.

June 6
An Arab revolt in the Hejaz becomes an added distraction for the Turks.

August 4
(to Jan. 9, 1917) The British drive the Turks out of Egypt and back into Palestine.

1917

February 24
A new British force retakes Kut and then pushes on to Baghdad (March 11).

July 6
T.E. Lawrence and the Arabs capture Aquaba.

December 11
Jerusalem falls to the British as they drive up through Palestine.

1918

April 14
Turkish troops advance to occupy Batum. Only in the Caucasus, now Russia is out of the war, can the Turks make any gains. Everywhere else they are in retreat.

September 19
(to Oct. 25) Battle of Megiddo. Turkish forces in Palestine are routed by the British and Arabs. Damascus, Beirut and Aleppo are captured during the pursuit.

October 30
In Mesopotamia the Turkish Sixth Army surrenders to the British.

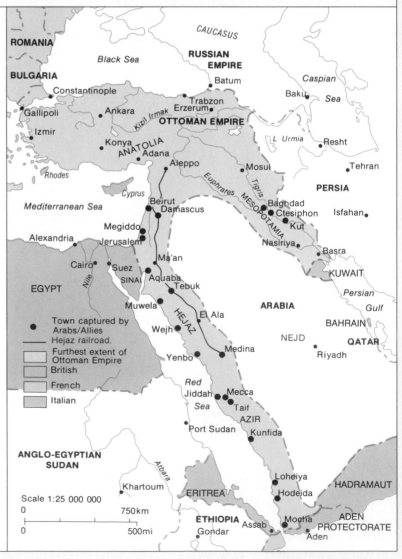

Scale 1:25 000 000

- Town captured by Arabs/Allies
- — Hejaz railroad.
- Furthest extent of Ottoman Empire
- British
- French
- Italian

▲ T.E. Lawrence – "Lawrence of Arabia".

◄ Arab troops photographed by Lawrence.

The Allied campaign against Turkey took three forms. The first was the direct assault at Gallipoli (see pp. 82–83). The second was a series of loosely coordinated attacks involving British troops in Mesopotamia and Russian troops in Persia. The third was the revolt of Arab tribesmen against Turkish rule. The Mesopotamian campaign grew out of the British defense of the oil pipeline from Persia. From Basra near the Persian Gulf, British forces advanced toward Baghdad in early 1915. After initial successes, the British were forced back to Kut-al-Amara, where they were besieged and surrendered in April 1916.

A second campaign in 1917 was more successful. The Arab revolt arose out of Arab aspirations for independence from Turkey, recognized with some ambiguous qualifications by the British after long negotiations. Consequently, Hussein, the grand sharif of Mecca, led an attack on 5 June 1916 on the Turkish garrison at Medina. By December 1916 Hussein was recognized by the British government as king of Arabia. In association the British launched an offensive through the deserts of Egypt to Palestine, supported by guerrilla actions led and popularized by T.E. Lawrence, who has entered historical mythology as Lawrence of Arabia. He succeeded in capturing the tiny port of Aquaba on the Red Sea in July 1917, and later took an active part in the British advance through Palestine and Syria.

While recognizing Arab political aspirations, the British also stated in the Balfour Declaration of 2 November 1917 a commitment to "view with favour the establishment in Palestine of a national home for the Jewish people" without prejudice to "the existing non-Jewish communities in Palestine". Thus the present-day Arab–Israeli conflict was born out of subversion of the Turkish Empire in World War I.

from the Western Front was never given primary consideration. The emphasis in planning and priorities returned to France and Flanders, where the bulk of British, French and Allied troops were located.

The "core" of the war remained in northwest Europe. Events in the "periphery" were dramatic, but indecisive. Military action in this phase of the conflict seemed to lead only to new stalemates. For example, the Brusilov offensive against the Austrian Eastern Front in June–October 1916 was at first massively successful. A group of four Russian armies, commanded by the veteran general Alexei Brusilov, took over 400,000 Austro-Hungarian prisoners, and although the Central Powers quickly formed a new line, Brusilov had demonstrated sufficient military prowess to bring Romania into the war on Russia's side. This turned out to be a disaster for Romania, since Falkenhayn himself led a punitive expedition into that country, which in effect was knocked out of the war by December 1916.

Few clear-cut developments emerged from the fighting in other sectors in 1916–17. The Italian army had trouble holding the Austrians on the Trentino river, and on Austria-Hungary's southern border Sarrail advanced in Macedonia. In the Middle East, where the Allies were mounting a two-pronged attack on the Turkish Empire, British forces captured Beersheba (31 October 1917), Jerusalem (11 December) and Baghdad (11 March), which helped to weaken the Turkish Empire. None of these operations seriously shifted the balance of power in the conflict.

In the naval war, a similar stalemate followed the only major engagement of the war between the German and British high seas fleets. This took place at Jutland, off the Danish coast, on 31 May 1916. The British fleet lost more ships, but the German fleet clearly broke off the engagement to avoid being lured into an even bigger confrontation. On balance the battle secured British strategic supremacy, since German commanders would not again risk their fleet and kept it bottled up in the North Sea and the Baltic for the rest of the war. The Germans placed their hopes even more fervently on submarine warfare. Yet it also demonstrated to the British that another major confrontation might not end with a British victory.

After lunch with the Emperor [of Russia], the meeting began. Our Imperial President was even more absent-minded than he had been at the previous session. He was constantly yawning and took no part in the discussions. In spite of his self-confidence, Gurko, who was acting as Chief of Staff, had some difficulty in conducting the meeting, for although normally level-headed he had not sufficient authority. It came out that the problem of supplies for the troops was likely to increase in difficulty, for there were constant changes of Ministers, who were superseded before they could bring any proper organization into being. Most of them were appointed to offices of which they had no knowledge whatsoever, and had to begin by learning the duties they were supposed to perform. They really had no time to do anything, for they were kept constantly fighting with the Duma or with public opinion in order to keep their posts. It is not to be wondered at that in such circumstances the machine of government functioned less and less efficiently, and the Army suffered proportionately and directly.

GENERAL BRUSILOV

Alexei Alexeivich Brusilov 1853–1926

Brusilov had a long military career – he first saw action in the Russo-Turkish War of 1877–78. By 1914 he was a veteran soldier of 61 and commander of a Russian army. He gained some successes in East Prussia and in 1916 was appointed commander of four Russian armies south of the Pripet Marshes. The offensive he launched on 4 June 1916 and which bears his name brought relief to the hard-pressed Italians by compelling the Austrians to withdraw forces from the Italian Front to the Eastern Front. Lack of munitions caused the offensive to peter out with heavy losses. It was the last successful Russian offensive of the war. A year later the Russian army, to use Trotsky's phrase, voted with its feet for peace.

TANKS AND TANK WARFARE

The tank, an armored vehicle capable of crossing difficult terrain, was conceived by the British army journalist Lt-Col. Ernest Swinton as a means of breaking the state of siege that existed on the Western Front following the onset of trench warfare in late 1914. Trials with a variety of commercial tractors in Britain resulted, early in 1916, in the appearance of an effective machine. It had all-round caterpillar tracks which gave an excellent performance over rough ground and weapons mounted in sponsons at the sides. Two types were produced: "male" tanks, to tackle enemy strongpoints and machine gun positions, which mounted two 57mm guns; and "females", which carried four machine guns instead and were designed to deal with infantry. These original machines were slow, difficult to steer and foundered on soft ground but they could crush barbed wire and were impervious to small-arms fire and shrapnel.

The British employed tanks for the first time on 15 September 1916 on the Somme, but with inexperienced crews and impossible ground, their effect was minimal. Things hardly improved for 12 months but then, on 20 November 1917, at the Battle of Cambrai, everything changed. Over 400 of the new Mark IV machine were employed. After three days they had driven a salient 8km (5mi) deep into the Hindenburg Line for a fraction of the normal casualties. It was judged a striking, if short-lived, success.

Early French developments paralleled those of Britain but the need for good cross-country performance was underestimated. The French heavy Schneider and St Chamond machines were based on modified tractor chassis. In action they were inhibited by poor trench-crossing ability, and the Schneider was a death trap.

The initial German reaction to the Allied tanks was to denigrate them as a sign of martial weakness. This, in turn, created a state of mind at all levels which was resistant to the whole idea. Thus, German attempts to develop a tank were compromised by a late start – their only operational model, the A7V, did not enter service until March 1918.

As might be expected, the Americans adopted the tank idea with enthusiasm. They chose the French Renault and the British Mark V for their own tank corps. However, it took so long to get production under way that no American tanks were ready before the Armistice. Russia and Italy only managed to produce prototype tanks.

Early in 1918 the British Mark V entered service. It featured a more powerful engine than earlier models and was much more maneuverable. It was followed by the Mark V*, a stretched version capable of crossing wider trenches without artificial aids like fascines. Both types took part in the Battle of Amiens on 8 August 1918, in which the lessons of Cambrai were employed on a larger scale. It marked the start of a successful offensive which finally sealed the fate of the German Army. It would be wrong to claim that tanks won the war, but they did provide an answer to the stalemate of trench warfare.

▼ British Mark IV tanks and infantry advance through the German line toward Cambrai, 20 November 1917. The attack was made across firm ground and produced the war's only major breakthrough on the Western Front. But it could not be exploited because of insufficient reserves.

◄ "Auld Reekie II", a Mark IV (female) tank of the 1st Battalion, British Tank Corps. Stowed above the cab is a fascine, which the tank would use as a stepping stone to cross wide trenches. The Mark IV was, numerically, the most important British tank of the war and fought in all the major actions from June 1917 until the end. It weighed 28 tons and had a top speed of about 6 km/hr (4 mi/hr). Its crew of eight (below) had to endure cramped, hot conditions.

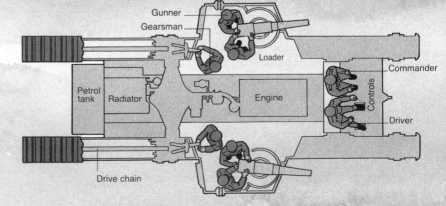

Gunner
Gearsman
Loader
Commander
Controls
Driver
Petrol tank
Radiator
Engine
Drive chain

▲ The Hornsby caterpillar tractor of 1909 (top) was the first tracklaying vehicle to be purchased by the British army. It helped sow the seed for the concept of the tank. The Schneider (center) was one of three types of French tank to see service during the war. The Germans introduced their own tank, the A7V (above), in 1918. It proved to be cumbersome and unstable in action and required a crew of 18. Only 20 were completed by the end of the war. For the remainder of their tank force the Germans relied upon captured British machines, which were generally preferred.

◄ Conditions at the Third Battle of Ypres were more suited to naval than tank warfare. G46, commanded by Lieutenant D.G. Browne, stuck in this shell hole near Kitchener's Wood on 1 August 1917. The damage to the track occurred later.

recently pacified if not peaceful, the army simply ran out of reserves when it reached the zenith of its advance in the summer of 1918. When the Allies proceeded to counterattack, the German troops they encountered were exhausted, poorly supplied and convinced that the promised victory had slipped through their fingers.

In this battle the Allies' overwhelming material advantage was finally demonstrated. The symbol of this gap between the two sides was the tank, first used in strength by the British in the Battle of Cambrai in November 1917. Six months later the Allies had learned to press home the advantage of armored warfare, curiously underdeveloped in the German army during the conflict. In the Allied counterattacks of July and August 1918 tanks were deployed in strength and used in coordination with infantry, artillery and air power, thereby keeping up unremitting pressure on the retreating German army. For the first time in four years the Front was moving, and no lull in the fighting gave the defenders a chance to rest, regroup and successfully counterattack.

The losses on both sides were heavy, but those of Germany could not be made up. It was this combination of fast-diminishing resources of men, materiel and morale which made the setbacks of 1918 so serious and the growing American presence so ominous.

Furthermore, by the time the German armies in the west were checked, the situation on the home front had become critical. In March 1918 the *Burgfrieden*, or political truce of 1914, was re-created, in anticipation of the impending victory on the Western Front: the deprivation and anxiety of the previous three years were eclipsed by a last surge of social solidarity and patriotism. But after the initial "victory" had turned into a massive and unmistakable retreat, the moods of Front and home front changed abruptly.

The line between the two should not be drawn too sharply. New drafts were constantly arriving at the Front, and the steady stream of wounded returning to Germany announced what most people knew but preferred not to admit: the war was going badly. Soldiers were not unaware of the food shortages, the black market and the profiteering that went on behind the lines. When advance in March turned into retreat from August to September, they and their families at home began to ask what positive reasons there were for going on with an unwinnable war.

▼ The German Spring offensive of 1918 was based on the same misconception as the Allied campaigns of 1916–17: that a successful military breakthrough on the Western Front would bring victory in the war. But even had the British and French armies crumbled in 1918, even had Paris itself been taken, Germany would still have had to face the enormous strength and resources of the non-European Allies. After 1917 there was no way that Germany could win this war of endurance. The German campaign of March 1918 was a remarkable feat of military skill, but in terms of influencing the course of the war, it was doomed from the start.

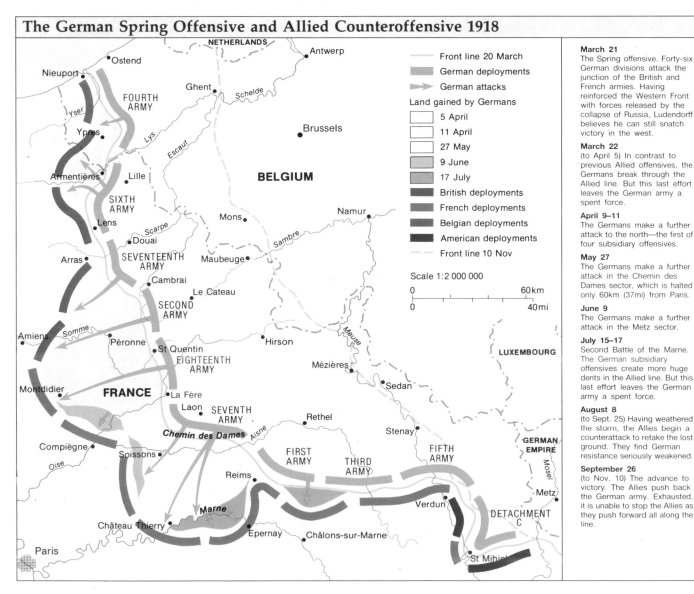

The German Spring Offensive and Allied Counteroffensive 1918

Front line 20 March
German deployments
German attacks

Land gained by Germans
- 5 April
- 11 April
- 27 May
- 9 June
- 17 July
- British deployments
- French deployments
- Belgian deployments
- American deployments
- Front line 10 Nov

Scale 1:2 000 000

0 — 60km
0 — 40mi

March 21
The Spring offensive. Forty-six German divisions attack the junction of the British and French armies. Having reinforced the Western Front with forces released by the collapse of Russia, Ludendorff believes he can still snatch victory in the west.

March 22
(to April 5) In contrast to previous Allied offensives, the Germans break through the Allied line. But this last effort leaves the German army a spent force.

April 9–11
The Germans make a further attack to the north—the first of four subsidiary offensives.

May 27
The Germans make a further attack in the Chemin des Dames sector, which is halted only 60km (37mi) from Paris.

June 9
The Germans make a further attack in the Metz sector.

July 15–17
Second Battle of the Marne. The German subsidiary offensives create more huge dents in the Allied line. But this last effort leaves the German army a spent force.

August 8
(to Sept. 25) Having weathered the storm, the Allies begin a counterattack to retake the lost ground. They find German resistance seriously weakened.

September 26
(to Nov. 10) The advance to victory. The Allies push back the German army. Exhausted, it is unable to stop the Allies as they push forward all along the line.

Ferdinand Foch 1851–1929

Aged 63 when war broke out, Foch had behind him a brilliant career as a military teacher. He played a vital role in the opening phase of the war, at the First Battle of the Marne (1914), and later as general commanding the group of armies of the north. His star was eclipsed for a while after the failure of the Somme offensive. However, in March 1918 he was made, almost four years after the outbreak of war, the first commander in chief of the Allied armies in France. With Pétain, Haig and Pershing formally subordinate to Foch, grand strategy could at last begin to emerge. The failure of the German offensive in the summer of 1918 allowed the initiative to pass to Foch. He never lost it, until the Armistice was signed. After the war Foch was weighed down with honors.

John Joseph Pershing 1860–1948

When the USA entered the war early in 1917 President Woodrow Wilson appointed Pershing commander of the American Expeditionary Forces. Pershing was 57 years old and could look back on a distinguished military career in Cuba, the Philippines and in Mexico. In Europe he resisted requests from British and French commanders for American units to be dispersed among the hard-pressed Allied forces. The American army remained independent and under its own command, with the exception of the critical period after the German offensive of March 1918. His forces achieved some notable successes in the Allied counteroffensive, in particular with the capture of the Saint-Mihiel salient and in the Meuse-Argonne offensive at the end of the war.

On the 20th (July) I visited the commanders of our units engaged and found all roads west of the salient greatly congested. No one who has not been an eye-witness can visualise the confusion in traffic conditions that exists immediately behind the lines during the progress of a great modern battle. It is a most difficult problem to regulate circulation over the roads and keep them from becoming seriously blocked, especially at night, when vehicles must travel without lights and frequent halts are necessary due to accidents of various sorts.

GENERAL PERSHING

▼ The mass surrender of German units near Amiens after the "black day" of 8 August 1918 signaled the beginning of the end of the war. But the German army itself remained intact until the Armistice, and could have gone on fighting, had the German people still believed in victory. But a disillusioned and hungry population had had enough. Both army and people knew that the war had to be brought to an end.

From August 1918 the German high command received increasingly serious reports of mass surrenders and a collapse in morale. They were confronted by what may be described as a soldiers' strike against the war – which was also reported on the home front. Thus military retreat fueled civilian hopelessness and anger at the regime that had got them into a cul-de-sac.

All this coincided with the surrender of Germany's allies. The Bulgarian, Turkish and Austrian armies all collapsed in September and October. By then Ludendorff had given up hope of an outright victory; his aim was to keep his army intact and the enemy off German soil. After all, the Germany army had not been broken; it had retreated, and could still inflict substantial casualties on the advancing Allies. Even as late as October 1918 Ludendorff played with the idea of fighting on, should peace negotiations break down. Such resistance would at least help to stop the spread of "Bolshevism" at home.

But such grandiose schemes of a final gesture – echoed in the German navy (see p.158) – were but pipe dreams. Everyone with eyes to see knew the war was over and that further bloodshed was pointless. Ludendorff resigned on 26 October. The Kaiser abdicated 14 days later. On 11 November 1918 hostilities ceased on the Western Front, where after all the war had come to an end.

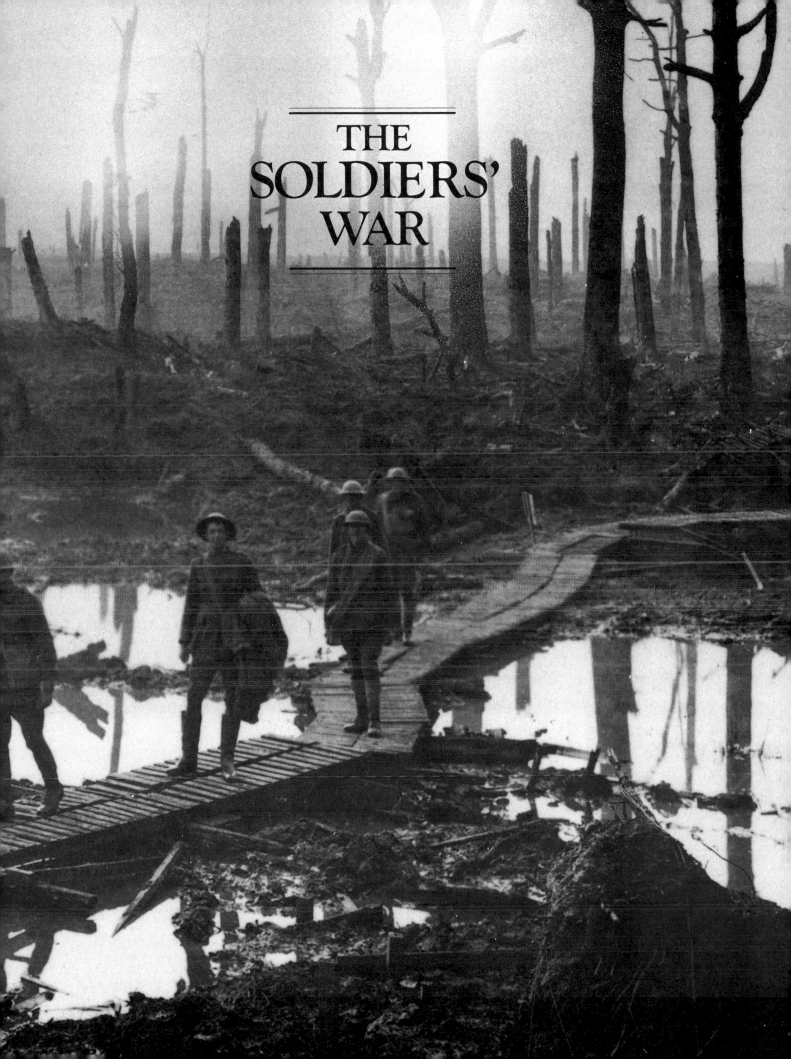

THE
SOLDIERS'
WAR

Datafile

The most important questions about the impact of the war on ordinary soldiers are how many served and what was their fate?

Surprisingly the answers to these questions have been wildly inaccurate and, on occasion, deliberately misleading. Manpower statistics were closely guarded secrets, and casualty figures were used as part of the propaganda war. To judge by some of the more extravagant claims of the press on both sides in 1914 (as well as later on in the war), the entire enemy army had been killed several times over. After the war military statistics were "adjusted" periodically to show that the other side suffered more, as if suffering can be reduced to a simple comparison of almost unimaginable totals of deaths. Consequently, we have no clear guide to the demography of the war. All we can do is provide a rough outline of the dimensions of the conflict.

If numbers alone defined power, then Russia – with a population of over 150 million, equal to that of France, Germany and the United Kingdom combined – was preeminent in Europe. But in terms of manpower trained for military service, Germany was the most powerful nation in Europe. France, Austria-Hungary and Russia had about 4 million men who had been in uniform, compared to 5 million in Germany. Again absolute numbers gave little indication of the true military strength of the Kaiser's army, demonstrated both in the sweep through Belgium and France and in the stunning victory at Tannenberg in 1914.

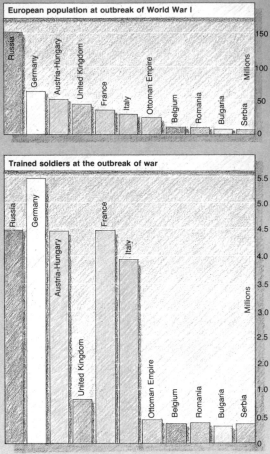

European population at outbreak of World War I

(Bar chart, in Millions: Russia, Germany, Austria-Hungary, United Kingdom, France, Italy, Ottoman Empire, Belgium, Romania, Bulgaria, Serbia)

Trained soldiers at the outbreak of war

(Bar chart, in Millions: Russia, Germany, Austria-Hungary, United Kingdom, France, Italy, Ottoman Empire, Belgium, Romania, Bulgaria, Serbia)

◄ The military implications of population growth in the 19th century were worrying to the French. From being the most populous nation in western and central Europe in the 18th century, France had fallen behind Germany, Austria-Hungary and Britain by 1914. Census information of declining fertility fed perceptions of waning political power.

◄ Conscription provided the major powers with unprecedented large reserves of trained manpower in 1914. However, totals of men who had undergone military training were no sure guide to a country's military might. Germany's superiority as a military power was due to quality, not quantity. Its enemies lacked both Germany's sophisticated professional officer corps and the infrastructure of industrial supply and railway lines which enabled it to fight a two-front war. Manpower totals also understated British power. To note only the small size of Britain's volunteer army – equal to the forces of Romania and Bulgaria combined – leaves the Royal Navy out of the equation.

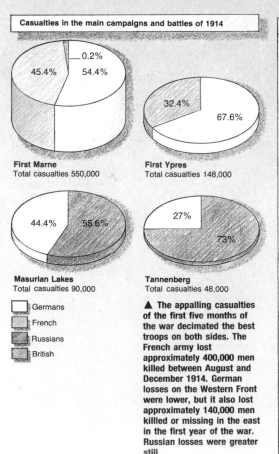

Casualties in the main campaigns and battles of 1914

First Marne
Total casualties 550,000
0.2% / 54.4% / 45.4%

First Ypres
Total casualties 148,000
67.6% / 32.4%

Masurian Lakes
Total casualties 90,000
55.6% / 44.4%

Tannenberg
Total casualties 48,000
73% / 27%

☐ Germans
▨ French
▧ Russians
▨ British

▲ The appalling casualties of the first five months of the war decimated the best troops on both sides. The French army lost approximately 400,000 men killed between August and December 1914. German losses on the Western Front were lower, but it also lost approximately 140,000 men killled or missing in the east in the first year of the war. Russian losses were greater still.

Chronology

June 28
Assassination of Austro-Hungarian Archduke Franz Ferdinand in Sarajevo

July 23
(to Aug. 4) War crisis in Europe

July 24
AH: Partial mobilization begins in Austria-Hungary

July 30
RUSS: General mobilization begins in Russia

July 31
FR: General mobilization begins in France

August 1
GER: General mobilization begins in Germany

August 3
German invasion of Belgium begins

August 7–16
British Expeditionary Force is landed in France

August 11
Goeben and *Breslau* enter the Black Sea

August 21
UK: Government issues orders for raising the first "New Army" of six divisions of volunteers

August 24
Main German armies enter France

August 26–30
Battle of Tannenberg: German victory in East Prussia

September 5–10
First Battle of the Marne: German advance halted

September 6–15
Battle of the Masurian Lakes: German victory in East Prussia

September 8–12
Battle of Lemberg: Russians capture Austria-Hungary's fourth-largest city

September 11
UK: Government issues orders for raising the second New Army of six divisions. Australian Expeditionary Force lands on the German Bismarck Archipelago

September 15
First trenches of the war are dug

September 17
(to Oct. 18) "Race to the Sea": front in the west is extended to the Channel coast

October 3
First units of Canadian and Newfoundland Expeditionary forces leave North America for UK

October 12
(to Nov. 11) First Battle of Ypres: inconsequential conflict between German and Allies

October 17
First units of Australian Expeditionary Force embark for France

November 1
Russia declares war on Turkey.

Battle of Coronel: German Pacific Squadron defeats British naval force off coast of Chile

November 11
(to early Dec.) Germans force Eastern Front further to the east

December 2
Austro-Hungarians capture Belgrade (capital of Serbia)

December 8
Battle of the Falkland Islands: British fleet defeats the German Pacific Squadron

December 11
Serbians recapture Belgrade

1914 THE WAR OF ILLUSIONS

The most important consideration in military affairs in 1914 was how to get as many men as possible into uniform and into the field. This required a close scrutiny of three independent determinants of manpower: first, the size and age-structure of the male population; secondly, the propensity of men to join up, either as conscripts, as in most countries, or as volunteers, as in the cases of Australia and New Zealand throughout the war, in Canada until 1917 and in the British case from 1914 to 1916; thirdly, the physical fitness of recruits. Later a fourth factor would weigh heavily in discussions of manpower. This was the need to balance industrial and military requirements. In 1914, though, this point was not seriously considered, because the consensus was that the war would be over by Christmas.

Prewar population growth
The murderousness of World War I was made possible by rapid population growth in the prewar period. This made available to all warring countries the largest population of adult males in their history. But growth was not uniform before the war, and there was much discussion of manpower problems among writers and churchmen,

▼ "Who hasn't seen Paris today and yesterday", exclaimed the poet Charles Péguy, "hasn't seen anything". He was referring to the send-off given to soldiers such as these. Six weeks later Péguy was dead; his romantic view of war took a little longer to die.

as well as military and political commentators.

French strategists – generals and journalists alike – were particularly worried about the implications of differential population growth rates. The source of their anxieties was the fact that the French population of about 40 million was substantially smaller than the German, which was about 68 million.

The censuses of 1910 for Germany and 1911 for France made dolorous reading to the French. They revealed that while there were over 13 million Germans aged 20-49, there were only about 8 million Frenchmen in the military age range. To make matters worse, the French birth rate was substantially lower than that of Germany. Low fertility was a strategic threat and led many commentators to forecast the ultimate disappearance of the French race.

The implications were also serious for military planners. Conscription long antedated the war in both countries. In 1906 Germany had called up over 1.2 million men. In the same year France could muster only 368,000 new soldiers. Having about three times as many men available as their French counterparts, the German army could afford to select the fittest and send home over half of those who came forward, on the grounds that

they were needed as wage earners by their families, or for a number of other reasons.

The true strength of the German army was its quality in command, logistics and *esprit de corps*. But it still had to face the prospect of a war on two fronts, which meant having to cope with Russian armies drawn from a population of 153 million, of whom 40 million were of draftable age. Even with the aid of the Austro-Hungarian armies, the Central Powers could not match the Russian potential. This is in part what lay behind the Schlieffen Plan. It aimed to defeat Germany's less populous (though militarily stronger) western enemy before its less dangerous (though more populous) eastern enemy had fully mobilized its massive armed forces and entered the war.

Germany's initial advantage compared with the French in command, materiel and in manpower was insufficient to bring it victory in 1914. Without a decisive and early outcome, all the combatant countries still had the manpower to fight a major war in 1914, and to continue to fight it for years.

Who went and why?

Of course this was true only if all the men required or eligible to join up actually did so. To the great surprise of some military men, they did. The French army had reckoned on over 10 percent not showing up; the actual figure was closer to 1 percent. In the case of a country facing invasion, this may not be surprising. But in Britain the

▶ Family photographs of men going off to do their national service were nothing new in countries where conscription was a long-standing practice. In Germany a reserve officer's uniform was a badge of honor among the middle and upper classes; all the more reason to capture for family albums the call to arms as a moment of masculine pride.

To my mind, the most typical and most moving case of such honest and at once insane ecstasy, was that of Ernst Lissauer... When the war broke out, his first act was to hurry to the barracks to enlist. I can well imagine the laughter of the sergeants and corporals when this fat body came puffing up the stairs. He was promptly rejected. Lissauer was in despair but, like the others, he at least wished to serve Germany with his muse. Everything that the newspapers and the German army communiqués published was gospel truth to him. His country had been attacked, and the worst criminal – as cast by Wilhelmstrasse – was that perfidious Sir Edward Grey, the British Foreign Minister. This feeling, that England was the arch-enemy of Germany and responsible for the war, found expression in his "Hymn of Hate"...

STEFAN ZWEIG

◄ In Russia, mobilization was greeted with the same outward display of national and imperial pride as in the West. These Russian troops are on their way to the central railway station in Petrograd (now Leningrad) with a marching band at their head. Ahead of them was a war far worse than anyone had imagined.

Recruitment in Australia

On 30 July 1914 the prime minister of Australia, Joseph Cook, said, "Remember that when the Empire is at war so is Australia at war". The next day he pledged that if the United Kingdom went to war, "Australians will stand beside our own to help and defend her to our last man and our last shilling".

Recruiting immediately began for an Australian Force. Enlisting stations were set up. The call to arms met a powerful response. Men left jobs, walked off farms, and risked their lives to tramp or ride hundreds of kilometers through outback drought to reach the enlistment centers in the cities. Many would-be recruits were rejected as unfit. Those accepted were exceptionally fit, which encouraged them to believe they were superior to recruits from other countries. Their motives for joining up were various. Younger men said they enlisted for adventure, older men out of duty. Some were attracted by the pay of 6 shillings a day. Many thought they had to prove themselves as men; others feared for the Empire. But all were united by a passion to halt barbarism and punish the Germans for a war that was happening far away. They were patriots of the empire.

The strong enlistment rates lasted until April 1915. Thereafter they only surged in times of crisis or when Australian soldiers were heavily committed in battle. When they fell the Federal government had to appeal for recruits. They resorted to films, advertisements and streetcorner orators.

By late 1915 the enlistment rate had fallen so low that the defense department could not make up numbers to replace casualties. In response the Federal government adopted two procedures. In September 1915 it took a census to identify by name men eligible and fit enough for military service. Men unwilling to serve had to explain why. At the end of 1915 Australia was divided into 36 recruiting areas and each area was given a quota-target for recruits. These measures prompted an increase in voluntary enlistment, but the rates fell below target in 1916, partly because of the high casualty rates that were sustained. Now the government concluded that voluntary enlistment had failed and had to be replaced by conscription.

Australia's recently appointed new prime minister, W.M. Hughes, already supported conscription for service in Australia. In mid 1916 (after a trip to the UK) he agreed to support conscription for service overseas. This was proposed in a public referendum in 1916 and rejected by electors. Hughes was expelled from the Labour Party. The government then again tried the most modern means of mass persuasion, and recruitment levels rallied again, but briefly. In late 1917 a second and milder proposal for conscription was put to electors, but fared worse than the first.

The referendum campaigns proved divisive and left a bitter legacy. Trade unionists and the country's large Irish Catholic population were accused of resisting conscription and thereby favoring the enemy and deserting the men at the Front.

But despite the hostility to conscription and the government's constant complaints about the shortages of soldiers, almost half of Australia's eligible men between the ages of 18 and 45 volunteered to serve in the war. Four-fifths of these fought overseas, of whom one-fifth died and half were wounded or maimed.

The Last Call

▲ An Australian recruiting poster by Norman Lindsay: a wounded bugler calls for help on the Western Front. The appeal to the British Dominions struck a powerful chord in Australia, where about 330,000 men voluntarily enlisted. Of these, about 59,000 were killed and 120,000 wounded.

response to the call to arms was equally impressive. In fact it was so great that many new British recruits had to train with umbrellas instead of guns, which were in short supply in the first months of the war.

If there was a limit on military manpower, it was not because of popular attitudes. Throughout Europe and in colonies and dependencies in every continent, ordinary people accepted military service simply as something they had to do – for a time. On the European continent they went because military service was required by law and because they believed their country was in the right. In the British Empire volunteers streamed into recruiting centers – from Canada to Australia – for the usual mix of reasons: the glamor of a uniform, the prospect of steady pay, escape from monotony, even, on occasion, altruism. In Britain, as much as in Germany, they joined up out of loyalty to their community, nation and Empire, probably in descending order of importance. The British way of expressing these commitments took the form of "protecting little Belgium", or "showing the Kaiser where to get off". Propaganda on both sides mobilized similarly oversimplified justifications for war.

But the key to mobilization in 1914 lies in one simple word: duty. Duty tempered, that is, by a sense of adventure. Millions of men were ready to join the ranks for an expedition into a totally imaginary war: one that armies would wage until a decisive breach in the enemy's lines was forced, leading to victory. If you asked how long this would take, the likely reply was a few months at most. The men of 1914 therefore thought of military service as a brief interlude in their lives. This was as true among the various national groups in the Austro-Hungarian Empire as among nationalists in Ireland.

In the same spirit, the white dominions of Australia and Canada answered the call to arms, as did India, Algeria and Senegal. Here again propaganda played a part, but the volunteers of 1914 must not be thought of as automata who simply responded to the mechanical appeals of their leaders. Some were fooled by recruiting slogans, but others joined up out of a real belief in the cause, or out of solidarity with their friends and acquaintances who had already joined up.

The sole problem in raising the volunteer armies from August 1914 onward was therefore neither men nor motivation. It was rather how to discover who could stand up to military life and who was physically unfit. To induct unfit men would cause trouble, since they were bound to break down either in training or at the Front. How many were likely to do so, no one knew, for there was no agreement as to the medical criteria for military fitness. Besides, few medical officers had the time to conduct rigorous medical examinations on the deluge of men who presented themselves at recruiting offices in 1914. The rule at the outset of war was: when in doubt, let him in. Of course many infirmities precluded front-line service – presenting the irony that ill health saved the lives of millions of men in Europe during the war. This was true throughout the conflict. Of the 2.4 million British men who were medically examined in 1917–18, over one million or 40 percent of those tested, were either totally unfit for army service, or capable of noncombtant duty only. They were the lucky ones.

Recruitment patterns among volunteers

In the British case, after the "August madness", the pattern of recruitment for the army revealed some important social variations. The highest rates of enlistment were among middle-class men employed in finance, commerce, the professions and the entertainment trades. About 40 percent of the men in these sectors volunteered between 1914 and 1916, compared to about 28 percent of men in industry.

In August 1914 a broad consensus stood behind the British declaration of war. A few months later strong support still existed, but those prepared to act rather than simply cheer were more likely to come from the better-off sections of the community. Why was it that men in middle-class or white-collar employment tended to join up in greater numbers earlier in the war than their working-class compatriots? The reasons were both cultural and material. Some were from families with military traditions; others had received the rudiments of military training at school or college; virtually all shared the culture of empire and national assertiveness, as well as the prevailing illusions, common to all classes, as to what war was all about.

Willingness to enlist was not the sole property of any one class in 1914 in Britain. But those among the less prosperous who were ready to show the Kaiser a thing or two still had to think twice before joining up. Who would look after their families? Would their jobs be there when they returned? These were very real questions in 1914 and caused more than a few working-class patriots to hesitate. In textile areas, enlistment was relatively low. This was probably related to the fact that the livelihood of families in these towns depended on both men's and women's work, which were threatened initially by the

▲▶ In the UK Lord Kitchener's index finger, immortalized in a famous war poster (shown here in its original version), pointed the way to the recruiting office; by December 1914, one million British and Irish men had joined up.

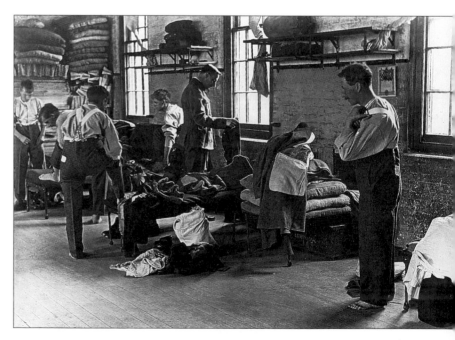

outbreak of war. Given the dislocation of international trade after August 1914, many people in the cotton and woolen industries were laid off. In some sectors of employment the direct substitution of wives for their husbands kept family incomes intact. But in the temporarily depressed textile trades this was out of the question. Men in these areas had every reason to ask, therefore, how their families would manage if they left for the army.

Some employers were prepared to help. Well before the British government passed legislation to provide separation allowances for soldiers' and sailors' dependents, individual entrepreneurs did the same on their own. Some were also prepared to band together with their trading associates to promise the men who went to war that their jobs would be waiting for them on their return. Employers even helped to provision new recruits in 1914, before the war office could house, clothe and feed them.

Special groups

This is the origin of that quintessential British institution of World War I, the "Pals' battalions". These were composed of men who joined up together and who shared an association at work or in their communities. Some were made up of middle-class men, like the Public School Battalions of the Middlesex Regiment and of the Royal Fusiliers, or the "Grimsby Chums", formed by some old boys at Wintringham Secondary School in the Lincolnshire port of Grimsby. Others were made up of working-class men who worked together, played football together, drank together and eventually fought together.

Another reason why working-class enlistment rates were lower than the national average was that some were told not to go. This was especially so in the case of railwaymen, but the need to keep others back to provide munitions was apparent from very early on. By 1916 these distinctions would be regularized by law; in 1914 they were established only informally, and in many cases were ignored. Witness the case of coal miners, among the most class-conscious, and also patriotic, of all British workers. By mid-1915, perhaps one-quarter of the workforce had enlisted. Later on miners had to be "combed out" of the army, so that coal production could be maintained.

The social structure of British enlistment

Given the different pressures on different parts of the community, it is not surprising that there was a social structure of voluntary enlistment in Britain between 1914 and 1916. The higher up a man was in the social scale, the more likely it was that he would join up early and serve throughout the conflict. This was bound to affect the social composition of casualty rates in British forces during the war – a point that will be discussed later. At this juncture what matters is that, whatever the propagandists said, the British army was not the nation in arms.

Roughly 6 million British men served during the war. Given that working-class enlistment rates early in the war were 10 percent below average for other classes, differential enlistment

▶ No one knew how to measure medical fitness for military service during the 1914–18 war. In the British army, which did not have the experience of dealing with millions of recruits, a haphazard system was initially adopted. Medical examinations were cursory and inevitably incomplete. Later on, a more systematic approach was introduced, but medics still passed thousands of men with ailments which made them unfit for active service.

◀ The new uniform and kit contributed to the holiday spirit of the first phase of army service.

The St Helens Pals

In 1914 the UK was faced with the need to expand its small standing army. Among those who took the initiative in recruiting were the leaders of local communities. Their efforts led to the formation of military units drawn exclusively from a particular place: so-called "Pals' battalions." A number of "Pals' battalions" were composed mainly of middle-class men, like the Public Schools Battalions of the Middlesex Regiment and the Royal Fusiliers. Many more were exclusively working class. The formation of these units provided a perfect occasion for the expression of civic culture. Municipalities vied with each other in their support of these units.

Prominent among landowners who led recruiting drives was the 17th Earl of Derby, who owned large parts of the English county of Lancashire. On 3 September 1914 he held a meeting in the Lancashire glass-making town of St Helens. Flanked by local religious and political leaders, Derby appealed for local men to volunteer and form a local battalion. At that meeting about 200 men volunteered. Another 800 men from St Helens and neighboring towns were then recruited. According to one of the last survivors of the battalion, Richard Hesketh, the battalion consisted of coal miners, clerks, and workers from the St Helens glass factories, and a vast array of other young men from the town and its area. Lacking uniforms and weapons, they trained with broom handles instead of rifles, until the army was ready to equip them.

In November 1915 the St Helens Battalion of 1,000 men sailed for France and the Western Front. Though trained as infantry, they were also assigned to digging trenches. In three years they served in most of the major British campaigns. On 1 July 1916 on the Somme they were in the third wave of infantry that attacked the German lines. Twenty percent of the original members were killed or wounded in this battle. In 1917, 15 percent were killed or wounded in the Ypres salient and 10 percent in the Third Battle of Ypres. In the German offensive of spring 1918 the battalion met the full force of the German onslaught. The result was that effectively 50 percent of the (replenished) force became casualties.

The remnants of the battalion returned to St Helens at the end of 1918. They had gained 31 honors, including a Victoria Cross (the highest award for gallantry). At home they attempted to pick up the threads of their lives and put their war service into some kind of perspective. In the 1918 general election prime minister David Lloyd George spoke of making "a fit country for heroes to live in." In the 1920s and 1930s St Helens' registered unemployment rate was 25 percent. The town had both above-average infant mortality and below-average housing. The political rhetoric faded and the reality of deprivation returned.

▲ Lord Derby's initial success in raising men from the Northwest of England in 1914 gave him the job of Director General of Recruitment a year later. But by then the flood of volunteers had shrunk to a trickle. Conscription became law in January 1916.

▼ The men of St Helens Pals' Battalion in February 1915, on their way to war.

lowered the possible number of soldiers Britain could place in the field early on by 600,000. Another 10 percent were declared permanently unfit for service, which does not include those who should never have been in uniform in the first place. Another 600,000 men were spared due to temporary unfitness. Medical officers were unanimous that the bulk of them were working-men from the major towns and cities.

From 1916 restrictions were placed on the recruitment of workers in essential industries, thus further distorting the social composition of the army. But even if we discount this matter, which did not become a serious factor until later in the war, we are still able to conclude that British forces would have constituted a cross section of British society only had they contained over one million more working-class men.

However, because the majority of the male population were manual laborers, Britain's army in World War I was still preponderantly working class. Initially the officer corps was decidedly middle class, being staffed either from the old professional army, the territorial army, or the finishing schools of polite society – the public schools and the universities of Oxford and Cambridge. Later on, casualties forced a partial and grudging broadening of the social base of the officer corps. This was bound to affect the social composition of casualties. Initially elites suffered a disproportionate share of war losses, since officer casualty rates were significantly higher than casualty rates among the men in the ranks. Later in the war this differential casualty rate was reduced, but still persisted.

Other less urbanized combatant countries had armies largely composed of peasants and farm laborers. This group also suffered the most in numerical terms. But despite this difference between Britain and continental countries, some similarities can be seen. For instance, there had to be a "comb out" of French iron workers from Le Creusot: they were needed more on the home front. And as in Britain, there was a progressive infiltration of lower-middle-class and working-class men into the officer corps, as the bloodshed mounted. Again casualty rates among officers, also drawn from more privileged groups, were higher than among those they led. Within a few weeks of the outbreak of war, the entire 1914 graduating class of the French military academy at St-Cyr was dead. The slaughter of the professional armies and of the class from which they were recruited was a unifying feature of the war experience of all major combatant countries in World War I.

War as adventure: the end of a myth

It did not take long for soldiers to recognize the emptiness of the notions they had formed as to what the war would be like. Shrapnel and machine-gun fire put paid to the cavalry charges of August, and turned the varied and colorful European uniforms of 1914 to various shades of khaki and gray. Above all, the men were changed. All descriptions of the early part of the war speak of the great divide represented by the first day of action, the first exposure to the smell,

▲ These German soldiers are on board "The Paris Express", direct from Leipzig to the French capital. Bedecked with flowers and graffiti proclaiming that the Germans were itching for a fight, these railroad cars poured millions of men into the 1914 offensives. By the end of the year, over 400,000 German soldiers had been killed.

the sound, and the chaos of battle. Consider this account of a French corporal, who saw service at Longwy near the Belgian-French border.

"August 22, 1914. A salvo bursts over the road. A horseman quits his stirrups, rolls off his mount, lies still. Quickly, going back from the effect to the cause, we become conscious of impending danger. This first victim, this hussar done away with in a second, disconcerts us. We knew there were some killed in every battle, and yet we were all in such a joyous state of unconcern that we were dumbfounded in the presence of this sudden misfortune. I see the smile congeal on the lips of my comrades. The bursts approach a hundred yards nearer. Now we look at these wicked little clouds less with curiosity than with apprehension....Suddenly shrill hisses which end in violent chuckles send us face against the ground, terrified. The salvo has just burst above us. Shot and splinters sail through the air, a big metal case comes whizzing and strikes the ground near my knee; instinctively, as if to ward off a blow, I had put up my arm to protect my face....More explosions. The balls rain, ricochet on the mess bowls, a canteen is pierced, squirts out its wine; a fuse hums for a long time in the air. With my head under my pack, I cast a glance at my neighbours; breathless, shaken by nervous tremblings, their mouths are contracted in a hideous grin, their teeth are chattering: their faces convulsed with terror recall the grotesque gargoyles of Notre-Dame: prostrate in this bizarre position, with arms crossed on their chests and heads down, they look like condemned men offering their necks to the executioner..."

As soon as the shelling ceased, this man's unit ran helter-skelter for a farmhouse 50 meters away, got over its wall any way they could, and then caught their breath and their nerve, after this, their baptism of fire.

Datafile

The stalemate of 1915 produced casualty totals of staggering proportions: 300,000 German deaths, 400,000 Russian, 300,000 French, and on and on. In Asia and on the Eastern Front, disease – the time-honored companion of war – took its toll. On the Western Front, disease was controlled, but machine-gun fire, artillery bombardment, and for the first time, gas warfare accounted for the bulk of the losses suffered on both sides.

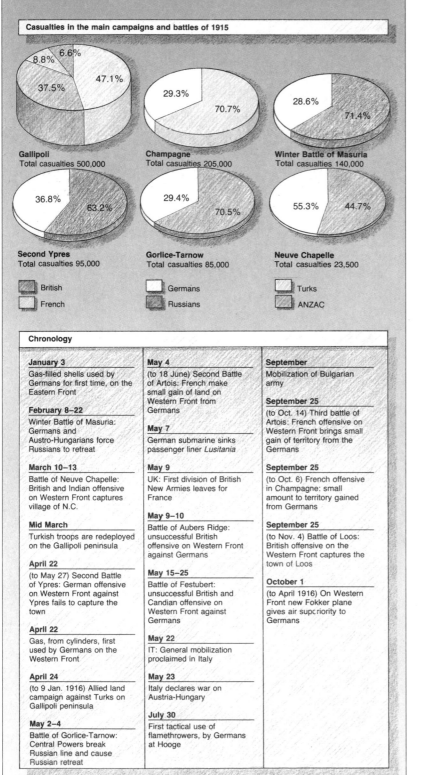

Casualties in the main campaigns and battles of 1915

Gallipoli
Total casualties 500,000
8.8% 6.6% 47.1% 37.5%

Champagne
Total casualties 205,000
29.3% 70.7%

Winter Battle of Masuria
Total casualties 140,000
28.6% 71.4%

Second Ypres
Total casualties 95,000
36.8% 63.2%

Gorlice-Tarnow
Total casualties 85,000
29.4% 70.5%

Neuve Chapelle
Total casualties 23,500
55.3% 44.7%

- ▨ British
- ▢ French
- ▢ Germans
- ▨ Russians
- ▨ Turks
- ▨ ANZAC

Chronology

January 3
Gas-filled shells used by Germans for first time, on the Eastern Front

February 8–22
Winter Battle of Masuria: Germans and Austro-Hungarians force Russians to retreat

March 10–13
Battle of Neuve Chapelle: British and Indian offensive on Western Front captures village of N.C.

Mid March
Turkish troops are redeployed on the Gallipoli peninsula

April 22
(to May 27) Second Battle of Ypres: German offensive on Western Front against Ypres fails to capture the town

April 22
Gas, from cylinders, first used by Germans on the Western Front

April 24
(to 9 Jan. 1916) Allied land campaign against Turks on Gallipoli peninsula

May 2–4
Battle of Gorlice-Tarnow: Central Powers break Russian line and cause Russian retreat

May 4
(to 18 June) Second Battle of Artois: French make small gain of land on Western Front from Germans

May 7
German submarine sinks passenger liner *Lusitania*

May 9
UK: First division of British New Armies leaves for France

May 9–10
Battle of Aubers Ridge: unsuccessful British offensive on Western Front against Germans

May 15–25
Battle of Festubert: unsuccessful British and Candian offensive on Western Front against Germans

May 22
IT: General mobilization proclaimed in Italy

May 23
Italy declares war on Austria-Hungary

July 30
First tactical use of flamethrowers, by Germans at Hooge

September
Mobilization of Bulgarian army

September 25
(to Oct. 14) Third battle of Artois: French offensive on Western Front brings small gain of territory from the Germans

September 25
(to Oct. 6) French offensive in Champagne: small amount to territory gained from Germans

September 25
(to Nov. 4) Battle of Loos: British offensive on the Western Front captures the town of Loos

October 1
(to April 1916) On Western Front new Fokker plane gives air superiority to Germans

---

The experience of ordinary soldiers in World War I was extremely varied. Indeed it makes little sense to talk about armies at all when surveying the conflict from the soldiers' point of view. Most men knew a lot about a very small sector of the front and virtually nothing about everything else. This was inevitable in a war of such an unprecedented scale.

The form and details of military organization varied substantially both between and within armies. But to appreciate the limits on the field of vision of the individual soldier, the organization and chain of command above him will be considered. The example to be used is that of the German army, but the basic point – that armies were enormously complicated and constantly shifting kaleidoscopes of forces – could be made equally well with any other combatant force.

The peace-time ration strength of the German army was 840,000 men. By December 1916 the German army had over 5.5 million men in active units. They were divided into 2,200 infantry battalions, 550 cavalry squadrons, 2,150 field artillery battalions, 1,950 foot artillery battalions, and 600 pioneer companies. Behind these units were the reserve, technical and auxiliary divisions. By the end of the war over 13 million men had served in the German army. The problem of organizing this force was staggering.

In peacetime the German army was divided into 25 corps. Each corps included two infantry divisions, with two cavalry brigades, one artillery regiment and one pioneer battalion in support. After 1914 the basic unit of tactical maneuver was the division. By February 1915 there were 51 active divisions in the field and 54 in reserve. By December 1916 a further 34 new divisions had been raised.

The size and structure of the component parts of infantry divisions varied considerably over time. Theoretically, the organization followed these lines. Each infantry division was divided into two brigades, led by major-generals. Divisions were made up of three regiments, each with approximately 80 officers, 3,200 other ranks, 200 horses and 60 vehicles. Regiments were commanded by a colonel, and were subdivided into three battalions, each commanded by a major and composed of approximately 25 officers and 1,000 men. Each battalion encompassed four companies, three infantry plus one machine gun company, led by a captain. Companies were broken up into three platoons, led by a lieutenant, and these in turn were divided into four sections led by a corporal. At the base of this gigantic pyramid was the squad – two to each section – made up of eight men and one lance-corporal.

This was the theory. In practice the situation was much more fluid. Units rarely maintained

1915 STALEMATE AND STAGNATION

prescribed ration strength for any length of time. In addition, junior officers frequently took on command responsibilities for larger units. Thus during the war it was normal for a regiment to be commanded by a major, a battalion by a captain, and a company by a subaltern. In addition a non-commissioned officer – for instance, the company sergeant-major or *Feldwebel* – could be promoted to a temporary officer's rank if he had seen 12 years' service before the war. A sergeant-major could also be given the rank of "temporary officer" of a platoon. This gave him right of command in the field, but none of the privileges of permanently commissioned officers.

For the vast majority of men the war was fought and remembered at the level of the squad, the section, the platoon, or company. Superior units were simply too large to impinge directly on the soldier's day-to-day life. With long casualty lists and the constant stream of new recruits flowing into military units, it was inevitable that the soldier's field of personal vision and attachments remained close to the relatively small group of men with whom he served.

The British army probably relied less on the leadership skills of noncommissioned officers. Early in the war recruitment of officers from the

ranks was infrequent in the British case, although the slaughter of 1916–17 led to a loosening of the criteria for promotion. Because the German army was a conscript force, it was natural that non-commissioned officers with previous training were given more responsibility than was the case in the all-volunteer British army of 1914–16. The result may have been a greater degree of flexibility in German units at group level, which may have operated with greater independence than could British platoons. It is possible as well that the British system, in which subalterns played a crucial role, was partly responsible for the exceptionally high casualty rates they suffered during the war. This is a speculative point, for casualty rates among German junior officers were also very high.

Supporting the front-line combat troops was a wide array of other forces. Particularly important was the artillery, in both the war of immobility of 1915 and the war of movement of 1918. The artillery of an active division in the German army was called a field artillery brigade. It was divided into two field artillery regiments, each of which was made up of two (and later in the war, three) detachments. In each detachment were three batteries. Thus each division was supported

▼ The first fully mechanized war still depended to a very substantial extent on horse power, as this photograph of an Austro-Hungarian supply column and pontoon bridge shows. For every taxi that brought supplies to the Marne, thousands of horse-drawn carriages connected railheads to every battle front.

by between 9 and 12 field batteries, each with its own array of vehicles and transport.

These supplies were in addition to those needed by the infantry regiment itself. Its transport consisted of 16 led horses, 58 two-horsed vehicles, and one four-horsed vehicle. They provided supplies from 12 small-arm ammunition wagons (one per company), 12 traveling kitchens (one per company), and three infantry medical store wagons (one per battalion). Further back stood the supply train, with each regiment drawing everything it needed from 16 baggage wagons, 12 supply wagons, three sutlers wagons and one tool wagon.

Specialist units also proliferated as trench warfare dragged on. Cyclist units and mountain units were formed. There were entrenching companies, tunneling companies, concrete construction squads, and labor companies. Men in these units were drawn from front-line companies, and returned to them when required.

By 1916 the German army developed new assault detachments or *Sturmtruppen*. Men of particular initiative were chosen for patrolling, trench raiding and other offensive operations. They were organized into assault companies of one officer and approximately 120 men, and were used first in 1916 at Verdun, and later extensively throughout the Western Front.

In addition to infantry units, front-line troops were supported by the machine-gun corps, detachments of which manned essential points in the front-line system. Attached to each infantry regiment were one or two machine-gun sections of 30–40 under an officer with three or four machine guns. By July 1916 approximately 11,000 machine guns were in use in the German army, irregularly scattered on both the Eastern and the Western Fronts.

Many books would be needed to describe the organization, function and deployment procedures of other major military units: cavalry, engineers, signal corps, communications troops, survey and map detachments, meteorological services, aircraft units and antiaircraft units, medical and veterinary units, and chaplaincies. The monumental scale of military operations made it inevitable that the different service arms knew very different wars. Furthermore, each soldier knew his own war, and could not have been expected to form an accurate or disinterested view of the whole.

Training and discipline

After the failure of the Schlieffen Plan and the inconclusive nature of the battles on the Eastern Front there was need for a drastic reappraisal of estimates of the probable duration of the war. Unfortunately it did not lead to a change in tactics, which still aimed at punching a hole in the enemy lines, to engage in the decisive war of movement required by strategical thought. This approach made no sense in the first three years of the war, and cost hundreds of thousands of lives.

Long after the men at the Front had learned the bitter truth about how static the conflict was, millions more were still being trained to fight a war of movement. All accounts of the 10-week

course for converting citizens into soldiers in Britain emphasize three essential features: monotony, bullying, and the inculcation of what was known as "the aggressive spirit". Contemporaneous photographs show how new soldiers were kitted out, but not how they were treated.

The French army too had its advocates of the breakthrough by sheer bravura. How was this *élan*, this martial spirit, to be inculcated? In the British case, apparently by marching, humiliation and bayonet drill: in effect, breaking down recruits to the lowest common denominator. The putative aim was to take away the awkward individuality of civilians and replace it with the anonymity of the common soldier, ready to follow orders without delay. Training also aimed to provide a routine of behavior which would help still nerves and prevent the instinct for survival from taking over in battle.

The insufficiency of this approach to creating soldiers was demonstrated by the complete compatibility of noisy informality and military prowess in the Anzac troops (from Australia and New Zealand). No spit and polish here, and a completely different attitude to discipline. Australians were also notorious for a quite un-British approach to the question of how officers and men

► When one surveys the complexity of the German army – or that of any other major combatant power – it seems amazing that any order promulgated at the top of the chain of command actually reached the "poor bloody infantry" at the bottom, who had to carry it out. This diagram shows the bureaucratic "flow chart" of authority, and also suggests the profundity of Clausewitz's dictum that in war all things are simple and the simplest things are infinitely complicated. What is equally remarkable is that the edifice remained intact and functional, even when the war was lost. The German army never collapsed. In defeat in November 1918, it remained an army.

▲ Three veterinary officers were attached to each cavalry and field artillery regiment in the German army. Here a surgeon, with the aid of a complement of soldiers, operates on a horse.

◄ German units engaged in prewar drill. All armies suffered from a glaring gap between the war for which they had been trained and the war they had to fight.

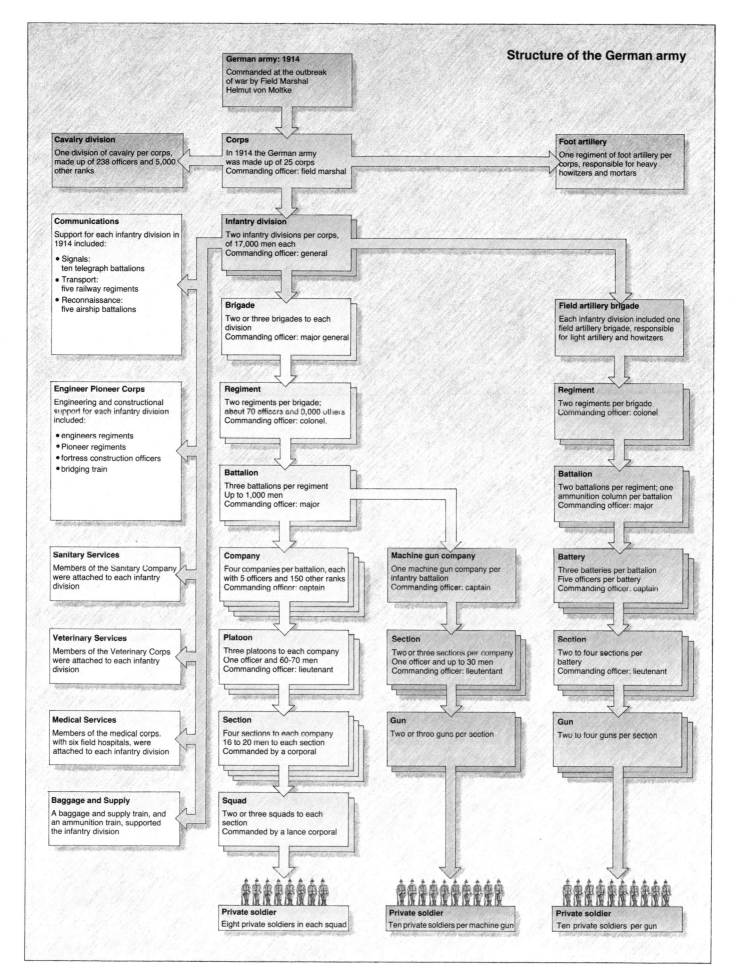

Structure of the German army

German army: 1914

Commanded at the outbreak of war by Field Marshal Helmut von Moltke

Cavalry division

One division of cavalry per corps, made up of 238 officers and 5,000 other ranks

Corps

In 1914 the German army was made up of 25 corps
Commanding officer: field marshal

Foot artillery

One regiment of foot artillery per corps, responsible for heavy howitzers and mortars

Communications

Support for each infantry division in 1914 included:

• Signals:
  ten telegraph battalions
• Transport:
  five railway regiments
• Reconnaissance:
  five airship battalions

Infantry division

Two infantry divisions per corps, of 17,000 men each
Commanding officer: general

Brigade

Two or three brigades to each division
Commanding officer: major general

Field artillery brigade

Each infantry division included one field artillery brigade, responsible for light artillery and howitzers

Engineer Pioneer Corps

Engineering and constructional support for each infantry division included:

• engineers regiments
• Pioneer regiments
• fortress construction officers
• bridging train

Regiment

Two regiments per brigade; about 70 officers and 0,000 others
Commanding officer: colonel.

Regiment

Two regiments per brigade
Commanding officer: colonel

Battalion

Three battalions per regiment
Up to 1,000 men
Commanding officer: major

Battalion

Two battalions per regiment; one ammunition column per battalion
Commanding officer: major

Sanitary Services

Members of the Sanitary Company were attached to each infantry division

Company

Four companies per battalion, each with 5 officers and 150 other ranks
Commanding officer: captain

Machine gun company

One machine gun company per infantry battalion
Commanding officer: captain

Battery

Three batteries per battalion
Five officers per battery
Commanding officer: captain

Veterinary Services

Members of the Veterinary Corps were attached to each infantry division

Platoon

Three platoons to each company
One officer and 60-70 men
Commanding officer: lieutenant

Section

Two or three sections per company
One officer and up to 30 men
Commanding officer: lieutenant

Section

Two to four sections per battery
Commanding officer: lieutenant

Medical Services

Members of the medical corps, with six field hospitals, were attached to each infantry division

Section

Four sections to each company
16 to 20 men to each section
Commanded by a corporal

Gun

Two or three guns per section

Gun

Two to four guns per section

Baggage and Supply

A baggage and supply train, and an ammunition train, supported the infantry division

Squad

Two or three squads to each section
Commanded by a lance corporal

Private soldier

Eight private soldiers in each squad

Private soldier

Ten private soldiers per machine gun

Private soldier

Ten private soldiers per gun

should treat each other. Master and servant was the essence of the British approach. Comrades in arms, with different levels of responsibility, was the Australian. This distinction was the point of a story (probably apocryphal) about an Australian officer telling his men how to behave before they were inspected by a British general: "Whatever you do, don't call me 'Alf'."

British soldiers managed to come to terms with their situation in many ways. Contemporary accounts repeatedly bring up three: the importance of regimental traditions, small-group loyalties and humor. The first gave men a sense of being part of history, of stepping into a formation that had been in battle before. Small-group loyalties gave them essential companionship. It usually involved two or three men in a platoon of a dozen, who went through it all together. This kind of camaraderie gave soldiers a powerful reason to stay the course: not to do so would be to

Songs of World War I

Soldiers traveling by train, on the march, drinking in bars, or idling in the trenches or behind the lines spent much time singing. Their songs came from various sources. France and Germany both had conscript armies with highly developed military musical styles. German songs, for example, often portrayed war as heroic and drew on traditional fears to encourage morale. Both aspects appear in the famous German song "The Watch on the Rhine" (below). In the British army, soldiers wrote songs to fit familiar tunes or simply sang old favorites. Some were humorous, often at the expense of high command. Others had more of a bite, such as the gallows humor expressed in the stanza from "The Old Barbed Wire" (right). The entry of the USA into the war in 1917 produced an outburst of patriotic songs. Songs written by professional songwriters usually did not find favor with soldiers, but an American exception to this was "Over There" by George M. Cohan. It was even recorded by the great Italian tenor Enrico Caruso.

From **The Watch on the Rhine**

There sounds a call like thunder's roar,
Like the crash of swords, like the surge of waves.
To the Rhine, the Rhine, the German Rhine!
Who will the stream's defender be?
   Dear Fatherland, rest quietly.
   Sure stands and true the Watch,
   The Watch on the Rhine.

To heaven he gazes.
Spirits of heroes look down.
He vows with proud battle-desire:
O Rhine! You will stay as German as my breast!
   Dear Fatherland, etc.

Even if my heart breaks in death,
You will never be French.
As you are rich in water
Germany is rich in hero's blood.
   Dear Fatherland, etc.

So long as a drop of blood still glows,
So long a hand the dagger can draw,
So long an arm the rifle can hold -
Never will an enemy touch your shore.
   Dear Fatherland, etc.

From **The Old Barbed Wire**

If you want to find the old battalion,
I know where they are,
I know where they are.
If you want to find a battalion,
I know where they are,
They're hanging on the old barbed wire,
I've seen 'em, I've seen 'em,
Hanging on the old barbed wire,
I've seen 'em,
Hanging on the old barbed wire.

Over There by George M. Cohan

Johnnie get your gun
   get your gun
   get your gun
Back in town to run
Home to run Home to run
Hear them calling you and me
Every son of liberty
Hurry right away
Don't delay go today
Make your Daddy glad
To have had such a lad
Tell your sweetheart not to pine
To be proud their boy's in line.

Over There
Over There
Send the word
Send the word
Over There
That the boys are coming
The boys are coming
The drums rum-tuming everywhere.
Over There
Say a prayer
Send the word
Send the word
To Beware.
It will be over.
We're coming over
And we won't come back
Till it's over
Over There.

◄ *Morning in the Cattle Truck* (detail), by Harold Williamson, shows what became a familiar form of transport during the war. Rail journeys were always slow; provisions were scanty and occasionally nonexistent; and the end of the line was usually the beginning of a lengthy march.

▼ This British motorized column moving through northern France is accompanied by cyclists and mounted traffic. The potential for traffic jams, even on paved roads and in clear weather, was almost limitless.

let down their mates. The third – humor – was a time-honored outlet for griping about the troubles and petty indignities of military life, and left in its wake some of the war's most popular songs.

In the line

Getting to the Front was certainly not half the fun. Most soldiers were transported by train: the rides were cramped and uncomfortable, and usually took a very long time to cover even short distances. It was said that on the Eastern Front a bicyclist would have done better. The problem was the sheer size of the units to be moved. A division of approximately 12,000 men, with its horses, stores and equipment, took up (according to some estimates) over 1,000 railway cars; getting it all on and off at appointed times were monumental tasks.

From the railhead followed the march: 50 minutes on, 10 minutes off every hour, with a 21–27 kg (50–60 lb) pack to carry. Fully disgorged from a train, a division took up fully 24km (15mi) of road, and it took about five hours for the whole parade to pass one spot. Fortunately northern France and Flanders are relatively flat, but those who served on the Italian and other Fronts frequently did a lot of climbing or desert marching. On the Western Front, for reasons of safety, the march up the line or to another section of the line, frequently took place at night. On the Western Front the destination could be anywhere from the English Channel to the Swiss frontier. In the east, the field of action covered a vast panorama from Poland to Palestine, not to mention the campaigns against German forces in Africa, and in Asia where the Japanese fought on the Allied side.

Trench systems and trench life

In France and Flanders the Front was not one line but many. The British system of trench warfare was fairly regular. Facing the enemy lines was the fire trench, built in a zigzag pattern to deaden explosions and prevent deadly fire from the flank from traversing the line. The trench was deep enough to eliminate the danger from shrapnel, though not entirely from snipers. Its floor was covered by wooden duckboards; a firestep (or ledge) brought the soldier to ground level.

At times the enemy front line was as close as 45m (50yd) away. Frequently "no-man's-land" was penetrated by what was known as a forward sap, or listening post, jutting out from the front line. In the British sector of the front the second line, built in the same way, was a support line, linked by a communication trench to reserve lines.

The disposition of forces in the French sectors was more irregular. Trenches with full components of men and equipment alternated with positions sparsely defended. No-man's-land was defined by two thick lines of barbed wire, punctuated by points of entry for patrols. Deeper dugouts lay beneath the support trenches, which were usually not backed up by a reserve line, as in the British case. Of course conditions varied enormously, and Verdun in particular was a special case.

The German trench system was more elaborate and, according to some reports, better built and maintained. This was due to the fact that for long periods the German army was on the defensive, and needed an environment which would enable their men to resist the massive bombardments and assaults of the Allies. German deep bunkers offered protection during the preliminary enemy bombardment that preceded most attacks, after which machine-gun crews and supporting soldiers could reemerge and annihilate the advancing lines of enemy troops.

The German line was much deeper than the British. At Neuve-Chapelle in northern France, for instance, the gap between the fully garrisoned front trench and the support trench was about 2,500m (8,200ft), with the same distance separating the support trench from the reserve trench behind it. In addition a chain of machine-gun emplacements, protected by concrete, was strung

▶ Boredom was a constant companion in the trenches. This, as much as the need for communication with one's family and friends, accounts for the volume of postal traffic from the Front during the war.

▼ An aerial view of one corner of the Western Front near Auchy-les-Labassée in France. The top right-hand quadrant of the photograph is German-held territory, marked by a clearly visible ribbon-like trench system. A three-line array of trenches, linked by communication trenches, can be seen just above no-man's-land, the devastated area in the center of the photograph. The round features dotting the center-right are mine craters. The left-hand side of the photograph shows the British trench line, which appears to be less extensive than the German line opposite it.

about 800m (2,600 ft) behind the front line. The interval between these lethal firing points varied, but could reach 600m (2,000ft).

By 1916 the Germans had developed a new approach, known as the system of "plane defense", which offered much greater flexibility to their men. In this the first line was lightly held, and easily evacuated in the event of an enemy attack. The second and third lines would then provide a massive counterattack, which would sweep back the exhausted enemy troops from their recently occupied, and expendable, positions. Ernst Jünger likened this system to a steel "sinew" or trap, flexible at first, but ready to spring shut after the initial pressure had been absorbed. But even Jünger – who wrote tactical manuals for the German army (and war memoirs after the Armistice) – admitted that this description provides too mathematical or architectural a view of the trenches. There was much greater variety in troop emplacement and liaison than is suggested in linear descriptions of the Front. Jünger preferred the image of a net, in which advancing soldiers were trapped at various points and depths.

The irregularity of a net suggests something of the vast and varied system of fortifications and trenches built by the French at Verdun. In 1916 these were involved in what was for soldiers the most difficult and murderous campaign of the war. Over the 10 months of the battle huge concrete blockhouses, such as Fort Douaumont and Fort Vaux, were defended by their own contingents, at times linked to other units, at times isolated and surrounded. This clustering of

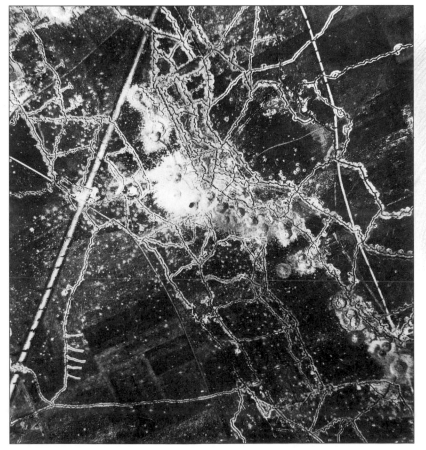

▼ The key to German resistance to the massive artillery bombardments which preceded the attack on the River Somme in 1916 was the construction of bunkers. Built to a depth of 3–9m (10–30ft), they could house up to a dozen men, who could withstand any barrage and still emerge rapidly to man machine-gun emplacements.

strong points was not unusual on the Western Front. What made warfare at Verdun unique was its absolutely monumental scale. By 15 July, five months after the Germans launched their initial attacks, fully 70 divisions of the total of 95 in the French army had passed through Verdun. They served on a front of less than 30km (48mi), on which were deposited the remains of over 650,000 men of both armies.

The average period in the line at this sector of the Front was eight days: soldiers could not take more. In the cold of February or the heat of July conditions were appalling, intolerable, perhaps unimaginable. A huge system of relief and reinforcement was therefore absolutely essential. This created what was dubbed – according to North African slang – the *noria* or the shuttle system. It meant that every unit in the French army had to take its turn, and that consequently new units knew very little about the terrain, conditions, or other minutiae of the battle. In effect the French army came to resemble a gigantic chain which passed through Verdun in a seemingly never-ending circle. Verdun was an extreme case of trench warfare at its most intense and horrifying. Fortunately few sectors had to endure anything like it for any length of time.

Let us consider some facets of life on relatively quieter sectors of the Front. One of the persistent myths of the war is that soldiers were in the front line all the time. This is simply untrue. In the British army, as a rule of thumb, out of every month an infantryman spent about one week in the two front lines, split equally between the fire trench and the support trench, one week in the

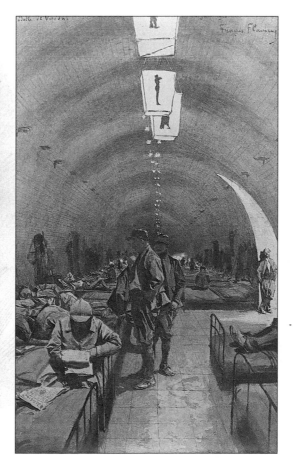

◀ This painting by F. Flameng shows French troops housed within the Citadel of Verdun on 6 June 1916. By then the German attack, begun in February, had reached its apogee. Forts Douaumont, Vaux, and Thiaumont were in German hands. There, outside the city of Verdun, they were held, at a cost of approximately 300,000 German casualties. French losses were higher still. Soldiers encased in concrete forts faced appalling conditions; the French defenders of Fort Vaux surrendered due to lack of water. This was siege warfare on a monumental scale.

In due course the prisoners arrived at Headquarters... The first was a great big ox of a 2nd Lieutenant who could have been hardly twenty... At his side stood a "Gefreite", a lance-corporal, small, stocky, with his hair close-shaven, a low forehead, and a shy look... He then told his story in passable French, continually putting on and taking off his leather gloves. Our front line, which had been the German second- or third-line trench, was naturally connected to the new German first line (their former third or fourth line) by old communication trenches choked up with sandbags and "chevaux de frise" – wooden frames covered with barbed wire. As it was night they had got lost and had finished up in our lines. "I haff come to the army," said the 2nd Lieutenant, " two veeks ago. I did not know the gutters" [the German Graben means both gutter and trench] "and I expected the Gefreite to guide me." As to the Gefreite, who was interrogated in German by the battalion sergeant-major, he winked and said, "Not my fault! the Offizier!" suggesting that he, as a simple soldier, was not responsible, that his job was to follow his officer. We felt that he had known only too well that the Lieutenant was going in the wrong direction, but he had held his tongue in the hope that in this way he would soon be finished with the war.

RENÉ ARNAUD

▶ These three cigarette cards, inserted in cigarette packs, show wartime British lorries. The top picture is of a revamped British postal van which was used in Russia; the center picture is of a portable bath; the third is of a mobile repair shop, also as used in Russia. The illustrations are striking in that they acknowledge some of the basic (and irregularly supplied) supports of morale: letters, hot baths, efficient maintenance of equipment. Even though the pictures are idealized, they spoke in a language soldiers understood. No doubt most were more interested in a smoke.

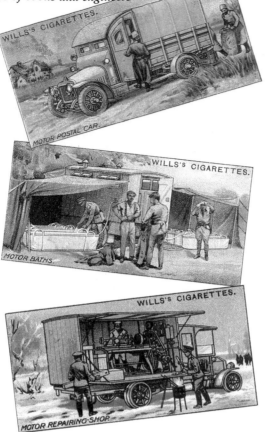

reserve lines. The rest of the time was spent behind the line.

Daily routine in the trenches was fairly predictable. The day began half an hour before sunrise, with the order to "stand-to". This would bring the whole platoon to the firestep, just in case an attack was in store. If it was not, sentries were posted and breakfast was taken. The next order of business was inspection, followed by more sentry duty and other mundane tasks, which usually involved repair work on the trench system. Rations arrived after a second "stand-to" of the day at dusk. Then the rotation of sentry duty continued.

This is the war most frontline soldiers knew most of the time. It was dreary, lice-ridden and very frequently wet and extremely muddy or dry and exceedingly dusty. But most of the time it was spent waging defensive rather than offensive warfare. It is true that raiding parties were organized to gather intelligence and cause trouble to the other side, and snipers were at work at all times. But these were interruptions in a war of endurance more than of bravado.

At some points a "live and let live system" evolved – a means of existence involving tacit cooperation between the sides, recognizing a rough parity of forces. Since neither was likely to dislodge the other, there were ways of minimizing

▲ A Bulgarian transport column passing through a Serbian town. The primitiveness of conditions on the Eastern Front made horse power (and other animal power) more reliable than motorized transport.

▶ It is best to leave to the imagination the cuisine dished out to soldiers from this French traveling field kitchen, shown at the front in 1916.

▲ One of the most time-consuming enterprises in a soldier's life was the repair, cleaning and replacement of his kit. Inevitable wear and tear, matched by endemic petty pilfering, made it almost impossible for a soldier to have all his regulation gear in order at any one time. Inspection required ingenuity and tolerance when items disappeared and reappeared before and after roll call. In addition to the equipment soldiers were supposed to have, most added all sorts of items to make their lives easier. The French *poilu* (literally "hairy one") shown right was notorious for carrying on his back the equivalent of a corner shop. Belgian troops (above left) fought as an independent force virtually throughout the war.

◀ A French military abattoir showing the slaughter of sheep, preparation of skins, and collection of meat and remains for food. The massive and never-ending task of provisioning armies began here and ended in the mobile kitchen opposite.

The Treatment of Prisoners

The most striking contrast between the two world wars was in terms of the treatment of prisoners of war. Atrocities were committed in both conflicts, but the systematic inhumanity of the 1939–45 war was by and large unknown in World War I. Prisoners' conditions varied considerably. Some did agricultural work, but most faced inadequate nutrition, miserable sanitary conditions, and boredom, rather than the degradation and extermination of camps on the Eastern Front in Hitler's war.

As the 1914–18 war dragged on, the numbers taken prisoner grew substantially. By June 1916 the Germans held 300,000 French prisoners, while the French held 95,000 Germans; 160,000 British soldiers became prisoners of war during the conflict. Of the total of 500,000 French

prisoners held in Germany between 1914 and 1918, 40,000 died there.

Partly to defray the costs of their upkeep, prisoners were put to work in industry, agriculture and public works. An agreement reached at Berne in December 1917, and ratified three months later, led to the exchange of prisoners aged over 48 who had been in captivity at least 18 months.

On both sides civilians were interned and treated as prisoners of war. Germans were held at Wakefield, Yorkshire, and a British community of 4,000 men were confined for the duration to the racetrack of Ruhleben, near Berlin. The treatment of Armenian civilians by the Turks, in contrast, descended to bestiality; about 600,000 Armenians were massacred.

▼ **All prisoners were alike, and yet each had his own story. This massive column of Russian soldiers taken prisoner in the Battle of Tannenberg in 1914 was full of soldiers with the same fatigue, fatalism, haunted eyes and fear masked by determination seen in the faces of all nationalities during the war.**

◄ This German prisoner holding his food containers was among thousands who lived a life of boredom, disease, and occasional dreams of escape and reunion with family and friends. The ranks were frequently thinned by outbreaks of epidemics including the terrible visitation of influenza in 1918.

the risk and discomfort of trench warfare. One was to have an unspoken agreement (worked out through trial and error) not to shell latrines nor to open fire during breakfast. Another was to make as much noise as possible before a minor raid, so that the other side could withdraw to their protected bunkers.

This limitation on hostilities did not exist everywhere and was stamped on by command when it came to light. But even such informal arrangements as survived could be quickly buried, along with men killed by snipers, by the odd shell, or gas. The fraternization that did go on briefly between the lines on Christmas Day 1914 did not characterize the way the war was fought in the trenches. Violence was always below the surface, ready to explode.

After sentry-duty was completed, any spare time that trench soldiers had was spent in a rough-and-ready kind of personal housekeeping, either of the delousing variety or patching and mending the poor-quality kit with which they were provided. This often became the art of finding essential uses for the most unlikely implements. Regulation equipment rarely sufficed for the running repairs that had to be done time and again. For this reason standard gear formed only the core of a soldier's personal effects.

In addition to a rifle, ammunition and a gas mask, French soldiers carried on their backs "their trunk and even their cupboard", as the French author Henri Barbusse put it. Their knapsacks – weighing up to 27kg (60lb) – contained the regulation "two tins of pressed beef, a dozen biscuits, two tablets of coffee and two packets of dried soup, a bag of sugar, fatigue smock and spare boots" as well as jam, tobacco, chocolate, candles, soft shoes, soap, a spirit lamp, a blanket, a waterproof sheet, some cooking utensils, a trenching tool and a water bottle.

In addition all sorts of odds and ends were carried around. In Barbusse's unit one man had 18 pockets stuffed with personal effects. In one pocket he had writing paper, an army squad book, maps, newspaper clippings, a folder of photographs from home; in another, mirrors, flasks of mineral oil, scissors, tubes of aspirin or opium tablets; elsewhere, he had his purse, pipe, pocket pipe-lighter, pack of cards and set of drafts, with a paper board and sealing wax pieces. Others in the same platoon had a German pay book, some phials of iodine, several knives, a revolver, string, nails, and a drinking cup. Clearly, provisioning was a very individual art in the trenches, entailing the storage for later use of items purchased, stolen, looted from enemy trenches, or taken from the dead.

Behind the line
When men were withdrawn from the front lines, they faced different problems. Since the war was originally supposed to end by Christmas 1914, members of the French army had been given little leave until 1915. It is therefore not surprising that French popular artists celebrated such moments of leave as there were with particular fervor. British enlisted troops were only occasionally given leave to return to Britain, but officers were

permitted to return home more often. Otherwise British soldiers were sent to the coastal enclave of Etaples, which housed a training camp to toughen up new drafts and keep older soldiers fit to return to the Front. This was the location of the notorious "bull-ring", where, for rest and recreation soldiers were treated to "square-bashing" (marching endlessly in squares), all sorts of onerous drills, and some of the nastiest sergeant-majors and military police in the army. For others the problem of billeting became crucial. Tact was needed to convince the local populace to offer shelter to what often appeared to be a band of brigands. Domestic scenes went on roughly as before, despite the presence of a large number of onlookers. Where houses were unavailable, other accommodation had to suffice. Once shelter and food were found there was still the minor problem of language, and enterprising business- men supplied pocket dictionaries and phrase books to the troops. One Belgian shipping company produced a guide to *The Language of Three Allies*, telling the British soldier all he needed to know about the Flemish and French equivalents and pronunciations of key phrases.

Life behind the lines was an important part of the soldiers' war and troops naturally looked to peace-time entertainments to occupy their time when away from the Front. The chief licensed recreations of British soldiers were sport, theatrical events and cinema. There was a vast proliferation of football leagues, and later on even baseball leagues for Americans. Countless plays were performed, by visiting entertainers or by the troops themselves, who often dressed up in drag to entertain their fellow soldiers.

Another wartime adaptation was humorous magazines, modeled among British troops on some of the more tasteless forms of schoolboy publication. But this gives them too little credit, for trench journalism was an extraordinary phenomenon in the British army, and had its equivalents in other forces as well. Virtually every brigade had its amateur journalists, who found ways to mimeograph and distribute several

▲▶ After the search for food, the search for shelter preoccupied most soldiers behind the lines. Billeting was a difficult and delicate operation, involving soldiers – at times resembling (and more than resembling) an armed band of thugs – entering the domestic world of peasants and townspeople. There was the universal language of children to mediate between hosts and guests, as shown above, but when household space was scarce, any available shelter had to do. These Canadian soldiers (right) had to make the best of a barn. Others were housed in overturned water towers.

▶ This rare photograph shows the production of a German trench newspaper. The soldier in the center is typesetting one of the hundreds of ephemeral journals produced by soldiers themselves in all major combatant armies. The mix of stories included humor, bad poetry, and swipes at those in authority, at home or at the Front.

hundred copies of an eight- or ten-page paper for a few weeks or months. The most famous was the *Wipers Times* ("Wipers" being the English slang name for Ypres), which was produced by a number of men of the Sherwood Foresters in a ramshackle office near the Menin Gate. It was printed on an abandoned machine salvaged by a sergeant who had been a printer before the war. Its first issue was 12 February 1916, and under different names it continued to appear for the rest of the war. The names of most of its contributors have faded away, but one, Gilbert Frankau, was a best-selling author in the 1920s. The tone of this paper, and of the many that tried to follow its success, was unabashedly rude in a public-school sort of way. On 31 July 1916 the paper (now rechristened the *SommeTimes*), printed an advertisement for a sure cure for optimism (an artillery barrage). Other articles sent up the absurdity of civilian attitudes toward and the reporting of the war. Chauvinistic nonsense of the kind produced by the journalists Hilaire Belloc and Horatio Bottomley was parodied under the by-line of Belary Helloc or Cockles Tumley. The peace camp also came in for a barracking. Such well-known Labour politicians as Ramsay MacDonald, Victor Grayson, and Arthur Henderson were caricatured as "Flamsey MacMonald", "Grictor Vrayson", and "A. Tenderson." They were portrayed as innocents who knew nothing about the war.

Staff officers came in for persistent ribbing. The *B.E.F. Times* of 8 September 1917 defined "a few more military terms." Among them was: "DUDS – These are of two kinds. A shell on impact failing to explode is called a dud. They are unhappily not as plentiful as the other kind, which often draws a big salary and explodes for no reason. These are plentiful away from the fighting areas."

Other issues had articles of a satirical kind which raised the delicate question of the faithfulness of girlfriends or wives back home. In one Biblical parody, the Book of Kings is rewritten: the plan of King David to kill Uriah the Hittite in order to get his wife, Bathsheba, goes seriously awry. On the whole, though, the subject of sex was very rarely broached.

These papers were successful largely because they showed that even in the exposed Ypres salient, some British soldiers managed to keep a sense of humor. This kind of insouciance was highly valued. But trench magazines had a wide appeal for other reasons. Partly, it was because of their tone of irreverence for authority; partly because soldiers had little to do and these papers helped to pass the time. The same sense of the ridiculous within the grimness of the war made Charlie Chaplin the most popular screen performer with the soldiers. His ability to survive against all odds in a storm not of his own making, and even occasionally to plant a boot on the seat of authority, translated easily to the landscape of war. His short film *Shoulder Arms*, made in 1918, was a masterpiece of this kind of soldiers' humor. It was this mixture of the sentimental, the frivolous and the mildly indecent which soldiers' songs also captured and which underlay the variety of soldiers' entertainments produced during World War I.

ARTILLERY WEAPONRY AND TACTICS

In 1914 the main artillery weapon was the light field gun, designed for mobile offensive warfare. All major combatant armies were equipped with field guns based on the French 75mm gun. These could fire up to 20 shells a minute with relatively high accuracy, and played an important role in the mobile warfare of 1914, but after the "race to the sea" stalemate set in along a 750km (475mi) front and, in effect, siege warfare took over.

One response was the development of heavier ordnance, to produce gaps in the enemy's barbed-wire entanglements and destroy enemy guns. In this the German army was at an advantage. Its general staff had learned from the Russo-Japanese War (1904–05) and had retained an emphasis on firepower. Each corps was provided with at least 12 150mm heavy howitzers – known for their noise and black smoke explosions as "Jack Johnsons" after the black world heavyweight boxing champion of 1908 to 1915.

As heavier howitzers and guns of longer range became available, all sides attempted to adjust to the new siege warfare. Trench mortars were devised to fire virtually straight into the air. The number of heavy guns grew exponentially. In 1914 the French had 300 heavy guns; in 1918 about 7,000, of which 400 were mounted on railway carriages. Of the 20,000 artillery pieces in the German army in 1918, about 8,000 were heavy guns. The gun with the longest range was the Kaiser Wilhelm gun which delivered a 108kg (238lb) shell to a target 148km (90mi) away. That destination was Paris.

Vast quantities of ammunition were spent on counterbattery work, the destruction of strong points, and wire-cutting operations. But heavy intensive bombardments before attacks sacrificed the element of surprise. The bombardments also blotted out not only the enemy defenses but also roads and identifying features and restricted the movement of infantry, guns and subsequently tanks alike. As tactics developed barrages were devised to protect infantry during their attacks. Guns were initially trained on enemy front lines and then lifted and moved on to support trenches. Later the more successful "creeping" or "rolling" barrage was introduced which moved in advance of infantry on a timed basis. But the absence of radio communications for control made these arrangements inflexible if the infantry were delayed or diverted.

The increased importance of artillery led to an enormous expansion of artillery forces. At its peak the British army's artillery men numbered 526,000 – a quarter of its total ration strength. The other side of the coin was that artillery and mortars caused the most casualties. In the British army artillery caused 58 percent of casualties, machine-gun and rifle bullets 39 percent.

Artillery did not win the war, but the noise and the surreal landscape it produced defined war on the Western Front. Nothing like it had ever occurred before.

▶ Artillery came in every conceivable size during the war. Guns on the Eastern Front (top right) were occasionally of Crimean vintage; newer models included a 6in BL 3-ton howitzer (second right, being dragged through the mud), and a 9.45in trench mortar (third right). The most compact French version of a trench mortar could be carried on a man's back. It was called *Le Crapouillot*, which was also the title of a celebrated trench newspaper. The biggest guns, like the German "Big Bertha" or the American 14in railway gun (fourth right), had a range of 50km (30mi) or more.

▼ Devised in mid-1916 for supporting infantry attack, the creeping barrage entailed a bombardment lifting forward short distances at fixed times, with the assault troops creeping forward as close as possible behind it. This was most effective when infantry stayed close to the shell bursts, no more than 100m (330ft) behind the point of impact. On the first day of the Somme (1 July 1916), this sheet of fire worked well with 7 and 18 Division of the British XV Corps. Of course, coordination between artillery and infantry was frequently difficult, and gas could disrupt the most meticulous planning. On its own, artillery was incapable of breaking the stalemate on the Western Front.

Barrage   1st lift   2nd lift   3rd lift

180 Pounder   Infantry   1st enemy trench   Support trench
Front line

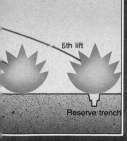

5th lift

Reserve trench

Datafile

Each of the great campaigns of 1916–17, Verdun, the Somme, Chemin des Dames and Passchendaele (Third Ypres), symbolizes the futility of the war. Taken together they present a catalog of offensive operations which went on for weeks or months after their initial failures, and succeeded only in cutting the heart out of the citizen armies which went to war in 1914. Total casualties in these offensives exceeded two million men.

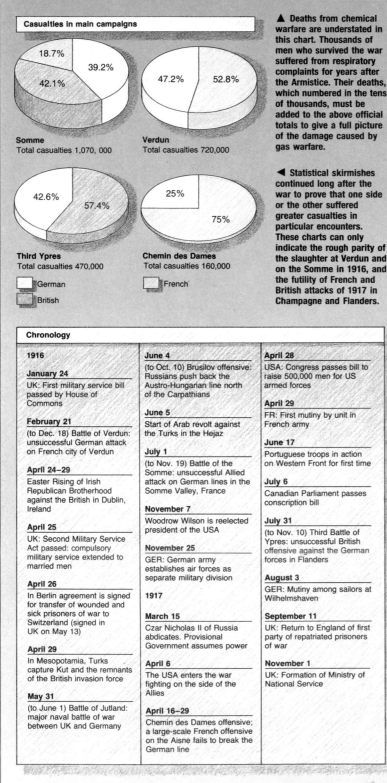

Gas casualties

8.5%
22.6%
33.3%
35.6%

Total 17,700

☐ German   ☐ US
☐ French   ☐ UK

▲ **Deaths from chemical warfare are understated in this chart. Thousands of men who survived the war suffered from respiratory complaints for years after the Armistice. Their deaths, which numbered in the tens of thousands, must be added to the above official totals to give a full picture of the damage caused by gas warfare.**

Casualties in main campaigns

18.7%
39.2%
42.1%

Somme
Total casualties 1,070, 000

47.2%   52.8%

Verdun
Total casualties 720,000

42.6%   57.4%

Third Ypres
Total casualties 470,000

☐ German
☐ British

25%
75%

Chemin des Dames
Total casualties 160,000

☐ French

◄ **Statistical skirmishes continued long after the war to prove that one side or the other suffered greater casualties in particular encounters. These charts can only indicate the rough parity of the slaughter at Verdun and on the Somme in 1916, and the futility of French and British attacks of 1917 in Champagne and Flanders.**

Chronology

1916	June 4	April 28
January 24 UK: First military service bill passed by House of Commons	(to Oct. 10) Brusilov offensive: Russians push back the Austro-Hungarian line north of the Carpathians	USA: Congress passes bill to raise 500,000 men for US armed forces
February 21 (to Dec. 18) Battle of Verdun: unsuccessful German attack on French city of Verdun	**June 5** Start of Arab revolt against the Turks in the Hejaz	**April 29** FR: First mutiny by unit in French army
April 24–29 Easter Rising of Irish Republican Brotherhood against the British in Dublin, Ireland	**July 1** (to Nov. 19) Battle of the Somme: unsuccessful Allied attack on German lines in the Somme Valley, France	**June 17** Portuguese troops in action on Western Front for first time
April 25 UK: Second Military Service Act passed: compulsory military service extended to married men	**November 7** Woodrow Wilson is reelected president of the USA	**July 6** Canadian Parliament passes conscription bill
April 26 In Berlin agreement is signed for transfer of wounded and sick prisoners of war to Switzerland (signed in UK on May 13)	**November 25** GER: German army establishes air forces as separate military division	**July 31** (to Nov. 10) Third Battle of Ypres: unsuccessful British offensive against the German forces in Flanders
	1917	**August 3** GER: Mutiny among sailors at Wilhelmshaven
April 29 In Mesopotamia, Turks capture Kut and the remnants of the British invasion force	**March 15** Czar Nicholas II of Russia abdicates. Provisional Government assumes power	**September 11** UK: Return to England of first party of repatriated prisoners of war
May 31 (to June 1) Battle of Jutland: major naval battle of war between UK and Germany	**April 6** The USA enters the war fighting on the side of the Allies	**November 1** UK: Formation of Ministry of National Service
	April 16–29 Chemin des Dames offensive; a large-scale French offensive on the Aisne fails to break the German line	

Verdun, the Somme, Passchendaele: these are the names of some of the major encounters of 1916–17, the third phase of World War I; they have come to symbolize the war as a whole. This is for two reasons. The first is the scale of the casualties in these huge battles. The second is that these operations, in effect, led nowhere.

Two questions immediately arise about this phase of the war, which have preoccupied historians and commentators ever since 1918. What was combat like for the men who fought in these fantastic and futile encounters? And, given the odds against survival, why did ordinary men, under no illusion as to what they were being asked to do, continue to fight in this kind of war? With respect to 1914, the historian asks: why did men go to war? By 1916, the question is really: why did they stay?

As if these questions were not hard enough to answer, the temperature of discussion has been raised by a few commentators who have set them in the context of the even more appalling carnage of World War II – slaughter not of soldiers but of civilians. To some observers the trenches were the concentration camps of World War I, in which a whole generation was slaughtered. This is an

1916–17 THE GREAT SLAUGHTER

The major campaigns of 1916–17 symbolize World War I

What was combat like?

How did men cope with the conditions?

The fog of war was made worse by gas attacks

Men had to live in a landscape of destruction for years

With the risk of being blown to pieces

Often in the company of the dead

extreme position, hard to accept in the light of the fact that millions chose to fight in 1914–18. However abused were their initial faith and commitments, they both killed and suffered; hence their status as victims is highly questionable. The noted French scholar Antoine Prost has found a better way to put the point. His remarks refer to Verdun, but have a bearing on many other facets of the war. "Like Auschwitz in World War II," he has written, "Verdun was a transgression of the limits of the human condition."

Prost's statement is profoundly true. This section will attempt to explore some of these claims by presenting three kinds of evidence. The first deals with the infantryman's landscape of battle. The second concerns his motivation. The third (in the next chapter) relates to the varied pattern of loss of morale, disaffection and mutiny, which was visible by mid-1917 and which grew irregularly over the following 18 months until it put an end to the war itself.

The fog of war

A persistent fog of confusion hung over the battlefields of World War I. Men in combat rarely knew what was happening or on occasion even

▼ French troops advancing through barbed wire entanglements on the Western Front. A direct hit by high explosives could completely obliterate all traces of a man; those hit by shrapnel risked being maimed or dismembered.

where they were. The front line was well enough marked, but as soon as an attacking force entered no-man's-land, which was usually an irregular terrain pockmarked with craters, the combination of terror, noise, bombardment, machine-gun fire, barbed wire, casualties and natural human error made it inevitable that men frequently lost their bearings and went forward, if at all, largely out of inertia.

All attempts must be abandoned to picture battle as a series of moves on a giant chess board – which is what military maps did, both at headquarters and in civilian newspapers. In battle, soldiers tended to move in every conceivable direction, and only occasionally in the one intended in the plan of attack. This was not a new feature of combat: witness the French writer Stendhal's accounts of the fog of war in *The Charterhouse of Parma* (1839) and Tolstoy's in *War and Peace* (1869). As in other wars, combat was a haphazard set of encounters, only some of which were planned. But the soldiers of 1914–18 did live through a war very different from those of Waterloo or the Crimea. In particular, three features of combat were unanticipated and very difficult to locate within any familiar frame of reference.

I wish those people who write so glibly about this being a holy war could see a case of mustard gas... could see the poor things burnt and blistered all over with great mustard- coloured suppurating blisters with blind eyes all sticky... and stuck together, and always fighting for breath, with voices a mere whisper, saying that their throats are closing and they know they will choke.

VERA BRITTAIN

The deadly cloud

The first feature is related to new weapons introduced in the course of the conflict. Most commentators describe the great battles of 1916–17 as wars of men against machines, with the men inevitably coming out on the losing end. This suggests that technical changes in weaponry prior to 1914 had transformed battle out of all recognition. To some extent this was true. The war in the west (but not in the east) saw the end of the cavalry as a key attacking force. It initiated soldiers into the use of camouflage, tank warfare, and aerial combat and reconnaissance. It produced artillery barrages on a scale never before known. And it presented a new and hideous kind of weapon: poison gas.

The onset of chemical warfare on the Western Front transformed the landscape of battle in a most bizarre and spectacular way. The first use of

poison gas there was at Langemark near Ypres on 22 April 1915. German troops opened 6,000 cylinders of chlorine along an 8km (5mi) front. The French and Algerian troops subjected to this attack either suffocated or fled. Two days later it was the Canadians' turn to be gassed. This attack was less successful, since the gas hardly rose above ground level, but the psychological effect was considerable, and the Canadians also retreated. On 1, 6, and 10 May 1915 British troops were gassed, but, due to a change in the direction of the wind, both sides suffered casualties.

This raises the key limitation of this innovation in warfare. It could cripple attacker as well as defender, and frequently did so. It also eliminated the possibility of a surprise attack. Hence it was rare for gas, or that other chemical device, the flamethrower, to do anything other than *stabilize* the lines. By 1915 the advantage in warfare had

▲ ▶ After their first appearance on the Western Front in 1915, gas attacks became a regular feature of the war (above). Box respirators or other antigas devices became standard field equipment, alongside impromptu means of defense against gas, such as that used by this Russian infantryman fighting near Baranovici in western Russia in 1917 (right). With luck, rain or damp would keep the gas below knee level; high winds would disperse it, or drive it back toward enemy lines. Gas shells were a greater menace.

► A makeshift gas factory. With the aid of a soldier, a German chemist is preparing a brew to be placed in bottles and laid near enemy lines for activation by sniper fire. Multiply this example by thousands, and it provides a rough idea of the demand for chemicals during the war. To meet it, huge industrial complexes were set up or expanded with government funds. These units provided a significant boost for the companies that became the industrial giants of the postwar years: ICI in Britain (formed by mergers in 1926), DuPont in America and I.G. Farben in Germany.

shifted in favor of the defensive. Relatively effective countermeasures were soon developed, in particular the box respirator, a device which kept soldiers alive at the minor price of making them look like invaders from another planet.

By 1918 roughly one shell in four fired by both sides on the Western Front was a gas shell. By then chlorine had been joined by the more lethal phosgene and by mustard gas, the antecedent of napalm, which blistered the skin in hideous ways. A gas alarm at any point on the Western Front would bring about a feverish transformation of faces into elephantine masks. After a time they became part of the scene. Soldiers drilled in them, read through them, fought in them, and on occasion kitted out their horses with them. Because of the range of German artillery, French schoolchildren were given gas masks too, but fortunately, few were needed.

▲ A German soldier carrying food to a dugout during a gas attack on the Western Front.

◄ These British soldiers were victims of a gas attack near Bois de l'Abbé in France in May 1918. The lucky ones would recover their sight within a few hours; the unlucky ones would have been blinded for life, or have had their lungs so badly damaged that recovery was extremely painful and very uncertain. Mustard gas accounted for some of the most severely wounded: blistering the skin as well as asphyxiating the men who inhaled it. Compassion rather than a cure was all that medical science could offer these men.

◀ Troops of the Canadian 4th Division holding the "line" at Passchendaele on 14 November 1917, at the end of Third Ypres. The water-logged landscape defined the conditions of combat and ensured the failure of Haig's attempt to break through German positions. In the March 1918 offensive, the Germans retook these craters, but gave them up again in the retreat of summer 1918.

Destruction

A second feature of the war on the Western Front was the extraterrestrial landscape of destruction produced by artillery fire, barbed wire and mud. The soldiers lived in a world where everything had been torn up and twisted, and where men could drown in mud. To the infantryman of 1914–18, Henri Barbusse remarked, hell was water. None of this was new in 1914. Many examples could be cited as precedents for the devastation of 1914–18: the destruction of Carthage in 698, the Dutch revolt of the 16th century and aspects of the Napoleonic wars (1800–15), among others. Closer still were the terrible battles of the American Civil War. The cornfields at Shiloh were said to have been yellow before the battle there; blood red after. But what made the landscape of destruction in World War I such an enduring feature in popular memory was that millions of men were forced to live in it, at times under it, for years. The paintings of the British war artist Paul Nash bring home the eerie unfamiliarity of the world the soldiers knew.

Of course, parts of the Front escaped the worst of the fighting. And even on the Somme or at Passchendaele wild flowers insistently returned, providing an enduring symbol of the war: the poppy, indigenous to northern France and Flanders, and liberally sprinkled, blood-red, across the battlefields of the war.

The company of the dead

The front-line soldiers of 1914–18 saw things that people should not see. Among them were hideously wounded men. Medical reports on the wounded make particularly harrowing reading, despite the language doctors used to distance themselves from suffering. But at least they had anesthetics to use, unlike surgeons in earlier wars. The butchery of battle was worsened by the

▲ British stretcher-bearers bring a wounded man back to a casualty clearing station through the mud of the Ypres salient on 1 August 1917. This man was a casualty of fighting near Boesinghe, a set of encounters dignified with the name of the Battle of Pilckem Ridge. For the wounded, the battle against infection was frequently hopeless.

▶ Detail of *Hell* by Georges Leroux. This painting suggests the truth of Henri Barbusse's assertion that for the front soldier, hell was water. As one trench newspaper put it, "This simple word, rain, which means next to nothing to the civilian, with a roof over his head, this word encapsulates the horror of the soldier in the field." (*L'Horizon*, July 1918.)

development of artillery, which could literally tear a man to pieces, even at times without leaving a single trace of his existence. On the other hand, medical advances meant that the ravages of disease were less severe in this war than in 19th-century conflicts. Appallingly wounded men were to be found on all fronts in World War I. Some were beyond help: others, whose minds had gone, were beyond communication. The wounded were evacuated to base hospitals and, when possible, back home.

Many veterans of 1914–18 spoke of their memories of the wounded. But what made at least as deep an impression was another and more unusual aspect of the conflict: the persistent presence of the dead. In previous wars battles had lasted a few days at most. They had had a beginning and an end, after which the dead of both sides, usually as complete bodies, were buried. But this war was different: combat went on for months; artillery fire dismembered men in a flash; and the front line hardly moved at all. Consequently, the line of trenches stretching from Switzerland to the English Channel was littered with the remains of perhaps one million men. Soldiers ate with the dead, made jokes about them, and rifled their possessions.

After the war attempts were made to provide the dead with dignified resting places. Remains were gathered and reburied with proper ceremony. Round Ypres, for instance, about 200,000 British soldiers killed in the war lie in well cared-for cemeteries. During the war no such measures were possible. Soldiers had to carry on in the presence of countless bodies of dead men, some familiar, most anonymous. Those buried would reappear during bombardments, and be reinterred, at times to help support, quite literally, the trenches in which they had fought. Many soldiers recalled the stench of decomposition, and

the swarms of flies on corpses, especially during the summer months. Everyone execrated the rats. It is difficult to imagine the nature of this ghastly environment. Human bones can still be found round Verdun to this day.

Coping with combat

It would seem to be the most natural thing in the world for men forced to live in this way to drop their guns and go home. This is no idle suggestion, and there was a steady trickle of deserters throughout the war. But aside from the desire to avoid being shot by your own side for cowardice,

◀ *"And have we done with War at last?*
Well, we've been lucky devils, both,
And there's no need of pledge or oath
To bind our lovely friendship fast,
By firmer stuff close bound enough".

Two Fusiliers
by Robert Graves

▶ Only those who had been through battle could really know how human beings could be squashed like ants or rearranged like "ghastly dolls", as the British writer Siegfried Sassoon put it. Many soldiers developed a defensive callousness after having seen dismembered corpses time and again. What ex-soldiers recalled in later years varied substantially. In R.H. Mottram's *Spanish Farm Trilogy* (1924–27), it was not a legless man but a headless man who continued to haunt the central character. Others blotted such images out of their conscious minds for ever.

there were other ways in which men came to terms with the stress of trench warfare.

The first was the human tendency to direct one's primary loyalty to very small groups. Such camaraderie made the war a very private affair indeed, focused on the survival chances of two or three men. These bonds, at times forged before the war, were reinforced by the isolation of platoons under conditions of bombardment or combat. To cut and run meant first and foremost to violate the trust of a handful of friends.

It also meant breaking faith with junior officers who shared the risks and whose casualty rates were even higher than those of the men they led. The English writer Robert Graves estimated that a subaltern's life expectancy at the front was about two weeks. Other evidence points to the greater risks officers faced: perhaps 20 percent of the men who held commissions and who served at the Front were killed, compared to a 10–12 percent death rate among enlisted men in combat units. There is evidence that many privates felt a bond of shared experience with officers with whom they served in the trenches, and whom they followed whatever the dangers.

There were other supports for the front-line

▼ This photograph captures the immediate aftermath of hand-to-hand combat between French and German troops in the Meuse region of the Western Front. This trench was taken by the French only an hour earlier. Under these conditions, the dead were left where they fell, or were simply added to the fortifications.

▶ **Mass or Holy Communion was said in the field of all armies. Here the Russian rite is observed in a forest in what is now Poland. The czar and czarina encouraged mystical religious fervor during the war. To what extent their sentiments were shared by ordinary Russian soldiers – overwhelmingly peasants – is difficult to say. All armies had their own version of the American saying that there are no atheists in a foxhole.**

▼ **The incongruous geometry of the steeple of Albert Cathedral was a landmark for British soldiers stationed on the Somme Front. Speculation was rife as to a supernatural reason for the suspension of Madonna and child.**

The harmonium has arrived... It has been wonderful to have it for Easter Day. Colonel Hooper allows me to have an ambulance to take it and me as near the line as possible... My barrel-organ, as it is called, causes great amusement. "Now, Padre," they say "all you want is a monkey." To which the obvious reply is, "well are you looking for a job?" At the South Wales Borderers headquarters, the Adjutant had got hold of some flowers, and had hung blankets round the shattered walls. We had four celebrations of Holy Communion, and after that a long round of services until late in the evening, but I have a very comfortable bed to come back to every day.

REVD H.W. BLACKBURNE
BRITISH ARMY CHAPLAIN

soldier. For those who wanted it, religious communion was available. On both sides chaplains went up the line with the rest of the army. Among them Catholic priests had a particularly strong reputation for bravery, and were seen frequently at the Front giving final absolution. Some clergy of other denominations also earned respect by sharing trench conditions.

Some soldiers lived in a different kind of supernatural world – a world of superstitious beliefs, which, like most prerational modes of thought, moved in two contrary directions. On the one hand superstitions arose out of the fatalistic belief that all was preordained, that a soldier was hit when the bullet "with his name on it" was fired. On the other hand they emerged out of the sense that the individual could change his fate by a carefully prescribed set of actions, or by touching a magical talisman. Superstition described a world in which men were both powerless and all-powerful: in which they could do nothing to alter their destiny, and could survive by touching a rabbit's foot.

Closely allied to this kind of mentality was the sense that supernatural forces were not far from the battlefield. There was the famous instance of the Angels of Mons, who appeared above and protected retreating British soldiers in August 1914. This idea probably derived from a short story published early in the war describing the return from the dead of the men of the medieval Battle of Agincourt, appearing luminously between the two armies. There was the Madonna of Albert – a statue of Mary and Child on top of a church near the British front line on the Somme. A direct hit had bent the statue to a right angle to the church's spire. British soldiers who passed this gravity-defying statue conjured up the idea that the war would end the day the Madonna fell. Potshots tried to hurry the day along, but without success. She fell under British bombardment after the Germans captured Albert in 1918.

Combat out of the trenches

The experience of the trench soldier in World War I has been emphasized primarily for two reasons. First his war was that of the majority of fighting men in the major combatant countries. Secondly the outcome of the series of skirmishes, standoffs, and battles in which he and his comrades were engaged on the Western Front determined the outcome of the war.

The Provision of Chaplains

All armies in World War I recognized the value of spiritual support for ordinary soldiers, but the provision and position of chaplains varied between armies according to national attitudes to religion. In 1914 there were no chaplains in the French army. They had been withdrawn in 1880 for fear of clerical opposition to the French republican constitution. The American army also omitted a corps of chaplains, as a consequence of the strict separation of church and state stipulated by the constitution of the USA. At the other end of the spectrum, the established churches of Britain (Anglican in England and Wales, Presbyterian in Scotland) dominated the British army chaplaincy department even though nonconformist churches were strong within Britain.

Because the French were fighting on their own soil they could draw on French clergy in the towns behind their front line. Army officers were happy to welcome clergy when they would consolidate discipline, but feared men who might undermine it. The American army allowed private supporters to pay chaplains and provide chapels. About 2,300 ministers served in France and were given the rank of first lieutenant, but to minister to troops required the goodwill of unit commanders and force of personality. The British army adapted to wartime needs by recognizing the "fancy religious sects" and providing chaplains for members of them. The proportion of Anglican clergy fell from 76 to 57 percent. Although the British army supported chaplains they remained adjuncts of the military machine. The British padres were shocked by the magnitude of religious ignorance in the army but saw that circumstances were inappropriate for attempting a religious revival.

▼ Chaplain T.R. White conducts a burial service over the common grave of 12 men who died in January 1918 at the American Red Cross Evacuation Hospital at Fleury-sur-Aire, in the Meuse region of France.

◀ Military life was full of ritual, some sanctioned, some not. This was as true of peasant armies in the east as of industrial armies in the west. Here a Serbian priest blesses a cake handed to officers and enlisted men, in the presence of priests and a choir in June 1916. By then most of Serbia had been overrun.

A large percentage of the (British) men were quite done for and could not possibly march another inch. They were lying on the ground (at Mosul, Mesopotamia) suffering from high fever and dysentery, and, needless to say, were smothered from head to foot in filth and covered with flies, the latter helping to make the sight, if possible, more sickening. Day after day we had seen men fall out of the columns on the line of the march, and after the escort had stripped the unlucky man of any clothing fit to sell, he had been given a final thrashing and left on the roadside to the mercy of the Arabs and Kurdish tribesmen. It had been a sickening sight, and one never knew when one might be the next one to fall out.

PRIVATE D. HUGHES

► Australian units served in Egypt, Palestine and Syria throughout Allenby's succesful campaign against the Turks. Conditions were harsh, particularly when camping in the Sinai, the Negev or Judean deserts. The temperature could plummet 30°C in a few hours. Water was always scarce: Allenby's troops and animals consumed 400,000 gallons per day. Disease was a greater threat than the Turks.

Other wars were fought by units scattered throughout the world. Here four of the "myriad faces of war" (in the words of the English novelist F.E. Manning) will be considered, to provide a greater sense of the variety of combat in World War I. The first is the doomed British expeditionary force in Iraq. After initial successes in 1915 against the Turks along the River Tigris, a combined British and Indian force under General Charles Townshend was forced to retreat to the fortress of Kut-al-Amara, where it was besieged. After 143 days the British and Indians surrendered. Over half of the men in the ranks then perished of disease and ill-treatment on a forced marsh over the desert to Aleppo in Syria.

Equally remote from the world of the trenches were the mixed African and German forces who led British, south African and Indian troops on a futile chase through East Africa between 1914 and 1918. The Germans were skillfully led by Colonel Paul von Lettow-Vorbeck, who managed to pin down Allied troops and keep them away from the European fronts for the duration of the war.

At sea it was inaction rather than action that caused most comment. Long periods of routine and drill were interspersed with rare moments of battle. After the anticipated major duels at sea had failed to materialize, other tasks awaited the navies. Among the Allies, protecting convoys was a hazardous and tense exercise. Similarly, running the Allied blockade of Germany or fighting the submarine war took skill, training, stamina and strong nerves.

The war in the air drew dare-devils to it and created instant heroes, like Baron Manfred von Richthofen, "the Red Baron", or the British aces Alfred Ball and Edward Mannock, all killed in

▼ This Indian soldier became a Turkish prisoner of war after the siege of Kut in April 1916. Men who were in this condition probably did not survive the desert march to captivity in Syria.

combat. What is less well-remembered is the huge backup that was required to keep these flyers in the air. The war of the mechanics was absolutely vital, although unlikely to produce decorations or headlines.

All the men engaged in these theaters of operations knew stress in many forms. Many suffered appalling privations: little need be added to the image of Townshend's defeated army struggling through the Iraqi desert. But their war (and their imprisonment) was in a way very traditional, as indeed was that of the bush warriors of Lettow-Vorbeck or the seamen patrolling the North Sea or the Atlantic. Even when the world of technical warfare is considered in the case of the war in the air, there was a curiously feudal flavor to combat, as if the most advanced form of aggression resurrected ancient and decorous codes of conduct. In contrast the war in the trenches was terrifyingly new. Not only were

there the innovations in weaponry but also the unprecedented degree of stress faced by hundreds of thousands of men. The British historian John Keegan has put it this way. To cope with fear a soldier in the Battle of Agincourt (1415) could ride or run to the safety of the next hill; his descendant at Waterloo (1815) could arrive a day late or take a wrong turn. But where could a soldier go when he had reached the limits of his endurance at Verdun or Passchendaele? It is true that most soldiers saw limited and intermittent duty in the trenches, but eight days could last a lifetime. And the fact of prior experience may not have made it any easier for a man to go back up the line, or to maintain morale during a retreat, as the German army did in late 1918. The world they knew was indeed unique. What is most remarkable is not that some broke under the strain, but that so many did not. Their resilience is one of the mysteries of the war.

▲ This German column of Askaris in East Africa passed through another desolate landscape of the 1914–18 war. Some jungle fighting took place, but combat in Africa stretched over arid plains and vast territories and involved relatively small units, mostly of African natives.

Datafile

Despite the fact that the war on the Russian Front ended with the Bolshevik revolution of November 1917, casualties in the last year of the war equalled or surpassed those of the previous three years. Partly this was due to the gigantic struggle which followed the German offensive of March 1918. Heavy fighting also continued in Italy, the Middle East and the Balkans. There was also the fact that an entire new Expeditionary Force entered the field – the Americans – who brought with them a formidable arsenal of weaponry. And we must not ignore the appearance of the "Spanish flu", a viral infection which struck down soldiers by the tens of thousands (and civilians by the millions) on both sides.

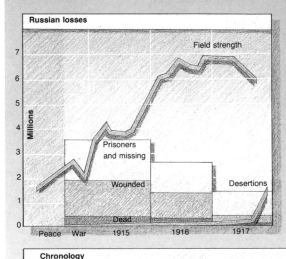

Russian losses

▶ It is one of the mysteries of the war how the German army remained unaware of the scale of disaffection which underlay the French mutinies of 1917 following the doomed Chemin des Dames offensive. Over one-quarter of the French army in the field was described as "seriously" or "profoundly" affected by mutiny. Equally surprising is the relatively light treatment of the mutineers: "collective disorder" occurred in 68 divisions; perhaps 61 mutineers were executed.

◀ Casualty statistics for the Russian army are even more unreliable than those available for Western armies. Estimates of total killed between 1914 and 1917 vary from 500,000 to 800,000. Less controversial is the steady rise in Russian prisoners of war. In 1914, on average 11,000 Russian soldiers were captured each month; in 1915 the figure had risen to 82,000; in 1916 it had reached 125,000. The desertion rate in 1917 describes the Army's final disintegration, which weakened the provisional government and led to the Bolshevik revolution.

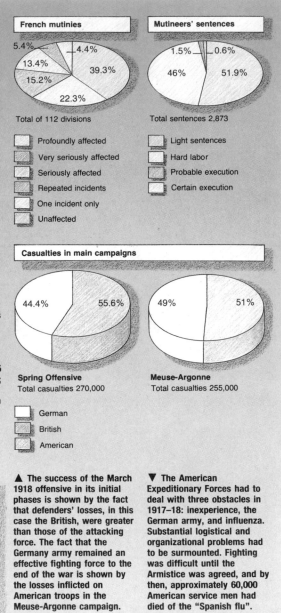

French mutinies

5.4% — 4.4%
13.4%
15.2%
39.3%
22.3%

Total of 112 divisions

- Profoundly affected
- Very seriously affected
- Seriously affected
- Repeated incidents
- One incident only
- Unaffected

Mutineers' sentences

1.5% — 0.6%
46%
51.9%

Total sentences 2,873

- Light sentences
- Hard labor
- Probable execution
- Certain execution

Casualties in main campaigns

44.4% — 55.6%

Spring Offensive
Total casualties 270,000

49% — 51%

Meuse-Argonne
Total casualties 255,000

- German
- British
- American

▲ The success of the March 1918 offensive in its initial phases is shown by the fact that defenders' losses, in this case the British, were greater than those of the attacking force. The fact that the Germany army remained an effective fighting force to the end of the war is shown by the losses inflicted on American troops in the Meuse-Argonne campaign.

▼ The American Expeditionary Forces had to deal with three obstacles in 1917–18: inexperience, the German army, and influenza. Substantial logistical and organizational problems had to be surmounted. Fighting was difficult until the Armistice was agreed, and by then, approximately 60,000 American service men had died of the "Spanish flu".

American troops

2.8%
38.6%
58.6%

April 1917
Total casualties 208,034

- Enlisted men
- National Guard
- Officers

American casualties

16.3%
20.4%
63.3%

by 1918
Total casualties 306,086

- Wounded
- Died of 'flu
- Killed

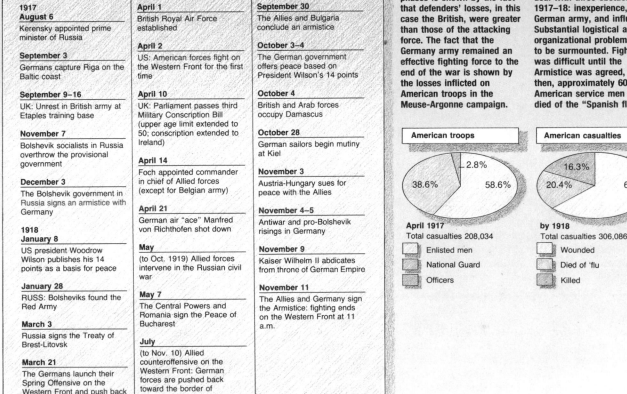

Chronology

1917 **August 6** Kerensky appointed prime minister of Russia	**April 1** British Royal Air Force established	**September 30** The Allies and Bulgaria conclude an armistice
September 3 Germans capture Riga on the Baltic coast	**April 2** US: American forces fight on the Western Front for the first time	**October 3–4** The German government offers peace based on President Wilson's 14 points
September 9–16 UK: Unrest in British army at Etaples training base	**April 10** UK: Parliament passes third Military Conscription Bill (upper age limit extended to 50; conscription extended to Ireland)	**October 4** British and Arab forces occupy Damascus
November 7 Bolshevik socialists in Russia overthrow the provisional government		**October 28** German sailors begin mutiny at Kiel
December 3 The Bolshevik government in Russia signs an armistice with Germany	**April 14** Foch appointed commander in chief of Allied forces (except for Belgian army)	**November 3** Austria-Hungary sues for peace with the Allies
1918 **January 8** US president Woodrow Wilson publishes his 14 points as a basis for peace	**April 21** German air "ace" Manfred von Richthofen shot down **May** (to Oct. 1919) Allied forces intervene in the Russian civil war	**November 4–5** Antiwar and pro-Bolshevik risings in Germany **November 9** Kaiser Wilhelm II abdicates from throne of German Empire
January 28 RUSS: Bolsheviks found the Red Army	**May 7** The Central Powers and Romania sign the Peace of Bucharest	**November 11** The Allies and Germany sign the Armistice: fighting ends on the Western Front at 11 a.m.
March 3 Russia signs the Treaty of Brest-Litovsk	**July** (to Nov. 10) Allied counteroffensive on the Western Front: German forces are pushed back toward the border of Germany	
March 21 The Germans launch their Spring Offensive on the Western Front and push back the Allied forces		

1917–18 REVOLUTION AND PEACE

In the last 18 months of World War I, in 1917–18, the bonds of commitment among both soldiers and civilians began to loosen, and in certain cases completely unraveled. In 1917 there was a crisis of morale in several combatant forces. In one sense, it is remarkable that it did not come earlier. But those who saw the way in which men wore out in battle like old clothes, as Lord Moran put it, knew that it was bound to come. When it did, it took different forms ranging from lethargy to brawls in base camps to mutiny. All arose out of a lowering of morale, and took on the distinctive features of armies made up of very different communities of men.

Morale has been defined in many ways, but in the memoirs of World War I three stand out. They are the maintenance of a belief in victory; the perpetuation of a will to fight; and the acceptance of duty and discipline. Morale broke down when men lost their belief that the war could be won in the way it was being fought.

▼ The "grumblers" shown here had much to complain about in 1917. It was simply too much to ask the men of Verdun to face another bloodbath a few months later in the Chemin des Dames offensive. The outcome was mutiny.

French, Russian and Italian mutinies
The first case in point was the French mutinies of 1917. They were precipitated by the Nivelle Offensive, a disastrous series of attacks on heavily fortified German positions in Champagne, east of Reims. The mutineers were drawn from units which had already fought well and suffered heavily in these operations. This was no minor incident. Between April and June 1917 250 separate acts of collective indiscipline were recorded. They occurred in 68 divisions or two-thirds of the French army. The mutineers had no formal organization and no clear-cut political objectives. They came from every walk of life and every part of France. Given the nature of French society, the majority were farmers or agricultural laborers. They were rarely violent. They had simply had enough: the most common form of mutiny was refusal to go back up the line.

Despite the attempts of military authorities to portray the mutineers as men led astray by

radicals and revolutionaries, they were non-political. Only one division of the 68 in turmoil had it in mind to march on Paris. The rest had more immediate demands: better leave arrangements, and an end to the murderous offensive. Some of these demands were met. Nivelle was replaced by Pétain on 16 May 1917, and the new commander made it his business to reduce casualties. Leave arrangements were improved, as were provisions behind the lines. Even the food got better, according to some reports.

Under the circumstances, repression was relatively mild. Military tribunals found 3,427 soldiers guilty of various acts of mutiny. The death penalty was set for 554 men, of whom all but 49 were reprieved. Those convicted of lesser crimes were imprisoned, half under conditions of hard labor, half under less severe conditions.

Mutiny of similar kinds happened in every other major army (bar those of Britain and the United States) between 1917 and the end of the war. On occasion it happened earlier, as in the mass defection of the Austro-Hungarian 29th Infantry from Prague in April 1915. In the Brusilov offensive of 1916 some Czech and Ruthenian units surrendered *en masse*. But the trouble got much worse in the third year of the conflict, when war weariness set in both at home and at the front. On 1 July 1917 the Russian army of the new Provisional government launched a

All the companies are in a state of turmoil; the men are receiving letters from friends informing them of the present spirit and urging them not to march; the ringleaders are becoming insolent; others are trying to influence their comrades.

HENRI DESAGNEAUX

American Troops in Europe

When the USA entered the war in April 1917 its army was small and unprepared for warfare on the Western Front. Within 18 months, however, conscription and a remarkable mushrooming of military organization had increased its size over 30 times, to about 4 million men, of whom 3.7 million served in France.

In the process of conscription some quintessentially American problems emerged. About 8 percent of conscripts were unable to speak or understand English. Many had no idea of what Germany and the Kaiser were. Then there were problems raised by American racism and the participation of blacks. The peace-time standing army contained 10,000 black soldiers and officers in segregated regiments. Whites feared that expansion would bring trouble, but nevertheless blacks were recruited and some 200,000 sent to France. They remained segregated and most worked as laborers, some as stevedores in the docks. But the black soldier did gain from his experience of the war: the French treated him for the first time as an equal and in Europe the racism of the USA seemed largely to fade away. The black regiments also brought their own music: jazz. Europeans were drawn to it, and the band of the 15th New Yorkers, led by Lieutenant Jim Europe, caused a particular sensation.

The American Expeditionary Forces entered the Western Front in October 1917. At the insistence of its commander, General John J. Pershing, they remained an independent fighting force and played a key role in the successful Allied counteroffensive in July and August 1918. By the Armistice they occupied 21 percent of the length of the Western Front. Over 100,000 American soldiers died on active service. A new generation of commanders emerged, including George Patton and Douglas MacArthur. The latter led American troops at the battle of St Mihiel.

In some ways the American forces of 1917 resembled the idealistic European armies of 1914. The arrival of millions of well-fed, confident young men at a time of crisis on the Western Front substantially bolstered the war-weary Allied armies. American optimism was well personified in a remark made by a marine sergeant. When told by a French officer to retreat in the face of a German attack, the American apparently responded: "Hell no. We just got here."

▶ Black American recruits at Camp Meade, Maryland, 1918.

► Whatever they said about the political sources of the 1917 mutiny, the French general staff knew that their men had simply been pushed too far. The reputation of Pétain (shown right) rested on the belief that he was miserly with the lives of his men and that he was responsible for improved conditions, both in and behind the lines.

major offensive and aimed to capture the city of Lemberg in Galicia (Austro-Hungarian Poland). Within a fortnight the attack had petered out. In the ensuing German counterattack the Russian army dissolved, its troops voting against the war with their feet, to use Trotsky's phrase. On 24 October 1917 the Austro–Hungarian army launched a surprise attack on Italian positions in the Isonzo Valley. The Austrians broke through the Italian line, and the subsequent Italian retreat from Caporetto turned into a rout. Three hundred thousand Italian prisoners were taken in the next 15 days. Many of these men were poorly fed and poorly led.

The resilience and defeat of German forces

One argument has it that mutiny was a function of attrition. When the ration strength of an army (the number in uniform) was reduced in number to the total number of losses it had suffered, it was likely to break. This happened in most armies in 1917. There were two exceptions. The first is the German army, which endured combat until very late in the war, well after its casualties exceeded its ration strength. The German army was one of the most remarkable military organizations ever created. The disturbances of 1917 in other forces did not affect it, although serious trouble broke out in the German navy during the summer.

But by August 1918 it was clear to many German fighting men that they could not win the war. High command was bombarded with reports of men refusing to go on, and of mass surrenders. These soldiers had lived for years with a belief in their invincibility, inculcated by a steady stream of propaganda. When the line began to move back in the summer of 1918 they finally lost the will to fight on.

The fact that the German army withstood the stress of war for more than four years was a remarkable achievement, placed in proper perspective by a brief glance at the history of wartime mutinies in the German navy. In July 1917 the first major set of disturbances broke out

in the fleet. The sources of trouble were manifold. The fleet was bottled up in the Baltic, and the sheer drudgery and monotony of life on ship were made worse by the propensity of inexperienced officers (the good ones were in the U-boat fleet) to enforce every petty regulation.

This was bad enough, but it would not have led to a breakdown of morale had the sailors' food been anything other than appalling. The contrast with the officers' mess was both evident and a source of increasing irritation. To defuse the situation, the navy ordered the formation of food supervisory committees on all ships. Some captains blatantly ignored this, and hunger strikes and other forms of action were organized to force them to do so.

No one could ignore the political context in which all this took place. The sailors were fully aware of the role their comrades had played in the Russian revolution, and openly discussed the Stockholm conference of socialist parties to be held (or so they believed) in a few weeks' time. Their representatives visited the offices of the radical Independent socialist party in Berlin, and so provided the navy with the evidence they sought to blame outsiders for trouble in the fleet.

But as in almost all mutinies in World War I, military grievances, rather than political agitation, were at the heart of the breakdown of discipline. On 31 July 1917 the recreation and cinema program of stokers on board the *Prinzregent Luitpold* was canceled, and the men were ordered to report for infantry drill. About 50 refused to do so, and left the ship, on which trouble had been brewing for months. When they returned 11 were arrested and imprisoned. A sympathetic strike by other sailors on their behalf did no good at all. Many were jailed and five were convicted of "treasonable incitement to rebellion", with the sentence of death. Admiral Scheer, chief of the high seas fleet, commuted the death sentences of three men, and confirmed execution orders on two others. They were shot on 5 September 1917.

A year later, repression of this kind was a thing of the past. On 27 October 1918 the German fleet at Wilhelmshaven and other ports received orders to put to sea for a final confrontation with the British. It never took place. Some sailors refused to weigh anchor; others extinguished their boilers at sea. The ships that had left harbor sailed back.

The reasons for the trouble were, as usual, complex. Partly it arose out of the same suspicion among ordinary sailors of the motives of the officer corps that had surfaced in July 1917. The sailors were in daily contact with disaffected workers in the major port cities. They all knew the war was lost. All the more reason to resist any desperate, last-minute attempt by the command of the high seas fleet to demonstrate their "honor" – and to do so against the will of the new government. Not only would peace negotiations be placed in jeopardy; so would the lives of thousands of sailors.

In the aftermath of the mutiny 47 sailors were arrested. But this time, peremptory courts-martial did not settle the issue. The changed political environment precluded that. A delegation of

▲ These sailors in Kiel are listening to an address by Gustav Noske, an emissary of the social democratic party about to take power in November 1918. Noske had come to Kiel to quiet the situation after 8 sailors had been shot by a naval patrol, in the wake of a successful mass mutiny against the high command's decision to fight one last (and hopeless) battle at sea.

My God – why did we have such criminal conscienceless officers? It was they who deprived us of all our love for the fatherland, our joy in our German existence, and our pride for our incomparable institutions. Even now my blood boils with anger whenever I think of the many injustices I suffered in the navy... on the Thüringen, the former model ship of the fleet, the mutiny was at its worst. The crew simply locked up the petty officers and refused to weigh anchor. The men told the captain that they would only fight against the English if their fleet appeared in German waters. They no longer wanted to risk their lives uselessly.

RICHARD STUMPF

sailors went to Berlin to explain their demands to the government. The demands were remarkably moderate: no reprisals; an end to meaningless discipline; recognition of the right of assembly; and an improvement in conditions on board ship. In effect this was the normal list of grievances found in most industrial conflicts. What turned such men to mutiny was the fear – not without foundation – that their officers were going to take advantage of their patriotism and launch a senseless attack on the British just to make up for the lackluster record of the high seas fleet in the war. "What price glory?" was a real question in the last weeks of the war.

This last hopeless battle never took place, and the mutineers who prevented it were finally released in the general chaos of the last week of the war. But the trouble was not over yet. On 3 November eight sailors were killed by a naval patrol. To quieten the situation, two political emissaries were sent to Kiel by the government. Sailors' councils joined workers' councils in taking over Kiel and other port cities. The revolt in the navy quickly spread to the home army and to the industrial working class, putting an end to both the monarchy and the war.

British loyal indiscipline and riot

The second exceptional case was the British army, which was the only European fighting force to avoid a major mutiny in World war I. But the absence of mutiny should not be taken to mean the absence of chronic and widespread indiscipline; on the contrary. Throughout the war the British army, like every other, had trouble keeping order among the troops. Regulations were so numerous that all soldiers were likely to break some of them; some soldiers insisted on breaking them all the time. The "good soldier Schweik" – that bulwark of the Austro-Hungarian army, who got away with breaking rules by feigned incompetence – populated all armies during World War I. Examples of failure to comply with orders could be found in every army and at all ranks. More

Naval Conditions

Life below ship decks has always been cramped and claustrophobic, with bunks shared by men on different watches and privacy absent. The German seaman diarist Richard Stumpf called his ship in World War I an "iron prison".

Consideration of wartime naval conditions must differentiate between submarine and surface fleets and between the surface fleets of Germany and the United Kingdom.

Submariners led a miserable existence. Enforcing the blockades required long tours of duty. The need to maintain radio silence resulted in isolation. Submarines were also exposed to the antisubmarine warfare of their opponents: over half of the 307 German submarines actively employed in the war succumbed to enemy action.

Examination of life in the surface fleets of the major belligerents reveals important social differences. The British navy went to war with a long tradition and volunteer ratings. Although there was the usual hierarchical divide between officers and men, both groups were provided for and they experienced the same dangers and engagements.

Stumpf's diary reveals how in the German navy, in the long periods of inactivity, tensions between officers and conscript crews grew into conflict. In the "turnip winter" of 1917–18 Junker naval officers dined on good food with fine wine while the ratings starved. To maintain some kind of discipline the officers imposed mindbending, brutal and, meaningless tasks. In July 1917 there was a naval mutiny. It should have been a warning to German authorities, but was not heeded. In late October 1918 German admirals attempted to mount a last-ditch attack on the British fleet: the response was another mutiny, which echoed civilian discontent.

Stumpf shows that a key to maintaining an impressive naval force was the provision of good living conditions. Without these the best crews were ineffectual. Germany's failure to understand this cost it dearly.

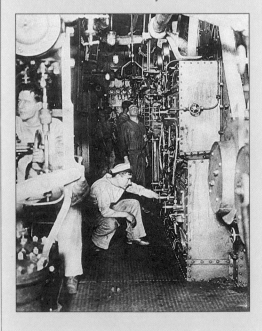

▲ The boiler room of a British man of war, 1917.

than this was necessary for mutiny, which in this context is best defined as a collective challenge to the chain of command, entailing a widespread and persistent refusal to fight the war the generals had ordered. While the British army was frequently beset by disorder and indiscipline of varying degrees of seriousness, at no time before the Armistice was it confronted by large groups of men who would not go back up the line.

The one incident that has been described as a mutiny was nothing of the sort. The trouble started at the base camp at Etaples – notorious for the harshness of its regime. On 9 September 1917 a New Zealander was arrested by police. Crowds demanding his release (which it appears, had already taken place) included Australians and Scots. They got into a brawl with some military police, one of whom panicked and fired his pistol. Two men were wounded, and one Scots corporal, an innocent bystander, was killed. Afterward men streamed out of the camp and into the town of Etaples. Some hours later, and somewhat the worse for drink, they returned to base. One regular soldier – who apparently urged the men to throw an officer, bound hand and foot into the river – was court-martialled and shot. Disturbances, apparently more unruly than violent, continued on 11 and 12 September. Men milled around the local towns; but there were no further shootings. The next day a contingent of 400 men from the Honourable Artillery Company arrived. By then the trouble was largely over.

In the context of 1917, it is stretching the term considerably to call this set of events a mutiny at all. These disturbances showed clearly that many of the British men in the camp had been abused long enough by the canaries (instructors) and redcaps (military police) – men whose jobs kept them away from the front. When one totally innocent man was killed, they took out their anger and resentment not on the officer corps or the army or the war, but rather on the military police.

This kind of violent protest against the appalling conditions in Etaples was a case of loyal indiscipline rather than mutiny. The men who rioted came from units which had seen considerable military action, and would do so again. But the men at Etaples did not refuse to face the enemy or to relieve front-line troops. They did not reject the way Haig was fighting the war. Rather they behaved as many other workingmen have done in the course of industrial disputes. They simply conducted their own private war with the military police.

The roots of British discipline

The question remains as to why the British army was able to avoid the more serious disturbances which at one time or another disrupted all other European armies. It is possible that there were differences in the speed and perceived impartiality of military justice among combatant forces in the war, but as yet no systematic evidence has been presented that this was so. Perhaps a more likely answer to the question "why did the British army avoid mutiny in World War I?" may lie in the social composition of the different forces. The French and German armies and, even more so, the Italian and Russian armies, were made up of peasants. The British army was largely manned by what was probably the most highly disciplined industrial labor force in the world. Just as in civilian life, men were prepared to defend themselves when they considered that they were being unfairly treated, or just pushed around. This is precisely what the protesters did at the Etaples camp in 1917. Afterward they went back to the war.

In surveying all these incidents, it is apparent that a much more disturbing question than why mutinies occurred is why so few took place between 1914 and 1918. Some reasons why soldiers carried on fighting after years of combat have been suggested, but it is important to note that the vast majority of the men who served simply did what they were told to do. It was their duty, because the state said so; and thus the bloodbath continued for four years.

▲ The base camps at Étaples on the French coast near Boulogne housed over 100,000 men in 1917, both new drafts from England and units recently returned from the front. The Ypres salient was a mere 80km (50mi) away, and in the closing months of 1917 the Third Battle of Ypres was still under way. The camp was infamous for the brutality of its military police (redcaps) and instructors (called canaries, for their yellow armbands) who pushed men around over a ten-day course in the "Bull Ring" or training ground. The violent incidents which took place at this base in September 1917 showed how morale could be undermined by a mindless regime behind the lines.

THE CIVILIANS' WAR

Datafile

Fear, enthusiasm and resignation or apathy marked civilian reactions to the outbreak of war. The first can be seen on the faces of the millions of refugees who streamed away from advancing armies in Belgium and France or in Serbia and East Prussia. The second was seen in cities where students paraded and recruits were sent off to war. The third dominated reactions in the vast rural areas of Europe where most people still lived.

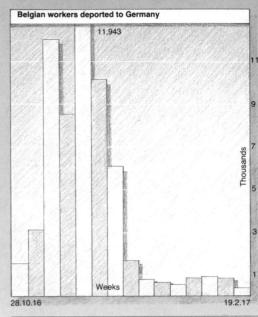

Belgian refugees

15.3%
1.2%
30.7%
52.8%
1914 Total 1,056,000
1918

Still in France
Still in Britain
Elsewhere

Belgian workers deported to Germany

11,943

11
9
7
Thousands
5
3
1

Weeks

28.10.16   19.2.17

▲ The flight of civilians from the front lines occurred on both the Eastern and Western Fronts. In the more densely populated regions of Belgium, the German army cut a path through urban and rural areas, from which over 1 million people fled. Most moved north to Holland, but many fled southward to France.

◄ The status of civilians living in occupied territories has always been unclear in wartime. All occupations have incidents such as occurred in Belgium, where those who resisted the Germans were shot. But more sinister was the forcible deportation of 60,000 Belgians to work in German arms factories in 1916–17.

Chronology

1914 **June 28** Assassination of Austro-Hungarian Archduke Franz Ferdinand in Sarajevo	**September 5–10** First Battle of the Marne: German advance halted	**November 11** (to early Dec.) Germans force Eastern Front further to the east
July 23 (to Aug. 4) War crisis in Europe	**September 6–15** Battle of the Masurian Lakes: German victory in East Prussia	**December 2** Austro-Hungarians capture Belgrade (capital of Serbia)
July 31 UK: London stock market is closed	**September 8–12** Battle of Lemberg: Russians capture Austria-Hungary's fourth-largest city	**December 8** Battle of the Falkland Islands: British fleet defeats the German Pacific Squadron
August–September BELG: One million Belgians leave their country	**September 15** First trenches of the war are dug	**December 11** Serbians recapture Belgrade
August 13 German invasion of Belgium begins	**September 17** (to Oct. 18) "Race to the Sea": front in the west is extended to the Channel coast	**December 16** UK: East coast towns of Scarborough and Hartlepool bombarded by German battle cruiser squadron
August 11 *Goeben* and *Breslau* enter the Black Sea	**October 12** (to Nov. 11) First Battle of Ypres: inconsequential conflict between Germans and Allies	**December 21** UK: South coast towns bombed in first German air raid on country
August 24 Main German armies enter France	**November 1** Russia declares war on Turkey. Battle of Coronel: German Pacific Squadron defeats British naval force off coast of Chile	**December 26** GER: Government places food supplies and allocations under its control
August 26–30 Battle of Tannenberg: German victory in East Prussia		
August 30 FR: First German aeroplane raid on Paris		

In 1914 popular support for the war effort was not universal, but the relatively few voices raised against the war were drowned by a chorus of approval in the popular press, in the churches, and even among organized labor. What the rest of the population thought is not so clear, but the masses in the towns and in the countryside took the war in their stride, thereby enabling the major belligerents to mobilize without the fear of internal popular opposition. Of course, the war they all supported was not the war they were to fight, but few had the prescience to realize what they were getting themselves into by rallying round the flag in 1914.

From peace to war

No one in 1914 had thought it would be so comparatively easy to shift from peace to war. But the transition to a war footing in the space of a few weeks went so smoothly throughout Europe that fears for the social stability of the combatant countries seemed to have been misplaced. Perhaps all the prewar talk of class fighting against class, of subject peoples unprepared to fight for their imperial rulers, was so much sound and fury, signifying nothing when a real or perceived threat to the nation appeared.

The faults in such a rosy analysis were exposed later in the war. But in 1914 this assertion could not be so easily dismissed. In effect, it posed three questions. First, why did socialists throughout Europe choose country over class? Secondly, why did intellectuals choose nation over reason? Thirdly, why did peasants and workers assimilate war into their normal routine of life? Each question will be examined in turn.

The fundamental reason why the socialist organization the Second International could not stop the war was that it failed to recognize the compatibility of patriotism with class consciousness. In 1914 one French pacifist trade union leader is reputed to have said: "French workers would not have permitted French soldiers to shoot anti-war activists; they would have shot us themselves." In the French case there was a long tradition of popular patriotism, drawing on the image of the citizen-in-arms of the French revolution and the defiance of the Parisian communards of 1871, surrounded by enemies on all sides. In the British case, patriotism was not so well grounded in working-class traditions, but it still commanded respect, especially among the better-off workingmen who flocked to the volunteer movement, the "Home Guard" (or civil defense organization) of its day, from the 1890s. The virtues of the British Empire and the monarchy were not anathema to the bulk of the working-class movement; on the contrary, loyalty to nation and loyalty to class went hand in hand.

1914 THE WAR OF ILLUSIONS

Why did support for war transcend sectional interests?

Enthusiasm for the war was real but transient

Flag-waving was a phenomenon of capital cities

Less enthusiasm in town and country

The press supports the war effort by self-censorship

And the spreading of atrocity stories

The churches face a dilemma

In Germany such a solution was specifically rejected by the most powerful socialist party in the world, the German social democratic party. This party was committed to an existence separate from the state which it would take over when conditions had ripened sufficiently to ensure the withering away of the old order. The central problem was that, although German socialists claimed to be untainted by the values and practices of the Wilhelmine state, they were in reality as German as their class enemies. They claimed to live in a separate society, a state within a state, with its own newspapers, social clubs, and welfare programs. But the very elaboration of functions and hierarchy which accompanied its growth helped to deepen the gap between theory and practice. In effect, their party had become a machine which in some ways replicated the bureaucratic features of German society. Ideologically, they remained apart; effectively, they were more assimilated – and patriotic – than they dared to admit.

This fundamental fact could be covered up in different ways. Marx himself had taken up the idea of socialists supporting their own nations in defensive wars, and there was very little sympathy for a czarist victory in the east. A party which stood out against the war also risked separating itself from the mass of its members, who believed that the conflict had been forced on Germany. However they tried to rationalize it, though, when their party voted in the Reichstag for war credits on 4 August 1914, German socialists stripped away the rhetorical veil of their prewar assertions that they would stop an act of fratricide among the European working class.

The psychology of war enthusiasm

The war showed that the culture of assimilation was deeper than the ideology of internationalism. This also helps to unravel our second question, about intellectual bellicosity in the autumn of 1914. The need to embrace (and perhaps more importantly to be embraced by) the community in arms at a moment of national danger accounts for much of the rash of war enthusiasm which spread in intellectual circles at this time. The novelist Thomas Mann asserted that "only the enemies of the spirit opposed the war which would leave Germany stronger, prouder, freer, happier." The composer Alexander Scriabin said "My Russian ecstasy is fulfilled." The dancer Isadora Duncan noted of her Parisian friends, "We were all flame and fire."

What many felt was an end to the isolation, the alienation from the masses that had been virtually an indispensable feature of intellectual life. Some accepted war as a great adventure; others saw it as a liberation from the decadence of a corrupt,

These students in Berlin were the enthusiasts of August 1914. Here they are shown marching off to join up. Their romantic bravado was matched in Paris, London, Vienna and Prague. Many of them left accounts of that fateful moment, which have colored our understanding of the outbreak of war. Consider these words of Stefan Zweig, an Austrian writer whose hatred of war did not blind him to the depth of feeling the war released: " I must acknowledge that there was a majestic, rapturous, and even seductive something" in the air, and "in spite of all my hatred and aversion for war, I should not like to have missed the memory of those first days".

commercial civilization. Still others believed it would cause a spiritual revolution, and some simply succumbed to the mystique of violence. Charles Péguy wrote a poem which expressed the emotional charge of the moment as well as its intellectual bankruptcy:

> Happy are they who die for they return
> Into the primeval clay and the primeval earth.
> Happy are they who die in a just war,
> Happy as the ripe corn and the harvested grain.

In effect, these writers were proclaiming their allegiance to a romantic war, the seductive force of which intellectuals were unable to resist.

In Britain some of these notions had wide appeal at the outset of the war; otherwise, it would be hard to explain the deluge of recruits who responded voluntarily to Kitchener's call to arms. On the continent, where conscription antedated the war, men joined their units out of a mixture of duty and conformity to the law. It may be useful to borrow an analogy of the philosopher Bertrand Russell which he used to describe the ambience of the early days of the war. Perhaps the trajectory of the "August madness" was a collective manifestation of a very familiar form of individual behavior, namely a love affair. In the first stages there is exhilaration and elation. Then comes a sense of contentment and identification with the loved one, followed by a return to normalcy. Next come inevitable tensions and attendant grumbling, followed in a few cases by separation, in others by resignation, quiet despair

or cynicism, in some, even by contentment, depending on circumstances and temperament. It may not be too fanciful to suggest that something like this happened all over Europe in 1914.

But in some areas there was little war enthusiasm at all. The most famous instances of flag-waving occurred in capital cities. This is unsurprising since these were also centers of rail traffic, and therefore staging points for mobilized soldiers, who were indeed given a noisy and emotional send-off when they went to fight.

But what about the villages and country towns where the bulk of Europe's population lived? There seems to have been much less to-do about the outbreak of war in such places. In France and Germany, Russia and Austria conscription was a "normal" experience; men who left were just doing what had been done many times before.

In addition, expectations of a short war directed anxieties to the need to bring in the harvest of 1914. Women, old men and boys did the job, as did unoccupied soldiers. Taken together with early measures in a number of countries to provide separation allowances for the families of conscripted men, the smooth gathering of the 1914 harvest ensured that the war would not bring severe economic hardship initially.

There were two institutions which helped to mold public opinion in the early days of the war: the press and the churches. Both journalists and clergymen helped bridge the gap between war and peace and allay whatever doubts surfaced as to the merits of each nation's cause.

The press

For the duration of the war most editors and their staffs were prepared to forgo the critical function of the press. This was true in all the major combatant countries and affected the style and character of journalism, both high and low. For instance, in 1914 the German satirical magazine *Simplicissimus* shelved its traditionally acerbic wit and adopted a patriotic line. This lasted well into the war. On a more popular level, the *Hamburger Fremdenblatt*, for example, previously a left-liberal paper, became the defender of the military high command and an opponent of defeatism, criticizing, for example, the Reichstag peace resolution of 1917. Such changes of attitude were common, and were not at all surprising in a country where the press was traditionally responsible not to the public but to a particular interest group or party. When the parties accepted the *Burgfrieden*, or truce of the fortress, so did the press.

Circulation figures in wartime Germany rose in a spectacular fashion, which is understandable at a time when so many lives were at stake. But what was printed was rarely reliable; and the effect of "a state of siege on truth" was ultimately to undermine the credibility of the press.

One difficulty in handling the evidence of the wartime press is that it was censored virtually from the first day of hostilities. Military authorities of course made efforts to stop the publication of information likely to be of use to the enemy, but a kind of self-censorship was also evident early on in the war. This took four forms. The first was simply not to report bad news. Very few

people knew of the scale of the carnage of the battles of 1914, when over 400,000 French soldiers were killed. In the British press a similar veil of silence was drawn over the loss of the battleship *Audacious* in October 1914.

Secondly, the press encouraged its readers to believe that victory was within easy reach. "Berlin anxious. Vienna in a panic" read one headline on 2 September 1914 in the Parisian paper *Le Matin* and the same kind of thing appeared repeatedly on the other side too.

Thirdly, newspapers made light of the dangers facing the men at the Front, turning them into happy-go-lucky daredevils. One correspondent assured readers of *Le Petit Parisien* that "our troops laugh at machine guns now... Nobody pays the slightest attention to them". The same journal printed what purported to be a letter from a soldier who wanted to assure the readers that "The German shells are not nearly as bad as they appear to be." This seemed to be the sentiment of one wounded soldier, whose story appeared in *Echo de Paris* on 15 August 1914: "My wound? It doesn't matter... But make sure you tell them that all Germans are cowards and that the only problem is how to get at them. In the skirmish where I got hit, we had to shout insults at them

▲ This scene of an anti-German riot in High Street, Poplar, in the East End of London describes the release of xenophobia in the early days of the war. Russian and Polish families suffered from the indiscriminate hostility of crowds too ignorant or inebriated to distinguish between foreigners on "our" side and enemy aliens. All "strange-sounding" names were suspect in war. This was as true of the elite as it was of the masses; witness the conversion of one part of the British royal family from Battenburg to Mountbatten.

The Occupation of Belgium

On 20 August 1914 German troops entered Brussels. The king of Belgium and his government fled, as did one million other Belgians (out of a total population of 7.5 million). All of Belgium, except the Flanders region (behind the Allied line), was placed under the rule of a German military governor-general, who ruled by decree. Belgian provincial councils were suppressed; many burgomasters were deported; and in 1917 the indigenous judiciary was removed. The Germans also levied a tax to pay for the maintenance of the occupying army.

From the start the Belgian economy was shattered. The industrial base was deprived of raw materials and markets, and contracted. By July 1918 the occupying power had confiscated or destroyed 167 factories and what could not be shipped to Germany was systematically looted. The remaining industrial installations, including 26 blast furnaces, were razed. By the end of hostilities over 800,000 men were unemployed and one-third of the population was on public assistance.

By early 1915, the country faced famine. Aid was provided by a semiofficial "Comité Nationale de Secours et d'Alimentation". It had been formed to distribute supplies shipped to Belgium by the "Commission for Relief in Belgium". These relief organizations operated with the acquiescence of Britain and Germany, although in 1917 alone 12 ships bringing supplies were torpedoed by German U-boats. However nothing they did could fill the gap between prewar and wartime import levels. Total imports between 1915 and the end of hostilities in 1918 equaled the total of imports for 1913 alone.

The Comité did however succeed in establishing an effective distribution chain via soup kitchens and public assistance institutions and hospitals. But it was quite unable to prevent a flourishing black market,

based on domestic produce. By the end of the war, black market prices were estimated to be 1,200 percent above 1914 prices.

The result for the Belgian population was that people did without basic necessities. They reverted to preindustrial diets of bread and potatoes and were deprived of meat and dairy products. Wartime mortality rates were more than double those of peacetime. The birthrate fell by 75 percent, in part on account of severe malnutrition. The war, for Belgians, was a total disaster.

◀ The German treatment of Belgian civilians was the subject of much controversy during the war. Atrocity stories abounded from the outset; virtually all were pure fantasy. But what was true was bad enough. There were numerous accurate accounts of harsh German punishment and reprisals for Belgian harassment of their troops during the August 1914 offensive. Thereafter the specter of espionage made German soldiers, like the one in this photograph, suspicious of every civilian. But this image captures a wider truth: there were no noncombatants in the war. The conflict obliterated the distinction between civilian and military targets in wartime, a distinction which has never been effectively revived.

▼ The first economic crisis of the war arose at its outbreak. But once the harvest of 1914 was gathered in, it became clear that the war could become part of everyday life. Here we see two kinds of activity going on side by side in the Belgian countryside. Women carried on the fieldwork, while the civil guard and army dug trenches in the very same fields.

▲ To many Poles, and even more to Jews, the arrival of German troops in Russian Poland in 1914 was initially greeted with enthusiasm. This German band is playing on the streets of occupied Lodz in December 1914.

▼ The Bishop of London, Dr Winnington-Ingram, in uniform. His bellicosity was matched by churchmen in every combatant country.

to make them come out and fight." The fourth kind of propaganda journalists spread without any order to do so was most sinister. This was the portrayal of the enemy as a monster. Here the art of the caricaturist, used to feeding off the physical idiosyncracies of leading politicians, came into its own. The hideous German, more ape than man, was a constant preoccupation of Allied journalists; similar instances of an appeal to hatred appeared on the other side too.

In Britain and France, such images fed on atrocity stories about German "crimes" in Belgium which Allied propagandists were happy to perpetuate, whatever the truth of the claim. A good example of this is the famous case of the "martyred" clergymen of Antwerp, cited by Robert Graves to show how lies could grow.

Stage 1: A Cologne newspaper reports that after the fall of Antwerp in August 1914, bells were rung in churches throughout Germany.

Stage 2: The Parisian paper *Le Matin* reports that the clergy of Antwerp were compelled by victorious German troops to ring their churches' bells.

Stage 3: In London *The Times* reports that Belgian clergymen who had refused to ring their bells after the fall of Antwerp had been arrested.

Stage 4: The Milanese newspaper *Corriere della Sera* reports that recalcitrant Belgian priests hadbeen sentenced to hard labor for refusing to ring their bells to celebrate the Germans' victory.

Stage 5: *Le Matin* reports that Belgian clergymen who had refused to ring their bells after the fall of Antwerp were tied to the bells upside down and used as human clappers.

A stream of Belgian refugees both to France

and to Britain brought home to all who wanted to know the true horrors of warfare in their native land. But as if the reality of warfare was not enough to stir the imagination, journalists let their fantasies run wild in an effort to galvanize support for the war.

The churches

One might have expected clergymen to resist these tendencies to demonize the enemy. The fact that many did not was perhaps inevitable, for two reasons. The first was that most clergymen spoke for established churches. As such they were part of the moral and (in a broad sense) political leadership of their countries, and shared the educational and ideological background of those who had taken the decision to go to war. The second was that there was a fundamental conflict faced by the wartime churches in all combatant nations between their theological mission and their pastoral mission. Essentially their theological role pointed toward the reconciliation of enemies, the search for a road to peace, and the reassertion, especially in time of war, of the humanity of all people. This was repeatedly affirmed by Pope Benedict XV, who thereby incurred the wrath of sections of the French Catholic Church.

The problem was not just one of the blind patriotism of the clergy. It was also that in their pastoral work in wartime, clergymen faced a different set of tasks. More and more they were engaged in the consolation of the bereaved, the fortification of the anguished, the care of the widow and the orphan. After all, how were they supposed to react when they visited a family which had lost a son, and were asked whether

◀ The war made the use of passports a commonplace affair. But in occupied territory passes were obligatory. Here German soldiers are photographing French civilians in the occupied north of the country. The photographs were taken in groups, apparently to save time and money. Individuals were identified by a number in the group portrait in which they were placed.

▼ Twice in this century French roads have been clogged with grim families trying to escape from the battle lines by traveling south. These families from the Pas de Calais are on their way to a safer home. Belgian refugees traveled north to Holland, south to France, thus swelling the migratory tide, which also reached England.

their son had died for a just cause, or what kind of person could have torn their son from them?

Perhaps their upholding of the patriotic cause was simply a reflection of the dilemma of all national churches espousing an international creed. But some clergymen went further, and contributed to what can only be termed the moral pollution of the war. One such was the Bishop of London, Arthur Winnington-Ingram, who in 1915 let loose this sermon of hate: "And first we see Belgium stabbed in the back and ravaged, then Poland, and then Serbia, and then the Armenian nation wiped out – five hundred thousand at a moderate estimate being actually killed: and then as a necessary consequence, to save the freedom of the world, to save Liberty's own self, to save the honour of women and the innocence of children, everything that is noblest in Europe, everything that loves freedom and honour, everyone that puts principle above ease, and life itself beyond mere living, are banded in a great crusade – we cannot deny it – to kill Germans: to kill them not for the sake of killing, but to save the world; to kill the good as well as the bad, to kill the young men as well as the old, to kill those who have shown kindness to our wounded as well as those fiends who crucified the Canadian sergeant, who superintended the Armenian massacres, who sank the *Lusitania*, and who turned the machine-guns on the civilians of Aerschott and Louvain – and to kill them lest the civilisation of the world should itself be killed." The effect of such rhetoric may have been as minimal as that of clerical pleas for forgiveness. But the wartime bellicosity of some churchmen helped discredit them in later years.

Datafile

War meant hard work for most civilians. Women traded jobs in textiles or domestic service for munitions work or substituted for men in nonessential jobs. In the countryside, women took over the management and cultivation of farms. After work, married women had to cope with looking after families on their own, with eternal queues and shortages, and with the fear of the loss of husbands, sons, relatives and friends, or the problems of wounded veterans. Millions of families were separated. Those on the battle fronts scattered as refugees. Adolescent men and women migrated to towns and cities, as did foreign workers. This pattern of movement and upheaval led many to fear for the future of the family. Their anxieties were misplaced. Women did their share in the war for the duration only. Afterward they went back to their former lives and their subordinate positions at work and at home.

Living standards fell for most people on the continent. Inflation wiped out savings and canceled out wage increases in Germany and Austria-Hungary. In occupied Belgium, severe shortages of food led to malnutrition. Economic difficulties in Italy were worsened by a drop in income repatriated from Italians in America. Civilians in Britain and France fared better. After a period of dislocation in 1914, war industries grew rapidly. Unemployment vanished, and social subsidies in the form of rent control and separation allowances helped protect families from the full effect of rising prices and military mobilization.

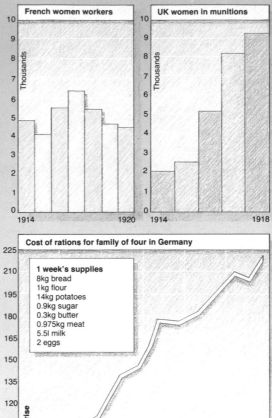

French women workers (Thousands, 1914–1920)

UK women in munitions (Thousands, 1914–1918)

Cost of rations for family of four in Germany (Unit rise, 1913–1918)

1 week's supplies
8kg bread
1kg flour
14kg potatoes
0.9kg sugar
0.3kg butter
0.975kg meat
5.5l milk
2 eggs

100=7.93 marks

◀ The majority of women-workers in the 1914–18 war had had paid employment before the war. The female labor force was redistributed, to substitute for male workers in uniform and to staff the expanding munitions sector. In France (far left), perhaps 40 percent of the workforce was female during the war. Roughly similar figures were registered for female labor in the west, while in the east agricultural labor became preponderantly female. After 1918 women left industrial work, but remained in the clerical and service sectors.

◀ The official statistics describing the rise in the cost of living, on which this graph is based, underestimated drastically the difficulties ordinary Germans faced in feeding their families. Official rations supplied only about half the minimal needs of the population. This meant that everyone had to find food on the black market, where prices dwarfed official maximum prices.

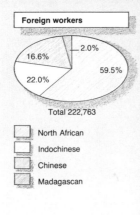

Foreign workers

59.5%
16.6%
2.0%
22.0%

Total 222,763

☐ North African
☐ Indochinese
☐ Chinese
☐ Madagascan

◀ During the war immigrant labor in France made up for the gaps created by both mobilization and low prewar birth rates. Roughly 500,000 foreign workers entered France during the war. One-third came from Spain; the rest (left) mainly from the French North African colonies of Tunisia, Algeria, Morocco and Madagascar, Indo-China and China. This influx of immigrant labor was not new; it merely constituted an accentuation of prewar trends.

Chronology

1915

January 4
UK: London stock exchange is reopened

January 19
UK: First German airship raid on England

February 8–22
Winter Battle of Masuria: Germans and Austro-Hungarians force Russians to retreat

March 10–13
Battle of Neuve-Chapelle: British and Indian offensive on Western Front captures village of Neuve Chapelle

March 21
FR: First German airship raid on Paris

April 8
Turkey begins massacres and deportations of Armenians

April 22
(to May 27) Second Battle of Ypres: German offensive on Western Front against Ypres fails to capture the town

April 24
(to Jan. 9 1916) Allied land campaign against Turks on Gallipoli peninsula

May 2–4
Battle of Gorlice-Tarnow: Central Powers break Russian line and cause Russian retreat

May 4
(to 18 June) Second Battle of Artois: French make small gain of land on Western Front from Germans

May 7
German submarine sinks passenger liner *Lusitania*

May 9–10
Battle of Aubers Ridge: unsuccessful British offensive on Western Front against Germans

May 15–25
Battle of Festubert: unsuccessful British and Canadian offensive on Western Front against Germans

May 23
Italy declares war on Austria-Hungary

May 31
UK: First German airship raid on London area

July 16
UK: National Registration Act requires registration of men eligible for military service

September 25
(to Oct. 14) Third Battle of Artois: French offensive on Western Front brings small gain of territory from the Germans

September 25
(to Oct. 6) French offensive in Champagne: small amount of territory gained from Germans

September 25
(to Nov. 4) Battle of Loos: British offensive on the Western Front captures the town of Loos

October 12
In Belgium Germans execute British nurse Edith Cavell for aiding the escape of Allied prisoners

1915 STALEMATE AND STAGNATION

In 1915, when the military lines stabilized, it became apparent that all belligerents faced a monumental task of clothing, feeding, housing and arming millions of men. If domestic industry were not to grind to a halt, the men who had joined up had to be replaced; if munitions orders were to be met, new workers had to be found, trained and set to work. This inevitably led to a change in the size and composition of the labor force in all warring nations. Of course these developments were uneven, and certainly not restricted to 1915; the process of recruiting new labor in industry, commerce and agriculture which began in the second phase of the war continued unabated until the Armistice.

The mobilization of a new labor force entailed four parallel sets of changes. First, the feminization of the labor force; secondly, a reduction in the average age of industrial laborers; thirdly, the tapping of new sources of labor supply, fourthly, dilution, or a change in the skill composition of the labor force.

The wartime employment of women

The feminization of the work force was the most important development and elicited much com-

> A long war of mass armies needs the support of a large work force
>
> Women take over their husbands' jobs and move into new areas of employment
>
> But the proportion of women in the labor force rises only marginally
>
> In France some soldiers are conscripted for factory work
>
> In Britain unskilled workers move into "skilled" jobs
>
> Living standards vary considerably

▼ In addition to traditional tasks in farming and textiles, women's war work included munitions production, clerical work, transport and all kinds of manual labor. This photograph of local women in a British ammunition dump in Italy may have suggested that women who should have been cradling babies were cradling bombs.

ment during the war itself. During the war women took on a myriad of tasks. Some took over their husbands' jobs, and became blacksmiths, paper-hangers and grave-diggers. Others were drawn into nonmanual trades where women rarely worked: witness women dentists, ambulance drivers, and switch-pillar inspectors. In addition, banks and offices employed women tellers and clerks to do jobs traditionally reserved for men. These were instances of substitution in the domestic economy. But women were also required to help out in munitions production. It must be remembered that munitions meant more than guns and bullets; the term came to encompass virtually everything the armies needed.

Some of the pride in the work of these new "munitionettes" is attested to by the displays that were made of the first shells produced by "lady operators" in one war factory. Photographs recapture the world of women's work in trades as diverse as the manufacture of army tropical helmets and airplane propellers, as well as in caustic soda works, coke works and the numerous filling factories which sprang up throughout Europe. These changes elicited much anxious comment at the time. Employing women on jobs

traditionally done by men presented a challenge to traditional sex roles. Some concerned voices were raised about the moral dangers of industrial work, the physical risks to the health of women, and the prospect of child neglect presented by the full-time labor of mothers.

These (usually male) commentators were right in pointing to the fact that the war efforts required the mobilization of women in the labor force. But they both understated the level of women's industrial work in the prewar period and overstated the change caused by the war. The French case illustrates this point. Early German successes required a major revamping of French industry. Women were drawn into new French factories, first by private employers and then by the state. They were concentrated especially in the chemical, wood and transport sectors, where they performed handling tasks of all kinds. Many specialized in running all sorts of machines: presses, furnaces, saws, cranes, paste grinders and lathes. In some areas, such as in metallurgy, fully a quarter of the labor force was female in 1918, compared to a twentieth in 1914. But this was the exception, not the rule. Elsewhere the proportion of women in the labor force did not go up much. Roughly 35 percent of the labor force was female in 1914; during the war, the figure rose to about 40 percent.

The same can be said of Germany. Women workers were recruited not from those previously unoccupied, but rather from those who had already been in paid labor elsewhere in the economy. Thus it is best to regard with considerable skepticism the numerous statements made during the war about its "revolutionary" effects on women's work.

After the Armistice, older patterns were restored in industry. In contrast, lasting gains in opportunities were registered in the clerical and commercial sectors. In Britain the female labor force in commerce rose by 400,000 during the war, and stayed high in the postwar years.

It is much more difficult to be precise about what war work meant to these women. Many recall the sociability of the job, and the satisfaction of learning new skills. But others recall the long hours and the double burden of paid work and unpaid child-minding and housework, which meant queuing up for scarce supplies either before or after working hours. German women ironically called these queues "polonaises", snaking their way slowly into a shoemaker's shop, a bakery or a butcher's shop.

Patriotism may have carried many along initially, but the glamor of war work faded very rapidly, as the second set of workers recruited to war industry – adolescents – also found. Here too we must be wary of attributing to the war what had long been a fact of industrial life. Whatever the law said about compulsory education, boys and girls were employed in marginal tasks before the war in both agriculture and industry. The war simply brought out into the open and tacitly legitimated what had long gone on in the shadows. The education of these adolescents clearly mattered less than providing the men at the Front with the tools of war.

◀ The war brought about a change in the distribution of the female labor force. Women replaced men who had enlisted in all kinds of labor, like this bill poster in Thetford in East Anglia, England (top), or the mechanic on the Parisian metro (center). Much of the work was dreary and unending. The working week for many war workers extended to more than 70 hours. The weight on the back of the woman coke worker (bottom) should help dispel any lingering romantic illusions about women's work during the war.

▲ These women workers in a German state munitions factory performed a variety of tasks. These are turners and lathe operators in a shell factory, doing the kind of skilled work denied to women before the war. Between 1913 and 1917 the total female labor force employed in metal works rose from 606 to 11,816, or from 5 percent to fully 28 percent of the labor force. The rise in women's wages was substantial. Before the war the average take-home pay for female metalworkers was about 2 marks per day; by 1917 they took home between 5 and 6 marks per day. A year later the figure rose to about 7 marks for a 10-hour day, an unprecedented wage for women's manual labor.

► This woman is planing a propeller in an aeroplane factory in Ipswich, England.

Women's Attitudes to the War

Many wartime propaganda images suggest that women stood firmly behind the war effort. Women's attitudes, however, were as varied as their lives. Certainly there were patriotic bigots – among them England's Mrs Pankhurst. Behind extreme patriotism often lay fear or anger. As one propagandist reported, of her visit to a munitions factory in England: "I speak to two High School Mistresses from a town that has several times been visited by Zeppelins. 'We just felt that we must come and help kill Germans', they say quietly ..." At the other end of the spectrum were the pacifists, who like the ardent patriots were in a minority. The views of most women lay between the two. Many realized that their labor would "release" men from their jobs to serve in the army, or that their work would help maintain the war. Some middle-class women soon gave up their new jobs, not wanting to support the conflict in any way; they could afford to do so. Working-class women had to work on, even though as one woman wrote: "Only the fact that I am using my lifes (sic) energy to destroy human souls, gets on my nerves. Yet on the other hand, I am doing what I can to bring this horrible affair to an end." The idea of women "doing their bit" has become a cliché, yet many women did feel they must do something to help the men.

Surprising as it may seem, there were also women who were left almost untouched by the war. Many very young or older women had no husbands or brothers in the trenches. They recognized the horror of the conflict but were personally unaffected. They threw themselves into war work – they were enthusiastic about the new jobs, new wages and new freedom. For them it was the twenties and thirties which brought poverty and misery.

► A pre-revolutionary Russian war worker.

Industrial recruitment and dilution

The third group of recruits to the war industries came from outside traditional channels. In France, foreigners, especially from the Mediterranean countries, and residents in French colonies were put to work. So were prisoners-of-war and disabled soldiers. In addition, in France (but not in Britain), soldiers were conscripted and then directed to work in factories, and did so under military discipline.

The need to intensify production and maximize output led to a series of changes that were summarized under the heading of "dilution". Essentially this meant the end of the demarcation of some jobs as skilled and others as unskilled. This divide had been the subject of long and bitter conflicts, waged over many years, to establish the right of artisans to a decent wage, protected by restricting entry into a trade and requiring newcomers to go through a period of apprenticeship. In Britain after 1915 skilled men gave up these privileges very reluctantly and only for the duration of the war. The result was to give the new recruits to labor – especially to women – access to relatively well-paid jobs denied to them

before the war. Given the additional earnings available for overtime and under piece-work conditions, where output determines pay, it should not be surprising that some munitions workers were substantially better off than they had been before the war.

Living standards in wartime

Early in the war most of these gains were wiped out by rapid price inflation. Some workers, for example the notoriously independent South Wales miners, were prepared to take industrial action as early as 1915 to defend their living standards. Most other workers at this time were very remote from this kind of militancy. But as we shall see, a substantial part of this new labor force was to show its discontent in very alarming ways, later in the war. One source of these disturbances was visible from early on. This was the phenomenon of "profiteering". The term "profiteer" itself had been coined to denote those who had made a fortune out of the Napoleonic wars (1800–15). A century later, rumors spread about similar practices in several European countries. We have only sketchy evidence to back up these claims, but

► These men of the Egyptian Labor Corps, stationed at Boulogne, formed part of a huge multinational and multiracial labor force backing up Allied units. By 1918 over 250,000 men from China, Vietnam, Egypt, India, the West Indies, South Africa and elsewhere were employed in all kinds of construction, maintenance and repair work. Given the endemic racial prejudice of the time, it is not surprising that they were segregated in special camps, and when they complained about conditions of wages, treated with the utmost severity. In September 1917, 23 Egyptian workers were shot after a strike at Boulogne. In the following months, 9 Chinese workers were killed in a similar disturbance. Such actions would have provoked a storms of protest had the victims been white; but no one in or outside the army spoke out against these brutal measures.

they did describe one feature of the wartime scene. In Germany the *declared* profits and dividends in joint stock-companies in 1915–16 were at the same level as in 1913. It will never be known whether or not this represented the normal sleight-of-hand tricks of accountancy, but there are many other indicators that show that profit margins rose in those sectors of industry supplying the war effort. Some firms in iron and steel did particularly well, as might be expected. As a rule, the larger the firm, the better were its chances of increasing its return on capital, whatever the inflation rate. Government agents appreciated the economies of scale to be gained by dealing with large units of production. Consequently, industrial concentration intensified during the war.

The benefits reaped by this well-to-do section of the population were not hidden at the time. Holiday resorts and spas still did a thriving business, and the luxuries some of the rich took for granted remained available, albeit at vastly inflated prices. The rest of the home population had a much harder time dealing with war conditions. The old, the retired, and those living on fixed incomes were impoverished by war inflation. Similarly affected were white-collar workers, particularly those in the lower grades. The position of manual workers varied according to the distance of their jobs from the war economy: the closer they were to the heart of the war effort, the better off they were. This may explain why so many women who had worked in the textile trades before the war moved into munitions work; they simply could not afford to stay put while the purchasing power of their wages diminished day by day.

Overall there was substantial variation in standards of living in wartime. In Germany average real wages for all employees dropped by ten percent in each wartime year. This covered a range of experience. Some munitions workers found that their pay kept up with prices; most did not. In France and Britain real wages were eroded early in the war, and picked up later. In occupied Belgium destitution was the fate of a substantial part of the population throughout the war.

Food supply

The food situation also varied considerably. Here we confront one of the fundamental errors of the German war effort. When it came to food supply the German high command was adamant in giving the army priority over civilians. This may seem common sense, but in a long war it was an invitation to disaster. By failing to organize civilian food distribution properly, the German leadership not only ensured chronic disaffection, it also undermined the efficiency of the munitions effort itself.

Making matters worse for the Central Powers was the combination of the Allied blockade and the run of poor and disastrous harvests in the middle years of the war in Germany and Austria-Hungary, leading to the infamous "turnip winter" of 1916–17. But bad management made a poor situation a critical one. Alongside absurd mistakes in pricing policies, which created a glut one month and a dearth the next, there was the shortage of men, horses and oxen needed to till the land. The result was an increasingly inadequate food supply, and eventually malnutrition. Some parts of Europe reverted to a kind of

▶ This photograph of the ruins of Termonde in Belgium gives some idea of the landscape of civilian life near the front lines. The widespread destruction of houses and utilities increased the risk of accidents to children and the spread of water-borne infectious diseases. From 1916 mortality rates throughout Belgium increased, reflecting falling conditions of housing, heating and nutrition. The average birth-weight of babies born in Antwerp during the war was about 750 grams (1.6lb) lower than in the prewar period.

We can get no potatoes again at present... The reason is this – a fortnight ago, the municipality idiotically announced that till the 1st of August potatoes were to cost 10 pfennig a lb – then each week a pfennig less, till they came down to 6 pf a lb. So to get that extra 1/8 of a penny, the growers before the 1st of August have pulled up masses of winter potatoes, which are not nearly ripe yet. They have put masses of these on to the market, and of course in a fortnight they went bad.

ETHEL COOPER, LEIPZIG

Food Shortages in Germany

About 19 percent of the average German's diet was provided by imported food in the prewar period; in addition, 27 percent of protein and 42 percent of fats came from abroad. These simple statistics show how vulnerable Germany was to the Allied blockade. The response of German administrators to this problem was inadequate. Most items of daily consumption including bread, were rationed by separate local authorities. Some set price ceilings, but dealers easily evaded them by sending their food to adjacent and uncontrolled areas. A war food office was set up on 1 June 1916 to rationalize controls, but chronic shortages persisted, leading to periodic food riots. Then came the disastrous harvest of 1916, which made potatoes scarce and established the turnip as a staple food.

Official wartime rations provided about half the calorific requirements of the population. The rest came from the thriving black market, which – at dizzying prices – prevented hunger from turning into starvation. From mid-1917 food supplies improved, but real scarcity returned again in June and July 1918, coinciding with the turn of the tide on the Western front.

▶ German housewives queue for potato peels, 1917.

economy unknown for a century, with city dwellers foraging in harvested fields for whatever they could find. Of course, these difficulties still paled in comparison with what faced the men at the front, which may explain why so many civilians put up with them.

Conditions on the Allied side were not nearly so bad. This was partly because, despite submarine warfare, the lines of naval supply were kept open. It was also due to a much more successful effort at increasing or maintaining home agricultural production in the UK and France. But the success of Allied food policy was ultimately grounded in the fact that, slowly and in an entirely unplanned manner, the Allies came to see that the only way to win the war was to defend *civilian* living standards, and to ensure that the distribution system did not break down. One of the keys to the Allied victory, therefore, was that they were able to mobilize and equip mass armies effectively without impoverishing the home population.

◀ This family portrait of 1916 was idealized in French graphic art in the style of the *Image d'Epinal*, reiterating the bond between Front and home front. In fact the joys of leave for the French soldier were few and far between. Better leave arrangements were among the first reforms introduced after the mutinies of 1917.

Datafile

Propaganda helped lengthen the war by steadying morale, silencing dissent, and bringing in wavering neutrals. Official agencies produced books, pamphlets, posters and films by the thousand to proclaim the virtues of the cause. Unofficial campaigns were waged through the press, which managed news in the interest of the war effort. Atrocity stories proliferated, as if the war's true bestiality was not enough.

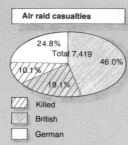

Air raid casualties

24.8%
Total 7,419
46.0%
10.1%
19.1%

///// Killed

///// British

[ ] German

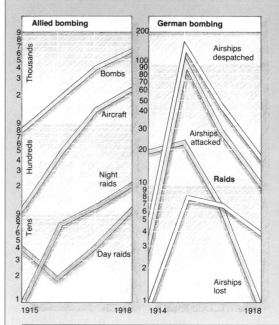

Allied bombing / **German bombing**

Thousands / Hundreds / Tens

Bombs
Aircraft
Night raids
Day raids

1915 — 1918

Airships despatched
Airships attacked
Raids
Airships lost

1914 — 1918

◀ Like military occupation, air raids obliterated the distinction between civilian and military targets in wartime. Approximately 1,400 people were killed and 3,400 injured by German air attacks on British cities and towns (left). The material damage these raids caused was substantial.

◀ Allied retaliatory air raids (far left) killed approximately 700 and wounded 1,800 German civilians. As German air raids diminished, Allied raids intensified. By 1917 the majority of attacks were night raids. In the last year of the war, 350 Allied air raids involving 2,319 aircraft dropped over 7,000 bombs on Germany.

Chronology

1916

January 24
UK: House of Commons passes first Military Service Bill

January 29
FR: Last German airship raid on Paris

February 21
(to Dec. 18) Battle of Verdun: unsuccessful German attack on French city of Verdun

April 24–29
Easter Rising of Irish Republican Brotherhood against the British in Dublin, Ireland

April 29
In Mesopotamia, Turks capture Kut and the remnants of the British invasion force

May 31
(to June 1) Battle of Jutland: major naval battle of war between UK and Germany

June 4
(to Oct. 10) Brusilov offensive: Russians push back the Austro-Hungarian line north of the Carpathians

June 6
Start of Arab revolt against the Turks in the Hejaz

July 1
(to Nov. 19) Battle of the Somme: unsuccessful Allied attack on German lines in the Somme Valley, France

September 2
UK: 14 German airships simultaneously attack locations in England

September 24
GER: British aeroplanes bomb Krupp works at Essen

October 28
(to 10 Feb.1917) BELG: Germans forcibly deport over 60,000 Belgian workers to Germany

November 7
Woodrow Wilson is reelected president of the USA

1917

February
In Central Europe the "Turnip Winter" reaches its depth with large losses of life

February 2
UK: Government introduces rationing of bread

March 16
Czar Nicholas II of Russia abdicates. Provisional Government assumes power

April 6
The USA enters the war fighting on the side of the Allies

April 16–29
Chemin des Dames offensive: a large-scale French offensive on the Aisne falls to break the German line

April 24
USA: Liberty Loan Act authorizes issue of war bonds

April 25
USA/UK: USA makes first loan, of 200 million dollars, to UK

July 31
(to Nov. 10) Third Battle of Ypres: unsuccessful British offensive against the German forces in Flanders

---

In 1916–17, as the great battles of Verdun, the Somme and Passchendaele proceeded to their bloody and inconclusive ends, a massive campaign of propaganda was launched on both sides to broadcast the virtues of the cause. By this period of the war it involved the presentation, by both private parties and government agencies, of four kinds of appeal, aimed primarily at, first, home civilians, to keep up their morale; secondly, enemy civilians, to undermine their morale; thirdly, enemy soldiers, for the same purpose; fourthly, neutrals, to bring them into the war. There is almost no way of telling how effective campaigns were in influencing opinion about the war, especially when most people, in and out of uniform, developed a kind of immunity to what was called in Britain the "eyewash" presented to them in the press. Until the very end of the war, propaganda probably had little effect on the commitment of civilians on either side. Ironically it may have made it harder for both soldiers and civilians in the Central Powers to accept the reality of defeat when it came in 1918.

A stronger case can be made with respect to propaganda aimed at neutrals, and in particular at the United States. It would be foolish to reduce American entry into the war to a response to the officially sponsored campaign to convince Ameicans of the virtues of the Allied cause. But the British appeal, much more skillfully managed than the German campaign in the United States, did strike an increasingly loud chord, especially after the propaganda disaster of the Zimmermann telegram (see p. 165) and the intensification of German submarine warfare in 1917.

French propaganda was under the control of the foreign office, the army and the navy. Press reports abroad were distributed through the Maison de la Presse liaison officer in foreign consulates. A useful and effective argument used in the USA by France was that the Frenchman Lafayette's contribution to the American Revolution should be repaid.

Many patriotic leagues and associations joined in the effort to win the war of words. The difficulties in France were less severe than in the case of Britain or Germany, for France had been invaded and could simply present its case as one of national defense. The variety of French propaganda was its hallmark. Some effort was made to organize French artistic propaganda under the aegis of the minister of education and fine arts. But of much greater importance was propaganda aimed at Germany, Alsace and Lorraine, and the occupied northeast of France and Belgium. A key figure here was the artist Hansi (see p. 229). He was a French patriot who escaped from Alsace in 1914 and helped broadcast anti-German messages to those who lived under occupation.

1916–17 THE GREAT SLAUGHTER

British and German propaganda

After the war at least one prominent ex-soldier was convinced that British propaganda had undermined the morale of the German fighting man in the war. This was Adolf Hitler. But for once in his life he probably paid his adversaries an unjustified compliment. The morale of the German army faded when it saw it could not win, not when it read Allied fly-sheets dropped on its lines. The despondency of German soldiers, for example at the battle of Amiens on 8 August 1918, was not induced by propaganda but by tanks. Still, it is significant that Hitler believed in the effectiveness of British propaganda, since this belief helped to establish the stab-in-the-back legend about why Germany lost the war: Germany's defeat was not due to material factors but to the subtle erosion of the soldiers' minds by enemies at home and abroad.

This situation Hitler would not allow to happen again. He consequently decided to use in Nazi propaganda what he took to be British methods of persuasion. This is how he put the

point in *Mein Kampf* ("My Struggle"), published in 1925:

"The great majority of a nation is so femine in its character and outlook that its thought and conduct are ruled by sentiment rather than by sober reasoning. This sentiment, however, is not complex, but simple and consistent. It is not highly differentiated, but has only the negative and positive notions of love and hatred, right and wrong, truth and falsehood. Its notions are never partly this and partly that. English propaganda especially understood this in a marvelous way and put what they understood into practice."

What Hitler could not understand was that the success or failure of propaganda is primarily a function of the willingness of people to listen to it and to believe what it has to say. British propaganda proclaimed the virtues of the war effort to a fundamentally unified society. It worked because of the already existing consensus about the legitimacy of the regime and the justness of the Allied cause. Similarly, few people in France needed to be convinced about the

▼ War loans were a device to which all combatants resorted in order to soak up excess purchasing power and thereby keep inflation under control. They were advertised by many striking posters. Among them was this cartoon, by the French artist Abel Faivre, showing the Kaiser humbled.

L'EMPRUNT DE LA LIBÉRATION

PICHOT. IMP. PARIS

Are **YOU** in this?

Gott strafe England

◄ The use of allegory and mythical figures in wartime propaganda was universal. The German poster "God punish England" shows Germanica defending her shores against the marauding British Royal Navy. The French female equivalent was Marianne, usually portrayed in neoclassical garb, striding bare-breasted into battle. One can appreciate the power of myth in wartime propaganda when such images are set against the more mundane portrait of the British nation at war, produced for the Parliamentary Recruiting Committee in 1915 by Lord Robert Baden-Powell.

Photography in World War I

World War I ushered in a new era in the control of information for publication at home and abroad by all combatants and in the formal organization of propaganda. Systems of official reporting, including photography, were set up. Professional photographers were appointed, given commissioned status and allowed privileged access to the battlefronts. The numbers employed varied considerably. Germany, anxious to present its efforts in the best possible light and generally speaking the technical leader in photography, maintained an average of about 50 official operators in the most important and controlled theater of war on the Western Front; France, concerned to sustain the national effort against the invader, had approximately 35; but Britain, less directly affected and chary of condescension to either the home or foreign press, maintained only an average of four.

Outside the Western Front in theaters such as the Eastern Front, control was less organized and there was considerably more scope for the professional reporter if his newspaper was prepared to finance him. Even so, although hard to assess accurately, the numbers of professionals engaged in war photography for any length of time remained small, probably no more than a few hundred altogether, including the official photographers. There were many incidents, particularly in naval warfare, where there was no room and no welcome for supernumeraries in actions, which were recorded by amateurs. A Kodak camera was frequently part of the equipment taken to war by the troops. Not only did these ordinary soldiers offer an occasional source of supply to the press but

they were also to contribute an important part of the full historical record.

As far as can be established, the professional and official photographers were guided as much if not more by the publishing standards of the day as by the military censors. They were concerned to reflect the fighting effort and its successes and treated the human cost of war with discretion because patriotism and contemporary standards of decency did not allow full disclosure.

▼ Despite considerable risks and technical difficulties, official photographers (like the Australian H. Baldwin seen here in France in 1917) provided invaluable evidence about the nature of the war. So did countless amateurs, who carried a Kodak camera as part of their equipment, and left a pictorial legacy which still exists in family albums and attics worldwide.

▲ The visual dimension of wartime propaganda took many forms, from stirring films of front-line troops (advertised on a Paris billboard, top) to posters, postcards and commercial ephemera. All combatants explored each of these media, and produced a vast array of designs and products. Some were aimed at an educated public. Witness the poster "In Deo Gratia", by the Frankfurt-based artist Fritz Böhle. It was clearly derived from the famous medieval woodcut *St George on Horseback* by Albrecht Dürer (1471–1528). In contrast, the message of Frank Brangwyn's British war poster "Put strength in the final blow" was more populist, realistic and accessible to a general audience.

need to throw the German army off French soil. In effect, Allied propagandists preached to the converted.

There is much more controversy about the character and persuasiveness of German propaganda. To judge by poster art, film and newsreel propaganda, as well as by pamphlet literature, the German campaign to influence opinion about the nature of the war differed little from that of its enemies. But some scholars disagree. The founder of the study of wartime propaganda, Harold Lasswell, showed that conflicts between civilian and military authorities hampered efforts to develop a smooth propaganda campaign during the war. No ministry of propaganda was established, despite repeated requests by the military authorities. Instead they set up their own press service, the *Deutsche Kriegsnachrichten* ("German War News") and broadcast patriotic appeals, with the blessing of Ludendorff himself.

Lack of coordination also marked German efforts to inform opinion abroad. Private groups proliferated, but little could be expected from

brochures produced by phalanxes of patriotic professors. Some of them mixed a defense of German culture with advocacy of racial prejudice, as in the letter signed by 94 prominent German intellectuals that countered Allied claims of German barbarity in Belgium in 1914 by pointing out that it was not Germany that let loose a black army on the white people of Europe. Signatories to this document included some of the most prominent figures in German intellectual life. The heavy-handedness of these and similar efforts has led other scholars to claim that in general German propaganda was elitist, condescending, unsubtle, and worked through coercion, rather than by characteristic British means of cooptation. In Germany public opinion was distrusted (especially in some army circles) as was the press. Consequently, propaganda was never geared to the language of the population: it spoke in the all-too-familiar tones of a Prussian officer or schoolmaster. It is claimed as well that this too reflected much deeper strains within the Central Powers. Propaganda simply could not recreate

Allied and German Propaganda in the USA

◀ **Rousing support: an American Liberty Loan choir.**

The declaration of US neutrality by President Woodrow Wilson in August 1914 accurately reflected the views of most Americans. Few knew or understood the causes of the war in Europe and in 1914 hardly anyone in America contemplated US involvement. But as soon as the guns began to fire across France and Belgium the major belligerents began to woo the greatest neutral power.

Germany spent over 100 million dollars in direct propaganda in newspapers and other publications. German-American groups were sponsored in many cities. Latent anti-British sentiment, specially among Irish Americans, was cultivated. Germany, however, could never overcome the taint of being the aggressor in Belgium.

The British propaganda effort, headed by Sir Gilbert Parker from the propaganda center at Wellington House, London, succeeded in building up a regular and remarkable correspondence with influential figures and institutions in the USA. By means of pamphlets, books and other tracts, Parker ensured that, for example, editors of American local newspapers received the Entente versions of news and opinion. This personal approach paid dividends in terms of forging trans-Atlantic ties with ordinary Americans. When added to the sinking of the *Lusitania* in 1915 and the USA's investment in the Allied war economy, it helped tilt the balance for war. When war came in April 1917, Parker could rightly claim the credit in helping to form the opinions and attitudes that underlay America's entry into the war. However, the Entente powers' greatest advantage was the ineptness of German propaganda, diplomacy and naval action against the USA.

Nothing strikes me so much to-day as the difficulty in arriving at the truth; there are so many statements and counter-statements from able people; but in all the propaganda, and in the German propaganda, and in the great "ouptut" of war documents which they are flooding the world with, in those I have seen there seems to me a great lack of candour... As for the propaganda here it has failed where they most desired it, doubtless, to produce an effect. The German-American, I suppose, the Fatherland counts to be loyal, but the American whom they have tried to convince, remains coldly unmoved by their every appeal in their pamphlets, their books, and their newspapers.

SARA NORTON DEC. 1914

social unity when much that was being done to the home population was divisive.

In effect, the argument is that deepening class divisions within wartime Germany made the working class more and more impervious to appeals designed by their class enemies. Similarly the hard-pressed middle class, squeezed by rampant inflation and chronic shortages of essential goods, had a difficult time squaring what they could see with what they were told about the war. The appeal of 1914 to take up arms in defense of their country was one thing; the call to carry on in a war enriching the few and impoverishing the many was another. Propaganda clearly failed to impress the increasing number of workers prepared to go on strike from 1916 on. High-sounding phrases simply could not compensate for a cut in the bread ration. Hungry families needed food, not more patriotic appeals.

Those who point to the difference between the propaganda efforts of Britain and Germany also emphasize the contrast in the nature of the press in the two countries. A strategy of cooptation required an already existing free and largely independent press fully prepared to lie for victory. This Britain had in abundance, since prominent newspapermen and proprietors were well integrated into the social and political scene,

and exercised real power in making and breaking coalitions and governments. Such newspaper proprietors as Lord Northcliffe and Lord Beaverbrook were prepared to put all their talents and resources at the disposal of the government. So were German newspapermen, but in Germany high politics were conducted in very different ways. The close association of German papers with particular interest groups and parties has already been pointed out. The press reflected but did not shape political events. In addition, German newspaper proprietors, many of whom were Jewish, were kept at an arm's distance by the men who ran the German war effort. Yet again social divisions that originated long before the war hampered the capacity of the belligerents to mobilize public opinion effectively.

The British conspiracy of silence

The techniques by which the British press early in the war either failed to report bad news or broadcast atrocity stories were developed later in the war into an art form. Reports from "our own correspondent" at the front were littered with euphemisms designed to obscure the reality of battles. Thus a retreat was called a rectification of the line; deaths became wastage; and heavy casualties were a baptism of fire. The conspiracy

◀ The British royal family distanced itself from many of its German associations during the war. King George V was, after all, first cousin of the Kaiser. In 1914 the first sea lord was Prince Louis of Battenburg, a descendant of German nobility. In 1917 the English members of the House of Battenburg renounced their German titles and anglicized their name to Mountbatten. Other members of the royal family were tireless in their efforts to encourage national unity during the war. They visited munitions factories and hospitals, and in 1917 King George V and Queen Mary visited the troops in France. Here the queen places flowers on a roll of honor for fallen servicemen in a working-class district of London's East End.

▲ General Hindenburg, the hero of Tannenberg, became a symbol of the immovable power of Germany during the war. His square features were instantly recognizable, and were reproduced in numerous posters and statues during the war. The graphic artist Louis Oppenheim created a widely disseminated war-loan poster of Hindenburg, and other artists and craftsmen did their bit to deepen the Hindenburg legend. There is no evidence that Hindenburg himself objected to such glorification, although it presented a clear challenge to the authority and prestige of the Kaiser.

of silence about bad news was usually maintained. Not surprisingly, a major effort was made in 1915 to keep the story of the Gallipoli disaster off the front pages. This would have succeeded, had it not been for the ingenuity of one young Australian reporter, Keith Murdoch (father of the current newspaper tycoon, Rupert Murdoch) who spilled the beans. British journalists would not have behaved in such an uncouth manner.

The story is an interesting one, since it shows that important and disturbing news got out only when it suited politicians to let it out. It was apparent from early on in the Gallipoli campaign that the enterprise was a disaster (see p. 82). But military censorship simply blocked the reports of the journalists who were there. One of them, Ellis Ashmead-Bartlett of the *Daily Telegraph*, passed to Murdoch some evidence of what was going on, in the hope that he could smuggle it back to Britain. Murdoch got as far as Marseilles, before another correspondent at Gallipoli, who was not going to let the *Telegraph* get the scoop, told the British authorities. Murdoch was arrested, and handed over all his papers. But on his arrival in London, he wrote down all he knew in a letter to the Australian prime minister, who duly notified Lloyd George, then minister of munitions, about what he had heard. Lloyd George was known as a man who had no love for the military leaders and saw that the story would help him get rid of the men responsible for the debacle. He passed the letter to Asquith, who put it on record in the parliamentary debate over the Dardanelles campaign. The upshot was the dismissal of the commander, Sir Ian Hamilton. This episode was, therefore, less an example of free reporting than a case of the use of a "leak" of military information as part of an ongoing battle between politicians and generals over who ran the war.

Misinformation

Misinformation, some of it calculated, was the stock in trade of many journalists. Some times they reported impossible casualty statistics. On other occasions they added yet another atrocity story to the existing stockpile.

One such invention is the famous story of the German "corpse factory", initiated in a report in London in the *The Times* on 16 April 1917. This noted that "One of the United States consuls, on leaving Germany in February, stated in Switzerland that the Germans were distilling glycerine from the bodies of the dead." This was followed later by a report from a German correspondent about a "Corpse Exploitation Establishment." This seemed to establish the validity of the story, which was repeated in cartoon form at home and in British propaganda around the world.

The author of this malicious lie was probably Brigadier-General Sir John Charteris, head of British military intelligence. Some years after the war he half-admitted that he had produced the story, simply by switching the captions of two photographs: one showing Germans removing their dead for burial; the other showing horses' cadavers on their way to a soap factory.

It is one of the ironies of history that the invention of this kind of lie prevented many from believing reports about the real "soap factories" constructed by the Nazis in the course of World War II. In this case, history appears to have happened twice: first as a farce, and then as a tragedy, which World War I helped indirectly to bring about.

Commercial propaganda

Journalists were not alone in presenting stylized views about the war. Commercial artists also moved into the propaganda game. There was a veritable flowering of kitsch, or sentimental art, in all combatant countries. In Britain, this took the form of advertisements for "Lifebuoy Soap: the Royal Disinfectant", or for the kitchen agent "Vim" set up like a motorized gun, or for Gibbs Dentifrice, apparently used by one airman who found it (so the advertisement claims) as "fragrant as the lofty air". In Germany too, the trade in patriotic mementos boomed.

In France some propaganda took on an earthier aspect. Lithographs, for example, showed the potential for mildly licentious propaganda in portraying French women seducing the enemy, apparently to keep them occupied while a French soldier slips away to carry on the fight. The caption of one card is so bold as to suggest in so many words that German artillery looks fine, but it never delivers the goods.

▶ The picture postcard industry boomed during the war. The French were particularly good at mixing patriotism with a commercial pitch on cards which soldiers and their families used for easy and cheap communication. Many of the images they bore were banal and full of simple sentimentality. The brotherhood of the Alliance, pictured right, inspired many such maudlin designs, clearly aimed at an international market.

▼ The Michelin company made sure that everyone knew that through their products they did their bit for the war effort too. The readers of the *Illustrated London News* of 2 May 1915 were told that the Michelin tyre, desperately needed by an ambulance or red cross vehicle, was a "rib of life" for the men waiting for medical help to arrive.

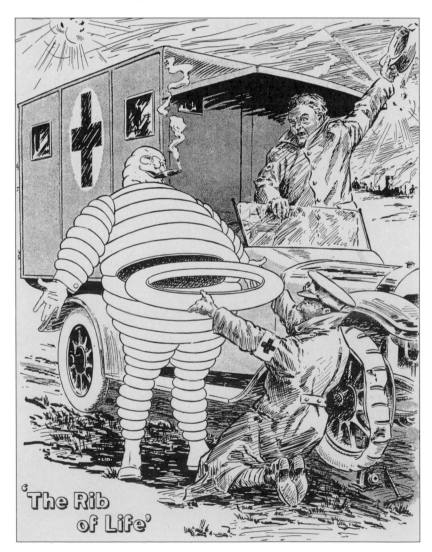

'The Rib of Life'

▲◀▼ Commercial artists domesticated the war in many ways. Septimus E. Scott sold Lifebuoy Soap as a "Royal Disinfectant" against the backdrop of a British military hospital (above). Other artists drew on stereotypes of women for their central imagery. In a typical German postcard (left), the loyal wife or girlfriend is daydreaming of her man at the Front. The returning soldier is spending "an exquisite hour which I will always remember" in bed with his girlfriend (below). The woman shown as the *"repos du guerrier"* (soldier's comfort) is found time and time again in this genre of wartime art.

The more respectable forms of French commercial art addressed themselves to the campaign to raise the French birth rate. The characteristic form was seen on one side of the postcards many soldiers used for sending messages home from the Front. Some show two French babies confronting five German ones, or have little boys emerging from cabbages and little girls, from roses, saying to a newly-married couple: "On your honeymoon, do not forget about us". Thus the producers of these postcards could do their bit for the war by selling a product which enabled people to indulge in a mixture of patriotism and light-hearted ribaldry. In Germany and elsewhere postcards expressed a mixture of uplifting messages of a patriotic and religious kind. Many highlighted the comfort women offered the men who fought for the Fatherland, but did so in a more discreet format than did some of their French counterparts.

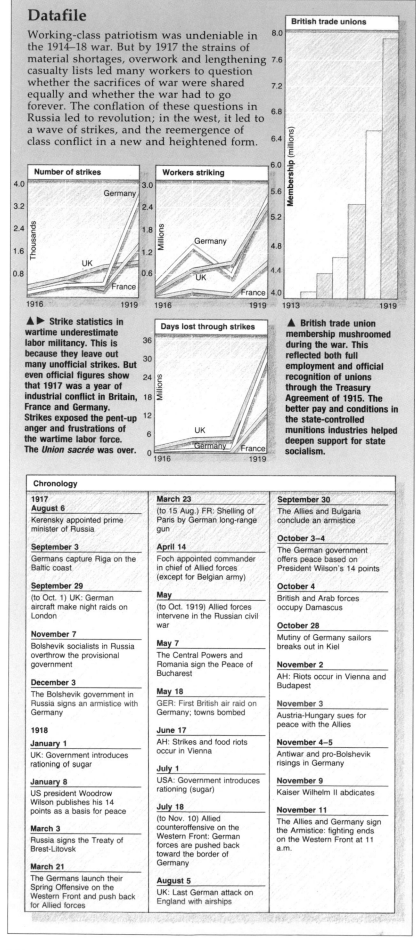

Datafile

Working-class patriotism was undeniable in the 1914–18 war. But by 1917 the strains of material shortages, overwork and lengthening casualty lists led many workers to question whether the sacrifices of war were shared equally and whether the war had to go forever. The conflation of these questions in Russia led to revolution; in the west, it led to a wave of strikes, and the reemergence of class conflict in a new and heightened form.

Number of strikes

(Graph showing strikes in thousands, 1916–1919: Germany, UK, France)

Workers striking

(Graph showing workers in millions, 1916–1919: Germany, UK, France)

British trade unions

(Bar graph showing membership in millions, 1913–1919, ranging from 4.0 to 8.0)

▲ ▶ Strike statistics in wartime underestimate labor militancy. This is because they leave out many unofficial strikes. But even official figures show that 1917 was a year of industrial conflict in Britain, France and Germany. Strikes exposed the pent-up anger and frustrations of the wartime labor force. The *Union sacrée* was over.

Days lost through strikes

(Graph showing days lost in millions, 1916–1919: UK, Germany, France)

▲ British trade union membership mushroomed during the war. This reflected both full employment and official recognition of unions through the Treasury Agreement of 1915. The better pay and conditions in the state-controlled munitions industries helped deepen support for state socialism.

Chronology		
1917	**March 23**	**September 30**
August 6	(to 15 Aug.) FR: Shelling of Paris by German long-range gun	The Allies and Bulgaria conclude an armistice
Kerensky appointed prime minister of Russia		
	April 14	**October 3–4**
September 3	Foch appointed commander in chief of Allied forces (except for Belgian army)	The German government offers peace based on President Wilson's 14 points
Germans capture Riga on the Baltic coast		
	May	**October 4**
September 29	(to Oct. 1919) Allied forces intervene in the Russian civil war	British and Arab forces occupy Damascus
(to Oct. 1) UK: German aircraft make night raids on London		
	May 7	**October 28**
November 7	The Central Powers and Romania sign the Peace of Bucharest	Mutiny of Germany sailors breaks out in Kiel
Bolshevik socialists in Russia overthrow the provisional government		
	May 18	**November 2**
December 3	GER: First British air raid on Germany; towns bombed	AH: Riots occur in Vienna and Budapest
The Bolshevik government in Russia signs an armistice with Germany		
	June 17	**November 3**
1918	AH: Strikes and food riots occur in Vienna	Austria-Hungary sues for peace with the Allies
January 1		
UK: Government introduces rationing of sugar	**July 1**	**November 4–5**
	USA: Government introduces rationing (sugar)	Antiwar and pro-Bolshevik risings in Germany
January 8		
US president Woodrow Wilson publishes his 14 points as a basis for peace	**July 18**	**November 9**
	(to Nov. 10) Allied counteroffensive on the Western Front: German forces are pushed back toward the border of Germany	Kaiser Wilhelm II abdicates
March 3		**November 11**
Russia signs the Treaty of Brest-Litovsk		The Allies and Germany sign the Armistice: fighting ends on the Western Front at 11 a.m.
March 21	**August 5**	
The Germans launch their Spring Offensive on the Western Front and push back for Allied forces	UK: Last German attack on England with airships	

A justly celebrated cartoon of World War I by Jean-Louis Forain shows two trench soldiers in conversation. One says, "Let's hope they hold out." The other asks, "Who?" "The civilians" is the tart reply. There was more than a grain of truth in this oft-repeated soldiers' jest, for the strain of the war began to tell on the home front at about the same time as it did in the armies. From the spring of 1917 the armies and noncombatants of most combatant countries became restless, war-weary and, on occasion, even rebellious. Here it is necessary to consider, first, the sources of popular discontent with the war and, secondly, what prevented it from spilling over into revolt until almost the end of the war.

Sources of disaffection

The first reason for disaffection with the war was material deprivation, which became critical from

1917–18 REVOLUTION AND PEACE

▼ **Parisian seamstresses on strike in May 1917. Their militancy in January 1917 touched off the most serious wartime French strike wave.**

early 1917. This was apparent to all observers of the Russian economy, and was a crucial factor in the collapse of the Russian monarchy. After three years of war, the turbulence of the Russian scene spread west, and for similar reasons. In the summer of 1917 there were bread riots in Turin, which left 41 people dead. The outcry heard in Italy over the yawning gap between deprivation and privilege, between the lot of industrial workers and the luxuries of the *pescecani* (sharks), was echoed virtually all over the Continent.

Between March and May 1917 prices of vegetables, coal and rice doubled in France. This was the single most spectacular increase in the cost of a basket of consumables at any time during the war. The outcome was the largest and angriest May Day demonstration of the war in Paris, followed by a series of bitter strikes, which started in the clothing industry but spread to bank employees, telegraph messengers and finally to munitions workers, especially in the aircraft industry. Similar disturbances broke out in Toulouse. As in Paris, women workers were prominent among the strikers.

Most of the evidence about these conflicts suggests that they concerned wages and were settled once increases were granted. Other motives may be detected in strikes which brought out 300,000 Berlin workers in April 1917. The trouble here started when, a few days after the Kaiser had made some vague promises about future political reform, it was announced that the bread ration would be cut. Strikers went back to work only on receiving assurances that their food ration – already at or below subsistence level – would be increased. Similar disturbances followed in Leipzig, Halle, Braunschweig and Magdeburg. A series of unofficial strikes broke out in British

▲ The arrest of a striker near a German munitions factory. Most wartime disputes were about wages and hours, but by 1918 strikes in Germany had a clear political content.

▼ Mass demonstrations were commonplace in Petrograd in 1917. This one denounced "capitalist lackeys" and hailed the revolutionary parties.

industrial districts at about the same time, prompting a commission of inquiry into industrial unrest. Again prices and wages headed the list of complaints. By the summer of 1917 the Kerensky regime was swamped by strikes. It is apparent that workers all over Europe were reaching the end of their patience with appeals for sacrifices on behalf of the war.

Even more ominous was the industrial unrest of early 1918. By then the food situation had deteriorated still further. In January, when the flour ration in Austria was reduced from 200 to 165 grams (7–6oz) per day, strikes broke out among munitions workers in Wiener Neustadt and spread to Vienna and Budapest. At the same time, Berlin again became a magnet for discontent. In all perhaps one million workers downed tools in many German cities in what was the biggest single protest of the war. New outbreaks of labor unrest were also registered in France, this time in towns unaffected by the 1917 troubles. What distinguished this second wave of militancy from the first was that by 1918 most strikes had an undeniable political content.

This is, not surprising in the light of the two major political events of 1917: American entry into the war and the Russian Revolution. The first brought the question of war aims to center stage. It was no accident that both the US declaration of war and the strikes of spring 1917 were soon followed by the passage of a resolution in the Reichstag in favor of peace.

Russian events presented the European working class with a new vision of the future, at a time when the old order was patently failing to deliver the goods: food and victory. This lay behind the long overdue split within the German social democratic party, and the appearance, in the form of the independent socialists, of a parliamentary bloc opposed to the war.

Sources of militancy

By 1918 it had become impossible to separate the political from the economic threads of industrial unrest. But there were other sources of strike action which account in part for the turbulence of the last year of the war. Five specifically war-related developments which affected each of the major European combatants help to explain the explosion of militancy in the last year of the war. They are: first, the changed character of the labor force; secondly, the leveling effects of the war; thirdly, the displacement onto the state of traditional hostility to the employer; fourthly, the release of bottled-up tension, contained too long by the constraints of the wartime social truce; fifthly, the creation of new aspirations and expectations.

As the war went on, the proportion of women and adolescents at work in war factories and workshops increased. In German heavy industry in 1913, 13 percent of the labor force consisted of women and boys under 16 years of age; in 1918, this group comprised 34 percent of the workforce

The "Spanish flu"

In the autumn of 1918, as the Allies were pushing back the German line, a further disaster occurred in most parts of the world: a virulent outbreak of influenza of pandemic proportions. The flu had first emerged in the spring of 1918. Its place of origin is unknown, but one widespread theory about its origin was reflected in its popular name. A first wave of the epidemic peaked in June and July 1918 and was followed by a more deadly wave which peaked in October and November and only abated in spring 1919.

Epidemic mortality was enormous. In France 166,000 died; in Germany 225,330; in Britain 228,900; in the USA 550,000. Worst hit was India, where perhaps 16 million people were killed. The flu had a particularly heavy impact on children and young adults. About 25 percent of its victims were 15 or under and about 45 percent between 15 and 35. Overall at least 20 million people died - more than were killed by the war itself.

Explanations for the flu abounded, but at the time its causal agent was not isolated. It had the character of a plague, so it was seen by some as divine punishment for the terrible man-made slaughter on the Western Front. Others pointed to circumstances that they believed (mistakenly) had been favorable to the virus: on the home front, poor health caused by rationing, food shortages, and the impact of blockade; on the military Front, insanitary, lice-ridden trenches and barracks.

Treatment of the flu was ineffectual and ignorance of its aetiology meant that a vaccine could not be prepared. The viral cause of the flu was not discovered until as late as 1933 and by then the mutant virus had largely disappeared.

▶ **A totally useless antiflu spray for London buses.**

in this key sector. This growth was eventually reflected in the prominence of women and young workers in strikes. These were people who had not been "tamed" by the disciplines of union membership and shopfloor routine. It was therefore impossible for the old guard to control incipient outbreaks of trouble, or to predict them.

The second arose out of the fact that wage differentials between well-paid and poorly-paid, industrial and agricultural, male and female workers were reduced during the war. This was in part a function of the need to draw as many workers as possible into the labor market. It was also an outcome of inflation, rent control and rationing, which tended to level social conditions, downward in Germany and Austria, upward in parts of Britain and France. This meant that workers in different trades faced similar problems and expressed in industrial action a widely-shared sense of resentment about their lot compared to that of their richer countrymen.

The third derived from the very prominence of the state in industrial life during the war. One consequence of the creation of wartime controls was that the paternalism of the state could rebound against itself. Once the state took upon itself responsibility for feeding as well as employing workers in essential industry, it was bound to

attract to itself the anger inevitably generated by the mistakes, the mismanagement and the arbitrary action of the petty tyrants and bureaucrats who proliferated during the war.

The fourth concerned the costs of the abrogation of the right to strike during the war. Normal outlets for letting off steam, so to speak, were blocked, and for three years no one had provided an alternative. Such mechanical metaphors are never very helpful in accounting for labor disputes, but there is considerable evidence that after three years of war, exasperation had simply reached breaking point. There is a wealth of comment on the part of observers of the industrial scene as to the irritability and progressively more assertive mood of industrial workers in the last phase of the war.

The fifth relates to the effects of the vast movement of populations during the war upon workers' attitudes toward what constituted an acceptable standard of living. People uprooted in this way tended to give up traditional ideas of what is a decent wage. They were less likely – especially under conditions of rapid inflation – to accept what their fathers or mothers had taken for granted or to act deferentially to anyone in authority. In a more general sense, too, the geographical mobility of the war changed the

For revolutionary propaganda the metalworkers' union was in the front line in Berlin. The first workers' rebellion, which bore an undercurrent of revolutionary grumbling, was the single general strike on the day that a war tribunal was dealing with Karl Liebknecht. 55,000 workers, both men and women, are said to have laid down their tools. In April 1917 200,000 workers allegedly went on strike in protest against the military conscription of one of their foremen, Richard Müller... One day after the outbreak of the strike, Müller was released from military service. The January strike of 1918 can be seen as symptomatic of the revolutionary feeling then current in Germany.

GUSTAV NOSKE

▲ On the whole urban workers were worse fed than were farmers or soldiers. In the last two years of the war, soup was dispensed on street corners to hungry urban crowds throughout central and eastern Europe. This scene took place in Russia in May 1916.

▶ The volume of Allied food purchases in the United States forced up the price of bread and led to shortages. In February 1917 riots broke out on the Lower East Side of New York when stores ran out of bread. This photograph shows an American food queue in 1918.

▶ In the last year of the war urban populations in Germany and Austria-Hungary were reduced to foraging for food, even, as this photograph shows, in refuse. Hunger forced people into the countryside, where they bartered whatever they had for food and kindling wood.

views many people had about whether they had to accept the world as they had found it. At least for a time, fatalism and passive resignation seem to have become two of the unintended casualties of the war.

Wartime militancy in the long perspective

These were the decisive features of the outburst of industrial unrest in the critical last year of the war. We must not lose sight, though, of some longer-term developments which underlay the wave of militancy which began in 1917 and lasted until well after the war. Let us consider just two. The first is related to the fact that in the late 19th and early 20th centuries strike waves appear in roughly regular intervals. They tend to follow periods in which previously unorganized workers join unions. This had happened in the late 1880s and seems also to have been the case after the growth of trade unionism in the early years of World War I. Secondly, the tendency for workers to demand political rights and to use political means to better the material conditions of their lives was certainly not created by the war. What the war did was to open a new phase in that struggle. This was largely because workers had come to see that in wartime all wage questions are political questions. By 1918 strikes had become a very effective political weapon in the wider campaign for political equality and a decent standard of living.

Restraints on militancy

It is therefore clear that new and powerful forces had appeared during the war which threatened to end it and topple the regimes engaged in it. What held this movement back? First, it must be reiterated that class consciousness and patriotism are not contradictory, but rather are compatible commitments. Most workers did want their country to win the war, and faced years of anxiety over the fate of loved ones in uniform. This helps to account for the lull in industrial action during the German offensive that began in March 1918. It also explains why workers waited so long before giving vent to their anger in strike action. It is also important to note that trade unionism still represented a minority of workers in all European countries. And even though joining a union in wartime was positively encouraged, many of those who did so had no interest whatsoever in disturbing the war effort. Furthermore, the growth of trade unionism during the war acted at times as a brake on militancy. Newly-organized workers may not have been well-disciplined, but they were loyal to their own unions, at least until conditions worsened to the point that any action was better than silence. Shop stewards, who were both union men and represented workers of different grades on the shop floor, usually took action on their own. But this was the exception rather than the rule in wartime.

Furthermore, in countries where living standards were maintained, trade unionism had achieved a recognition and an unprecedented degree of respectability. Workingmen had been brought into councils of state, and intended to stay there. The key roles played by Albert Thomas in France and Arthur Henderson in the UK were a pointer to the future.

The new situation was also recognized by the more far-sighted employers in both the winning and the losing camps. The way forward, in their view, was to perpetuate alliances between business and labor which had brought gains at least to the bigger battalions. This was the motive behind the famous Stinnes-Legien agreement, drawn up a few days after the Armistice, on 15 November 1918, whereby German employers and trade unions entered into a social partnership necessary for the transition to peace. In Britain similar intentions took the form of "Joint Industrial Councils", through which an ongoing dialog could be maintained. Such flexibility in the stance of big business helped stabilize its position in the uncertain conditions of 1918 and after.

For all these reasons the substantial turbulence of the last year of the war was contained. But only just. Had the war carried on for another year – which was indeed possible, had Ludendorff delayed or canceled his decision to win the war on the Western Front by just one more gamble — the outcome might have been very different, regardless of how many Americans were thrown into the fray. The ordinary people of Europe on both sides had been stretched to breaking point by 1918, and however great their patriotic commitments, many people, both high and low, heaved a sigh of relief when the German army at last accepted defeat.

◀ How far removed from the cheering crowds of 1914. Starving and malnourished children were a common sight in central and eastern Europe, both before the Armistice and in the following period up to July 1919 when the Allies continued their blockade of food supplies to the Central Powers.

▼ The numbers of losses – killed, wounded, missing and prisoners of war – were so huge that it was virtually impossible for the combatant nations to keep an accurate count of the human cost of the war. These women are shown in 1915 trying to account for German prisoners captured on the Russian and French Fronts. Each card told the story of World War I in its own way. It was a story of suffering, multiplied by many millions, which taken as a whole is comprehensible not in statistics but perhaps only in art.

THE HUMAN COST OF THE WAR

No one will ever know how many men perished while on military or naval duty in World War I. An estimate of about 9 million – the total population of New York City – may give some idea of the magnitude of the catastrophe. Over 70 million men were mobilized; thus over one in eight of those who served was killed or died on active service.

A statistical presentation of estimates of the losses in World War I hints at the sheer scale of the slaughter, but it is difficult to grasp the full meaning of such statistics: two million German dead, 1.3 million French dead, and so on; but anyone who wants to know what World War I brought about has to start at this point.

Some further inferences can be drawn from these appalling statistics. Although more Russians died than members of any other nationality, the greatest proportional losses were suffered by Serbians, Romanians, Bulgarians and Turks. The Western Front was where the war was won and lost, but the Eastern Front was, if anything, an even bloodier field of combat. American losses were relatively low.

What did casualties on this scale mean to those who survived the war? The answer to this question may never be known, but we can appreciate the poverty of accounts which fail to pose it. It is true, of course, that for those who fell the war was over. But when did it end for their parents, widows, children, relatives and friends? It is likely that by 1918 every household in most combatant countries had lost a relative or friend.

In the interwar years, special commemorative services for the fallen were begun. In Germany the Nazis used them to glorify the dead. But there was nothing intrinsically sinister about the belief that the living owed a debt to the dead, which could be acknowledged, if never discharged, in public ceremonies. A vast monument to the fallen of Verdun was erected in the interwar years; literally thousands of others dot the countryside of France, Flanders, Italy, Turkey and Palestine. Collective exercises in mourning and remembrance continue to this day – Armistice Day in France, Anzac Day in Australia and New Zealand, Remembrance Sunday in Britain, Memorial Day in the USA.

What did the war mean to the millions of men wounded on active service? Here diffidence must be adopted. For some, pensions helped compensate for injury, and they eventually recovered. For others, for example victims of shell shock, little could be done. After a while polite society shunned their company, but as the art of Georg Grosz and Otto Dix suggests, they were a familiar sight nonetheless. Similarly, the millions of widows and orphans produced by the war received some help from public authorities, but no one pretended this made up for their loss. And when consideration is given to the stories contemporaries themselves told of broken lives and marriages, lost careers and opportunities, we again confront the fact that the war lasted much, much longer than the conflict itself.

▼ The Cenotaph in London's Horse Guards Parade became the focus for British ceremonies of remembrance. Other monuments drew those who knew private grief, and who, like this Munich woman (bottom), sought a name on the list of the fallen. To touch a name engraved in stone was for many a necessary act of mourning. In France war memorials were placed in market squares, rather than in churchyards, to testify to the civic virtues of the 1.3 million men who fell.

▼ Over 240,000 British soldiers suffered total or partial leg or arm amputations as a result of war wounds (below right). Artificial limbs helped them try to resume "normal life". Less could be done for blind veterans, gas victims or tubercular men. Psychiatric wounds were untreatable. But in the UK and elsewhere, most disabled veterans suffered from less visible ailments. In postwar Aachen, in Germany, about half of the disabled veterans had orthopedic trouble.

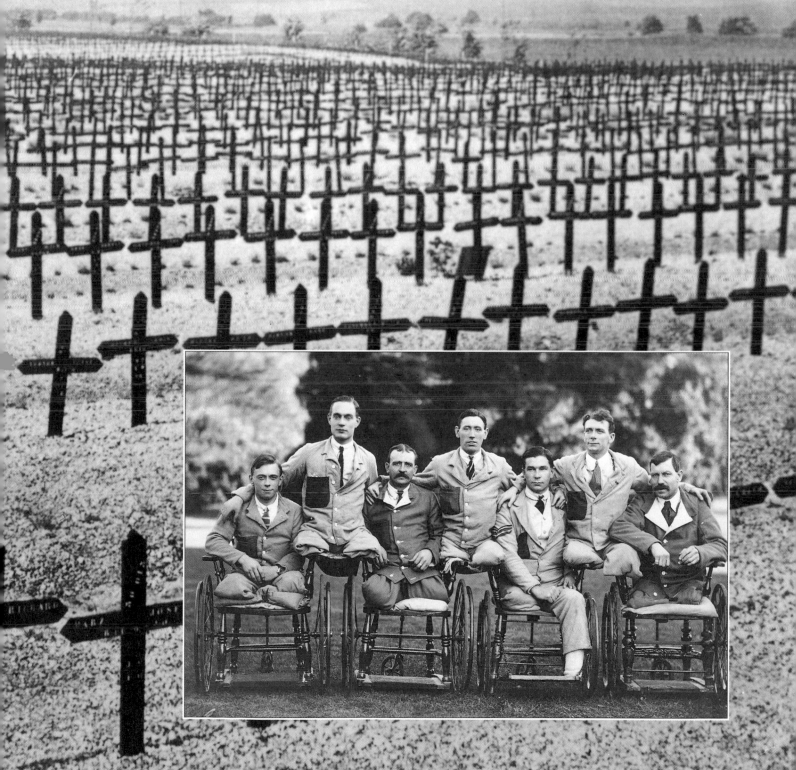

The "Lost Generation" numbered over 9 million soldiers who died in the war. About one in eight of those who served was killed. Turkey, Romania, Serbia, France and Germany suffered higher than average rates of loss. But those who mourned did so for people, not proportions. The great majority of the men who fell were under age 30. Most were ordinary workingmen: agricultural laborers on the Continent; industrial workers in Britain.

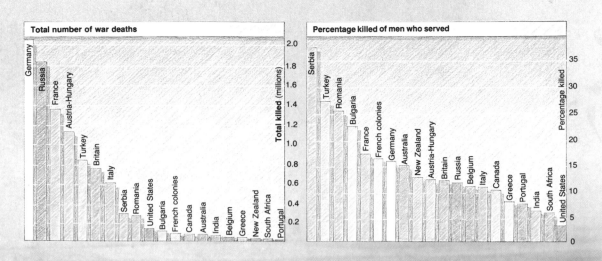

Total number of war deaths

Total killed (millions): 2.0, 1.8, 1.6, 1.4, 1.2, 1.0, 0.8, 0.6, 0.4, 0.2

Germany, Russia, France, Austria-Hungary, Turkey, Britain, Italy, Serbia, Romania, United States, Bulgaria, French colonies, Canada, Australia, India, Belgium, Greece, New Zealand, South Africa, Portugal

Percentage killed of men who served

Percentage killed: 35, 30, 25, 20, 15, 10, 5, 0

Serbia, Turkey, Romania, Bulgaria, France, French colonies, Germany, Australia, New Zealand, Austria-Hungary, Britain, Russia, Belgium, Italy, Canada, Greece, Portugal, India, South Africa, United States

ACKNOWLEDGEMENTS

Picture credits

1	British soldier and cross: IWM
2–3	Soldiers dragging howitzer: IWM
4	German prisoners, 1918: IWM
20–21	Czar Nicholas II (Russia) and President Poincaré (France): HPL
58–59	General Fritz von Below and staff (Germany): IWM
96–97	Australian troops at Chateau Wood near Ypres, 1917: IWM
140–141	Belgian refugees: NAW

7 RV **8–9** IWM **11** Historisches Archiv F. Krupp, Essen **17t** RV **17c, 17bl** IWM **17br** BDIC **23** EPA **24** Edimedia, Paris **25t, 25b** HPL **26t** PNL **26–27t** BSV **26c** HPL **26–27b** ADNZ **26b** EPA **27** HPL **28–29** BSV **29** Musee Royal de l'Armee et d'Historie Militaire, Brussels **30** ADNZ **31t** HPL **31c, 31b** RV **32** PF **32–33** HPL **34t, 34b, 34–35** HPL **35** EPA **38t** BSV **38c, 39** HPL **38–39** UB **40–41** IWM **40** HPL **41** RV **42** *Punch* **43t, 43b** HPL **45l** IWM **45r** NAW **46t** UB **46c** PF **46b** ADNZ **47** Institut für Marxismus-Leninismus, Berlin **48t** RV **48b** HPL **49** National Museum of Ireland, Dublin **51** PF **52** EPA **52–53** HPL **53t** HPL **53ct** Novosti Press Agency, London **53cb** Robert Hunt Library, London **53b** BSV **54** BDIC **54–55** BSV **55** HPL **56** RV **56–57** PF **57** EPA **61** HPL **62t** HPL **62cl** ADNZ **62bl** ADNZ **62br** BSV **64–65** HPL **64** PF **65** UB **66** IWM **67** ADNZ **68–69** BSV **69t** UB **69c** PF **69b** IWM **70** HPL **72t** HPL **72b** EPA **73t** HPL **73b** EPA **74** UB **75t** HPL **75b** RV **77tl** HPL **77bl** ADNZ **77r** BSV **78** UB **78–79** Librairie Larousse, Paris **79** Jean Loup Charmet, Paris **80t** EPA **80b** ADNZ **81** IWM **82** HPL **83** IWM **84, 84–85** IWM **86** IWM **87t** IWM **87b** EPA **88, 89tr, 89tc** TM **89br** NAW **89l** IWM **91** IWM **92l, 92r** EPA **93** BSV **95t** HPL **95b** IWM **99** Librairie Larousse, Paris **100** EPA **101t** PF **101b** EPA **102–103, 102, 103l, 103r** IWM **104t** EPA **104b** St Helens Public Library, St Helens, UK **105, 107** PNL **108t, 108b** PF **110** IWM **110–111** IWM **112t, 112b** IWM **113** Jean-Loup Charmet, Paris **114t** (cards) PNL **114c** PF **114b** HPL **114–115** Elsevier Séquoia, Brussels **115l** IWM **115r** Jean-Loup Charmet, Paris **116–117** Robert Hunt Library, London **117** IWM **118t** IWM **118b** EPA **118–119** IWM **120–121** BSV **121tr** HPL **121cr, 121br** IWM **121b** NAW **122–123** HPL **124t** PNL **124b** Novosti Press Agency, London **124–125** IWM **125t** PF **125b** ADNZ **126, 127t, 127b** IWM **128t** IWM **128b, 128–129** RV **130l** IWM **130r** HPL **131t** NAW **131b** HPL **132–133, 132, 133t** IWM **133b** Bundesarchiv, Koblenz **135** BDIC **136–137** NAW **137** Bibliothèque Nationale, Paris **138t** UB **138b, 139** IWM **143** RV **144** HPL **145t** BSV **145b** EPA **146t** PF **146b** *Illustrated London News*, London **146–147** EPA **147** RV **149** IWM **150t** IWM **150c** EPA **150b** IWM **150–151** UB **151** IWM **152, 153** IWM **154** UB **155t** PF **155b** RV **157** Phaidon Press Picture Archive, Oxford, UK **158tl** IWM **158tr** PNL **158b** IWM **159tl** BDIC **159bl, 159r** IWM **160** NAW **161l** EPA **161r** EPA **162** EPA **163l** PNL **163tr** IWM **163cr** BDIC **163br** BDIC **164–165** Edimedia, Paris **166t** PF **166b** Novosti Press Agency **167** HPL **168t** HPL **168c** BDIC **168b** IWM **169t** EPA **169b** EPA **170–171** UB **170t** HPL **170b** ADNZ **171** IWM

Abbreviations

AA	Andromeda Archive
ADNZ	Allgemeiner Deutscher Nachrichtendienst, Zentralbild, Berlin
BDIC	Bibliothèque de Documentation Internationale Contemporaine, Paris
BSV	Bilderdienst Süddeutscher Verlag, Munich
HPL	Hulton Picture Library, London
IWM	Trustees of the Imperial War Museum, London
NAW	National Archives, Washington
PNL	Pictorial Nostalgia Library, West Wickham, UK
PF	Popperfoto, London
RV	Roger-Viollet, Paris
TM	The Tank Museum, Bovington Camp, Wareham, UK
UB	Ullstein Bilderdienst, Berlin

t = top, tl = top left, tr = top right, c = center, b = bottom, etc

Editorial and Research Assistance
Steven Chapman, Mary Davies, Robert Dewey Jnr, Jackie Gaff, John Horgan, Louise Jones, Nick Law, Andy Overs, Mike Pincombe, Maria Quantrill, Graham Speake, Michelle von Ahn

Artists
Alan Hollingberry, Ayala Kingsley, Kevin Maddison, Colin Salmon

Design Assistance
Cyndy Gossert, Dave Smith, Del Tolton

Photographs
Shirley Jamieson, David Pratt, Joanne Rapley

Typesetting
Brian Blackmore, Catherine Boyd, Anita Wright

Production
Stephen Elliott, Clive Sparling

Cartography
Sarah Rhodes
Maps drafted by Euromap, Pangbourne; Lovell Johns, Oxford; Alan Mais (Hornchurch)

Color Origination
J. Film Process, Bangkok; Scantrans, Singapore; Wing King Tong Co., Ltd, Hong Kong

Index
Ann Barrett

INDEX